Stephen Bourne

Trade Population and Food

A Series of Papers on Economic Statistics

Stephen Bourne

Trade Population and Food
A Series of Papers on Economic Statistics

ISBN/EAN: 9783744646116

Printed in Europe, USA, Canada, Australia, Japan

Cover: Foto ©Suzi / pixelio.de

More available books at **www.hansebooks.com**

TRADE, POPULATION AND FOOD.

A SERIES OF

PAPERS ON ECONOMIC STATISTICS.

BY STEPHEN BOURNE.

. . . . "——a question which has given rise to great discussion of late, and which by some has been considered a most serious matter to our commercial position: I mean the great and growing difference between the value of the imports and exports of this country. I think the credit is due to Mr. Bourne, a valued member of our Society, for having first called attention to this phenomenon in a paper which he read last year. . . . . Though I do not share in the gloomy conclusions which Mr. Bourne draws from these figures, yet I think they are well worthy of consideration and require an explanation."—*Speech by Mr. Shaw-Lefevre as President of the Statistical Society, 25th June, 1878.*

LONDON:

GEORGE BELL AND SONS,

YORK STREET, COVENT GARDEN.

1880.

RIGHT HON. EARL GRANVILLE, K.G.,

SECRETARY OF STATE FOR FOREIGN AFFAIRS.

My Lord,

Having at an unusually early age become interested in the progress of political life during the stormy period which succeeded the Relief Act of 1829 and preceded the Reform Bill of 1832, I have never wavered in attachment to those great principles which later on dictated the Abolition of Slavery in the West Indies (where I resided during the transition period) in 1834 and the removal of Restrictions on Trade in 1845.

Having also in my boyhood been honoured by the patronage of the then Lords Holland, Brougham, and John Russell, and received my first appointment in the public service at the hands of Lord Melbourne, I learned to venerate the champions of that liberal legislation which raised our country to its proud position of prosperity at home and honour abroad.

In your Lordship I now recognize the connecting link between the policy of those days and the more recent development of the present times,—the able representative of British interests at the Court of our nearest neighbour for a

considerable portion of the interval between the two periods,
—and the enlightened administrator of our Foreign relations at the present moment.

Permit me, then, although personally unknown to your
Lordship, to thankfully accept your permission to dedicate
to you this volume, the result of many years of thought and
labour spent in the public service, in the hope that it may
be received with favour as a slight contribution to the
knowledge of the trading position in which the Empire
stands.

With much respect,

Your obedient Servant,

STEPHEN BOURNE.

LONDON, 16th October, 1880.

CONTENTS.

INTRODUCTORY.—THE PRESENT CRISIS IN TRADE.

I F it savour somewhat of presumption thus to place before
the public a series of papers which with a few exceptions
have already appeared in the published Proceedings of
various Societies, the apology to be offered is that in the
opinion of friends, the accuracy of whose judgment it would
be still more presumptuous to dispute, their appearance is
justified by the importance of the subjects of which they
treat. These friends know that the information they contain has been honestly and laboriously collected, and though
the conclusions which the figures are employed to support
may not altogether meet with unchallenged acceptance, they
think the facts are yet worthy of attention as evidence towards the working out of problems of the highest interest.

It was at first intended to rewrite the whole of the papers,
bringing down the figures compiled for the earlier to the date
of the later ones, and eliminating from each whatever had
been introduced into the others; so reducing the bulk of the
volume, and giving greater completeness to the whole. It was,
however, found that to do this would involve the preparation
of a mass of new figures which would not have altered the
reasoning of which they were the basis, involving great
labour without any corresponding advantage. On the contrary, that though in a few instances the repetition of figures

and the restating of results may be found in some degree
wearisome, yet as illustrating different branches of the subjects, and leading up to conclusions which harmonize and
support each other, the iteration is valuable for strengthening
the opinions arrived at through different channels on kindred,
yet not identical topics, all converging to the same end.
The papers, therefore, excepting that in some few instances
later figures have been added to some of the tables, and
here and there a verbal alteration has been made, are reproduced in the same state as they first appeared. They are
also ranged in chronological order rather than with reference
to their subject-matter; so that wherever similar points
are touched, the later paper gives contact with the latest
facts. It is hoped that in their collected form these essays
may not be altogether useless to those statesmen, political
economists, and leaders in philanthropic movements to
whom the present trading and social relations of the country,
whether home or foreign, must at this time be a source of
the deepest interest as well as keenest anxiety.

The mention of one other reason for publication may
perhaps be pardoned. It has been a source of much solace
to the writer during the many weary years through which
he has been officially engaged in the compilation of trade
statistics, to trace the information they afford backwards to
its sources, and onwards to its bearings upon the progress and
prosperity of the community : thus, by utilizing the labour
bestowed—beyond the mere results shown in the published
trade accounts—relieving the tedium of perpetually dealing with dry and uninteresting details. With this object he
has ever sought to improve and simplify the methods for procuring, recording, and compiling the various accounts ; and
had some share in bringing about the extensive changes of
system in 1870 which form the subject of the first of the

following papers. Since then, finding himself—whether from the accidents of official life, the results of political changes, or as the penalty of too great pertinacity in pursuing those plans of statistical reform which then received the highest sanction and have since obtained the highest praise—in a great measure shut out from the honour and responsibility of carrying them into practice; it has been to him no less a labour of love than of presumed duty to give the country which has paid for his services the benefit of such light, the result of long training and close observation, as it might be in his power to throw upon the various subjects with which the trade returns are so intimately connected.   It must, however, be understood that, whatever the shape in which the figures are condensed or reproduced, they rest upon official sanction only in so far as they emanate from the recognized official authority, and that the author is solely responsible for the forms in which they are presented in the following pages, as well as for the opinions expressed or the deductions which to him they appear to sustain.   With these explanations and in this spirit he desires to offer a few preliminary observations on the momentous trading crisis through which the country has been passing of late years, the end of which has certainly not yet arrived.

The subjects treated of in the following pages may be ranged under three heads: the progress of our Trade, the increase of our Population, and the supplies of Food which our commerce procures for our people to consume. The sequence in which they stand in the title-page of the volume indicates the order in which they claim consideration.

A retrospect of the early history of our foreign trade will show that it arose from the same cause which induced

Solomon to send ships to Ophir for gold and to bring home from thence the " silver, ivory, apes, and peacocks." Our ancestors desired to possess some of the treasures which travellers had discovered other lands to contain, and to consume the luxuries which their own soil and climate failed to bring forth. But very early the enterprise which took our discoverers abroad induced them to settle in the new-found countries, and by degrees to establish trading posts and colonies to an extent which no other nation has attempted, first, for the collection and transport of the articles produced by the natives, and then for themselves to cultivate or manufacture the goods they found to be in demand at home. This required supplies for their maintenance, materials for their fisheries, farms, and factories, which could only be obtained from home, and thus, in addition to the sending out of goods in payment for those we received from thence, there was a growing export of those things which formed the capital worked by the settlers, but mostly owned at home. To this, in process of time, became added goods purchased on credit or paid for by loans, stocks, and shares furnished by capitalists at home. There was thus a continually expanding export trade, furnishing employment to the growers, manufacturers, and traders at home. During this period the import trade had likewise been progressing, and was maintained, first, by the demand for articles wherewith to repay those who had furnished the foreign supplies for our own use; then in the return of interest, earnings, and profits on capital and labour bestowed both at home and abroad ; and, finally, for goods purchased by this country with the proceeds of repayments made by others. The remarkable development of this trade in both directions during the twenty years of its greatest prosperity, 1854-74, forms the subject of the second paper, that on

"The Progress of our Foreign Trade," read in 1875 ; its predecessor, that on the "Official Trade and Navigation Statistics," having given information as to the nature of the returns from which the particulars of this progress were derived.

It was then that the phenomenon alluded to by Mr. Shaw-Lefevre in the quotation on the title-page, that of the "Growing preponderance of Imports over Exports," was brought to view in No. III. paper of 1876 bearing that title. It will be seen however, from the concluding paragraph of the previous paper (p. 52), and still more from the notes on p. 223 that at a still earlier date (1873) the analysis to which the trade returns had been subjected, led to doubts as to whether the rapid rise in our imports was altogether compatible with the prosperity of trade, when unaccompanied by a corresponding expansion in that of our exports ; and from this arose the attempt in that paper, not so much to give the explanation of this phenomenon, which after its reading was in Mr. Shaw-Lefevre's opinion still needed, as to state plainly the circumstances of our trade, in order that its condition might be properly investigated. This paper was the precursor of many others, from the pens of Mr. Newmarch, Mr. Giffen, Mr. Mundella, and Mr. Shaw-Lefevre himself, all dealing with the various points suggested to account for this remarkable change in the balance of our trade. In truth, however, no satisfactory explanation has been afforded. In one quarter it was thought that the difference was more apparent than real, inasmuch as the values given were subject to deduction on one side, and addition on the other. This was admitted and calculated for in the paper itself, and after much discussion the degree in which these alterations affect the results is not a point on which there is much diversity of opinion ; and at best it does not explain the rapid transition from one condition of trade to the other, amounting to a change of nearly £100,000,000 as between 1872 and 1877. Another opinion was, that the difference was due to the large profits on our trade, and the greatness of our income realized abroad and remitted home; but there was no apparent reason why these sources should have so suddenly augmented, or the receipts from them have coincided with the setting in of a period of depression. It was then argued that the rapidity of our accumulations at home forbad the supposition that our importations were excessive. Subsequent experience, however, has shown that the appraisement of our national property was set too high, and a fresh valuation would now considerably lower the estimate. Again, the condition of manufactures abroad was thought to be such as to dispel any fears that our manufacturing supremacy was in danger; notwithstanding this, it must be admitted that progress in this direction at home has scarcely kept pace with its rapid strides abroad. Another idea put forth was, that those to whom we had lent money in our colonies and other places were paying off their debts ; but the figures proved that if this were so, payment was being made in articles of food, the consumption of which would not only cancel the debts but destroy the wealth they represented. A nearer approach to a satisfactory solution may be found in the suggestion that the discrediting of foreign loans which took place at this period had restricted sales for export. This, however, would show that in the measure that former exports had resulted from the expenditure of these loans in this country, the manufacturing interests had gained at the expense of the investing members of the community, and that the diminution of these transactions was beneficial. Yet it in no wise accounted for the vast increase of the imports which, but for our necessities, ought to have lessened with our diminished power to effect exchanges of our own produce. Nor does the supposition that we were ceasing our investments abroad at all support the argument that our continued increase in imports was advantageous. It simply shows that we were sending forth our money to purchase perishable commodities for consumption instead of for profitable investment. Neither of these views explains how we could fail to become poorer by buying more than we were selling. No. VIII., on " Excess of Imports," written though not published early in 1878, and No. IX., on the " Relation between Imports and Exports," late in the same year, are both of them efforts to discover some of the reasons for the existing state of things, and the principles which should guide to a right judgment regarding them. The two Papers XI. and XV. carry on the facts necessary to a correct understanding, by analyzing the figures for the worst year of the depression, and showing the " Decay of our Exports " in 1879, and those which manifest a partial " Revival in Trade " up to the present time.

The last paper to be mentioned in this section is No. X., " On the Silver Question," in which, besides dealing with the history of the production and prices of the precious metals, it was maintained that there had been neither such an appreciation of gold as to account for the depreciation of silver, nor such a scarcity of the superior metal as would either considerably enhance its value or impede trade transactions. The soundness of these opinions would appear to be shown in the subsequent rise in prices, and the absence of the anticipated drain of gold for the expansion of the circulation in other places. When that drain does take place it will occur, not because gold is wanted for use in

America or elsewhere, but because other means of settling balances have become exhausted.

On all these points there is room for much divergence of opinion, but the facts remain unaltered: that this preponderance of imports still exists, that though for the few intervening years the balance was reduced, it never before reached so high as it has done during the past year, and that as shown by the most recent returns—those issued whilst these sheets are passing through the press—its dimensions are still increasing.

Neither is there any room for questioning—whatever may be inferred from it as to the prosperity or adversity of trade or manufactures—that the cause of this continuous balance exists in "The Increasing Dependence upon Foreign Supplies for Food," the details of which are put forward in Paper No. IV., compiled early in 1877. Whilst manifesting that these had been trebled since 1857, it yet fails to show the still higher totals which have since been reached. In a subsequent paper, No. V., on "the Nature and Extent of our Food Supplies, and the sources from whence they are derived," information will be found which may serve as material for guiding to some conclusions as to the bearing of these facts on the welfare of the nation. Other papers contain figures also which may aid in the same direction.

The second division under which a portion of these papers may be classed is that which relates to Population. Just as our trade in its origin and growth has widely differed from that of other nations, so have there been peculiar conditions under which the inhabitants of the United Kingdom have progressed to their present numbers and social positions. In China and India we have examples of nations existing for ages in much the same condition, cultivating the land as their forefathers had done, trading more between themselves than with foreigners, but constrained by the pressure of increasing numbers to seek commercial intercourse with other countries—principally with England—and thus sharing in the benefits of Western civilization, enabling them to exchange the products of their industry in the shape of raw material and food for the finished articles sent from our own and other shores. In the United States we have an example of a different kind: a comparatively new people, occupying lands of great richness in agricultural and mineral products, increasing with great rapidity, by natural additions, consequent upon freedom of space and abundance of food, aided by the attractive influence of the same causes bringing immigrants from the older countries; employing itself mainly in agriculture, and so obtaining manufactured articles from abroad, mainly from the Mother country, although now endeavouring to rival her in both manufacture and trade. The same may be said with a great degree of truth of our own Australian and African colonies, who, like the United States, in becoming peopled have not only sustained themselves upon the food resources of their own lands, but have been able to produce large quantities both of this and of raw material for transport to the old world—again up to very recent times chiefly to this country. The soil has created the population, and with it the means of subsistence. Here, however, we for many years past, though rapidly adding to our numbers, have ceased to grow more of food or clothing, and thus are yearly becoming more dependent upon our manufacturing and trading operations for obtaining the necessaries of life. It is the trade which has created our population, and that in three ways—the natural increase which it fostered, the restraint it put upon emigration, and the immigration of those who found better employment here than in the places of their birth. On the maintenance and the rapid enlargement of that trade we depend for the life and the increase of our people. Hence the depression and suffering resulting from the lessening or decay of our exports, and the grave anxiety with which the present state of affairs must be regarded.

In Paper No. VI., "On the Growth of Population," &c., 1877, it was sought to be shown that up to the date when that paper was written there had been no increase outstripping the means of subsistence produced at home or procurable from abroad in exchange for our manufactures. In No. XII., "The Social Aspect of Trade Depression" as the status of the several members were affected by it was set forth, whilst in No. XIII. the necessity for extended colonization as a consequence of that depression was contended for; and in No. XVI., on the "Finance of National Insurance," the practicability of the proposed measures for the prevention of pauperism was investigated from a financial point of view. The objections to which this scheme lies open on the ground of expediency, as well as for social, moral, and even religious reasons, are numerous. There was not space for dealing with these, which may form the subject of future consideration should the National Club still be a candidate for public acceptance.

The third subject dealt with in these papers is that of Food, which besides having the two already alluded to devoted entirely to it, finds a place or places in almost every one of them; for the necessity of obtaining supplies of food forms so important a consideration in every trade question that scarcely any can be separated from it. To our trade we owe the increase of our population, and to the extent of that increase we owe the necessity for trading in food. It is thus the first, the last, and the all-important subject on

which hinges the continuance or advance of our national
prosperity, for herein we differ from almost every other
nation, and it is the end and aim of trade to remove the
existing consequences of that difference. We cannot avoid
supplementing our deficient home supplies by drawing upon
the superfluous growth of other countries; we must necessarily work for the production of something wherewith to
pay for those supplies, and we have no means of carrying on
the exchange but through the medium of the trading relations we establish or maintain with the rest of the world.
Closely connected with this are the facts spoken of in paper
No. XIV., on " Drinking and Depression," which deals with
the waste of money expended on alcohol, and the degree
in which this affects wages, and through wages the enhanced
cost of our manufactures, thus heavily weighting our commerce with the world.   Paper No. VII., though relating
solely to an article which can only be classed with food,
more properly belongs to the first group, that of trade, since
on the adoption of some satisfactory settlement of this matter
much of our trade, with France especially, depends.   Yet
it is impossible not to see that if we would dispense with the
consumption of that article we might save for devotion to
other uses all the labour expended in producing the goods
we have to sell or exchange for wine.   It will be noticed
how closely the principles, on which three years since it was
suggested that legislation should be based, are in confor-
mity with those proposed by Mr. Gladstone in his recent
Budget, but withdrawn to await an agreement with the
French Government.   Paper No. XIII., on Colonization,
enters more fully into the extent of our home supplies, and
from their proved deficiency points to the necessity for many
of our people to go forth and become food-producers for
themselves and for those who remain at home, in some or all

of the magnificent territories which form a part of the British Empire.

The needed explanation, then, of the phenomenon manifested in the growing expansion of our imports beyond that of our exports is simply this,—that with a prosperous state of trade and manufactures, the mouths we have to feed, and the food required to feed them, have increased beyond the powers of our own soil to provide for; and that other nations have been growing in intelligence, wealth, and manufacturing power, and so in the capacity for supplying their own wants, without increasing, but rather decreasing, their demands upon those products of our labour by which our ability to purchase food from them is largely maintained. Our necessities have been multiplied by continuous seasons of diminished produce from our own soil, whilst agricultural operations have been progressively advancing abroad; thus, concurrently with lessened crops, there has been a lower range of prices to remunerate our own agriculturists, and they have had less to expend with the manufacturers for the home trade. That we should have been able thus long to stem these adverse currents does, indeed, manifest the progress of our resources, and the accumulations of our past prosperity in trade; but it does not at all indicate that we may not now be expending more than our income, or at least ceasing to make those accumulations which have contributed to our wealth and given us the commercial standing which we still retain. Neither does it forbid the supposition that if that wealth and that supremacy in trade and manufacture is to be preserved, we must retrace our footsteps, in some directions, and advance with greater boldness and rapidity in others.

One feature in the present aspect of affairs appears to have been lost sight of, or not, at least, sufficiently appreciated—namely, the extent to which the wealth—not only the floating but the realized capital we have—may be held as bankers rather than owners, and how large a portion of our trade we carry on as agents rather than principals, earning commissions instead of realizing profits. It may be that during the years of depression through which we have been passing, this has been the most profitable position to occupy, for there seems to be a growing tendency towards increasing the rewards of the distributor rather than those of the producer. All the experience we gain from an insight into the methods by which fortunes have been accumulated by individuals, or dividends earned for shareholders in banks, shows that boldness in speculation by the one, and the almost unlimited expansion of credit in the other, have been the sources of success. It is amazing to see how vast a superstructure credit builds upon a slender basis; how little of actual available capital serves to carry on the most gigantic undertakings. It is thus that money held simply in custody, often enables its holder to obtain and expend so large an income. It may be that thus we have been enabled to tide over times in which we have certainly been spending more than we have been earning, and fortunate will it be for us if we thus sustain our commercial pre-eminence, until we can take the new departure—to use a nautical phrase—which the altered conditions under which the voyage must be pursued renders an absolute necessity.

What then are the steps we must retrace? Clearly those of individual and national extravagance, of deterioration in the quality of our manufactures, and the honesty of our trade—of undue exaltation of wealth, and dependence upon skill or smartness in obtaining the larger share of that which already exists, rather than upon industry and perseverance

in creating and preserving, not money alone, but all that
really adds to the wealth of the world. What, too, are those
in which we must advance? As individuals we must attach
more value to honest labour, whether of the hands or the
brains, employed in actual production, or the improved use
and lessened destruction of that which labour has already
created; and must use the hours reserved from laborious
occupation as opportunities for real recreation, not for indulgence in enervating pleasures or exhausting pursuits.
As citizens we need to set a higher value upon the powers
of life, by sanitary improvements to lessen mortality, by
hygienic measures to improve and strengthen the health of
the populace, and by police regulations to repress, so far
as these can possibly do, all interference with that which
wastes time or substance. As producers and manufacturers
we need to study and practise whatever may lessen the cost
of production and increase the power of labour; to cultivate those branches in which we have a natural or sure
superiority over other nations, and cease to increase those
in which it is certain that other countries must ultimately
excel ourselves. As traders we need to lessen the cost of
distribution, to discourage costly rivalry, to increase facilities
of transport, and to seek out new openings for the sale of
our goods and the bringing home new articles of utility,
whether as food or for manufacture. As labourers we should
cease from ruinous strikes and all interference with the
devotion of time, strength, and talent, wherever and for however long they may be profitably employed. As capitalists
we must cultivate those close and cordial relations with
labour through which alone money can be made to increase;
eschew all those speculations which merely seek to transfer it from one pocket to another, and even risk it wherever at home or abroad it may help honest labour to increase

production. As statesmen we must economize the national resources, and, so far as is compatible with the detection of crime or the prevention of pauperism, the spread of education and the preservation of healthy life, remove every restriction upon individual liberty. We must so regulate our intercourse with other nations as to avoid expenditure in war or the destruction of the life and property of those who by peaceful measures might be made our customers and friends. As disciples and teachers of Economic science, we must seek for the more universal diffusion of those principles of action which in our individual case or national experience have been proved to encourage labour and enhance capital in harmonious union. We must repudiate any attempt to revert to the policy of protection, or the imposition of reciprocal restrictions upon the fullest freedom in the interchange of commodities, in the utmost confidence that whatever of real utility is best produced or manufactured in any one part of the world, it is the best that every country should obtain at the lowest cost and in the readiest manner. We must seek to have all fiscal regulations so applied as to afford the greatest freedom in the handling, storing, and dealing with all dutiable goods which may be consistent with the safety of the revenue, so long as the exigencies of the State render the continuance of Customs or Excise duties absolutely indispensable.

It will be said, however, that all these are truths well known and generally approved. They recommend no specific measures, suggest no new courses of action. Is it not the fact, however, that in these days we are in danger of forgetting that it is just in proportion as we have put them into practice we have prospered in times past, and that because through their imperfect recognition on the one side, and their undue exaltation, as the means of rectifying every

natural or acquired disadvantage which wo find ourselves unable wholly to overcome, on the other, there is a growing disposition on the part of many to revert to a selfish and exclusive
policy ? This may only retard the progress of a young and
mainly agricultural country like the United States, but would
inevitably result in the speedy decay of an old country like
ours, whose prosperity has hitherto resulted from the advance
of its trade with the whole world. It is painful to have to
repeat the truths which should be accepted as axioms, to
refute those fallacies which were thought to be exploded-
but so long as there remains any considerable body of statesmen or economists who cling to protection or would restrict
freedom of trade, the compilation of statistics and the restating of the facts they substantiate can scarcely be deemed
a work of supererogation.

It is often unjustly charged on those who dwell upon
the admitted excess of imports, that they take unnecessarily
gloomy views of the trading condition of the country—at
least it was so charged when first the fact was brought to
notice in 1873 [1]—but it can scarcely now be said that any
unfavourable anticipations then entertained were worse than
the experience of the intervening seven years ; nor that the
present state of our trade is so satisfactory or encouraging
as to support the roseate hues in which their opponents
represented this preponderance of imports as our unalloyed
gain. It is unfortunate for those ardent free-traders who
yet doubted the soundness of all the trade which was then
being carried on, and who foresaw the adversity which has
since existed, that the facts they adduced have been
perverted to the support of Protectionist theories ; but this
would have been less the case had there been any disposition on the part of those who believed in the con-

[1] Page 223.

tinuance of unexampled prosperity, to admit that there was any cause for anxiety. The fact remains undisputed that the disparity between the two continues to exist, and that the years through which it has lasted have not been marked by a prosperous progress. Even now, whilst these words are being written, the trade returns which are being published show the increase of an adverse balance, and that the food imports very nearly swallow up the whole value of the produce and manufactures we export. Yet we do not hear that traders or manufacturers are reaping large profits, that labourers are able to command exorbitant wages, or that there is any plethora of work for those who are seeking employment, such as would naturally result were we truly advancing in wealth in the measure that the goods we receive from abroad exceed those that we are able to sell for export. Still there is no reason to doubt the strength of our natural position, or that there are abundant means for the comfort and happiness of all, and many more than, the present members of the Empire, if only we will discard our sense of false security, forsake the vices prosperity has engendered, and learn to practise the virtues which are taught by adversity. There may not be room within these islands for all who would like to remain at home, or for the employment of all the labour and capital which may be redeemed from unprofitable uses; but there is ample scope for all of the present and many successive generations in manufacturing for the yet uncivilized nations of the world, and developing the producing powers of the uninhabited portions of our own Empire.

The Official Trade and Navigation Statistics.[1]

[THE following paper was prepared soon after the extensive alterations in the methods and arrangements for compiling the statistical returns which took place in the year 1871. It was drawn up and promulgated, not without advice from competent authority that it was expedient to make the public acquainted with the changes which had then been made; and although the system then introduced has now become thoroughly established, it is perhaps more than ever necessary to detail its character, so that those who compare the accounts of one period with another may be made aware of the points in which the comparisons need correction. In subsequent papers the degree in which these changes affect the information collected from the published returns is more fully pointed out; and if these several alterations are borne in mind, they will serve to correct many erroneous deductions from figures which are not so fully in concord as they would have been had one uniform plan been in use from the earliest to the latest period.]

It was my intention, in the paper I have the honour of laying before you this evening, to have grouped the several articles of import and export, as shown in the trade returns for the past year, into distinctive classes—according to the use for which they are brought here, or the purposes to which they are to be applied—and to have instituted a com-

[1] Read before the Statistical Society, 21st May, 1872. Vol. xxxv.

parison between the quantities thus shown and those of one
or more former years similarly classified. The classification
proposed for the imports would have embraced the distinctive headings of articles of food and personal consumption,
of fuel and lighting, of clothing and habitation, of works of
art and the gratification of taste and amusement, of raw
materials for manufacture, of those for agricultural operations, and any others which might appear of a sufficiently
distinctive character to be worthy of forming a separate
class. The years chosen for comparison with 1871, would
have been 1861 and 1851, and possibly another decennial
period ; selecting those in which the census was taken, as
being convenient periods for considering the figures so obtained in connection with the growth of our home population, and thus showing our increasing dependence upon the
supplies we obtain from abroad. We should thus have seen
the extent and the several degrees in which our comfort and
happiness—if not our very existence—depend upon the
maintenance and growth of our commercial relations, and
have had, as I venture to think, a more distinct view of the
wide-spread benefits of the unrestricted intercourse we are
enabled to carry on with every producing and manufacturing
country throughout the world. In like manner, by a similar
classification of our exports, but varied in accordance with
their character and origin, rather than with their appropriation by those to whom we send them, a comprehensive view
might have been presented of the various commodities which
enable us to pay for the goods we import, whilst at the same
time furnishing employment to so large a portion of our industrial population, and adding so greatly to our stores of
material wealth. A further statement of the articles drawn
hither, simply as to a depôt, from which other countries may
obtain their supplies, would have shown how large a proportion of our foreign trade results from the facility with which
its operations are here carried on—the consequence of our
wealth, our intelligence, our industry, and the undisturbed
peace we have so long enjoyed.

In the process of this investigation I should have had to take into account the extensive alterations which have recently been made in the substance and form of our statistical returns, whereby the comparison between different periods is much disturbed and often rendered difficult. This would have led me to notice the nature and extent of those changes, to have reviewed the history of our statistical progress, and to have given some consideration to the character and scope of our present arrangements for collecting, recording, and publishing the information obtained through their instrumentality. In pursuing this plan, I should have had to derive my facts from the various tables compiled for public use, and though in dealing with them I might have had some advantage from having through many years of official engagement become conversant with their details and uses, the conclusions to which I might have been led would have been entirely of personal authority, and have been in no way invested with official sanction. In like manner, for any opinions I may now express or inferences I may draw—myself, and myself alone, must be held responsible. Having, however, proceeded some distance in the path thus marked out, I became aware of two serious difficulties which stood in the way of a satisfactory completion of the task on the present occasion. In the first place, an unlooked-for delay in the compilation of the annual statement, which it was fully expected would have been in the printer's hands at the termination of last quarter, prevented the necessary figures from being available. Had the reading of this paper taken place earlier in the session it might have been well to have dealt with the figures for 1871, published in the December monthly account, imperfect and insufficient as they might be ; but since those of the revised and perfected annual accounts are so near being ready, it seemed a pity to employ any considerable amount of time or labour upon those which are subject to correction ; and still more undesirable to place on record quantities or calculations which would, though even in minor particulars,

differ from the final results of the year's transactions. And
in the second place, my object being to put before you such
a statement of the principles upon which our collection of
statistics rests, of the sources from whence they are derived,
of the manner in which they are dealt with, and the results
which these labours produce, as may in some measure
explain their value and aid in their employment, I found it
impossible to compress these remarks within less space than
is afforded by the limited time that I am privileged to ask
your attention. I am, therefore, most reluctantly compelled
to fail for the present in the first part of my self-allotted
task, and to seek your indulgence for confining myself to
such observations as it may be in my power to offer upon
the latter portion of the subject. Should I in so doing over-
step the line which separates matters of public or special
interest from those of purely official importance, you will, I
trust, make allowance for the difficulty of getting out of the
groove in which the thoughts of an official are so apt to
traverse. If, again, I may seem to enter upon details which
are of too trivial a nature to warrant being brought under
your notice, I would ask you to bear in mind that the
integrity of the accounts depends upon the care which is
taken to secure accuracy in the original rendering of small
particulars; and seeing to what an extent the official department must be dependent upon the public interest in the
attainment of this object, I would hope to enlist your sym-
pathy with such an end, and to provoke your individual and
collective influence towards its attainment. It must be quite
needless to enlarge upon the advantage to a great commercial country like ours, of having all the information which
can serve to illustrate the progress of its commerce collected
together; neither can it be requisite to dilate upon the
necessity that such information should be as full and accurate
as it is possible to make it; but it may not be unimportant
to familiarize the minds of those who furnish the materials
for, and those who make use of, the publications of this kind,
with some of the processes by which they are prepared, and

tho means by which their completeness and truthfulness may
bo secured.

I.—*Methods Adopted for Collecting Statistics.*

The earliest attempt to obtain anything like a systematic
collection of authentic commercial statistics, would seem to
have taken place in the year 1697, when the office of Inspector-
General of Imports and Exports was established on a system,
by which "provision was made that an account should bo
kept of the trade carried on by England with each foreign
country and each of the British settlements and possessions
abroad, showing the goods imported and exported, methodi-
cally enumerated and classified ; their quantities by weight,
tale, or measure ; and their equivalent in money, computed
at certain official rates of valuation then first assigned."
The necessary information was obtained and condensed by
tabulation into prescribed forms at the several ports throughout the kingdom, and being transmitted to this office by the
different collectors of customs, was then collected into the
required records.   From these, as occasion offered, extracts
were made and collections formed in obedience to requisi-
tions from the proper authorities ; or periodically presented
to Parliament and issued to the public by the Board of
Trade. In later years it was found that the Examiner's—an
office originally created to exercise a check upon the correct
receipt of the revenue—could conveniently collect the statistics for the port of London, by a system which computed
the duties due upon each article of import in the process of
bringing them together for the use of the Inspector-General.
In 1849 this plan was extended to the out-ports, which, instead of framing accounts each for itself, transmitted to tho
Examiner duplicates of the original entries passed by the
importers. Thus his books of record contained the particulars for the whole kingdom, and it became his duty to forward the whole of the periodical accounts to the Inspector-
General, by whom they were again transcribed into tho

various appointed forms and books. This concentration of
the preliminary work under one head was a decided step in
the right direction. It ensured greater uniformity in dealing with all matters of detail, lessened the time employed in
its performance, and considerably diminished the expense.
But there still remained the three offices—Examiner's, Inspector-General's, and Board of Trade, all engaged in the
same duty. It became apparent that " to arrest the work
at a certain stage of advancement in one office, for the purpose of committing its completion to an entirely different set
of workmen, involved a considerable sacrifice of both time
and strength, for which no corresponding advantage was
gained," and " that the union of the two Customs' depart-
ments would permit an earlier rendering of the periodical
returns, and result in a marked advancement of the service
in efficiency and economy." Yet it was not till 1870 that
effect was given to the recommendations made so far back
as 1857. Towards the close of the latter year, directions were
given for the fusion of these two offices into one ; that of
Inspector-General of Imports and Exports as well as that of
Examiner ceased to have an independent existence, and the
new " Statistical Department " undertook the whole duty ;
the Board of Trade ceasing to have any share in the production of the accounts, but retaining its control over their
nature and form. This change, so long anticipated and
laboured for, has, notwithstanding the temporary confusion
incidental to a period of transition, been attended with marked
success, and gives promise of still greater satisfaction in its
further progress.

This office having thus become the depository for all the
information bearing upon commercial statistics, which it is
in the power of the customs' officers to collect; it is evident
that its work will resolve itself into the three branches of
recording facts, compiling accounts, and publishing returns;
and that, though these duties are primarily undertaken for
the service of the Government, they are intended ultimately
for the benefit of the public, and must, therefore, be so shaped

as to meet the wants of those for whom they are performed. It may not be without interest to trace the successive processes by which this is effected, and, in so doing, to take first those which relate to the importation of foreign and colonial goods.

II.—*Imports.* 1. *Sources of Information.*

There are three sources from which information regarding these can be obtained: the report by the master of the vessel of the cargo she brings; the entry by each importer of the precise portion of that cargo which belongs to himself; and the accounts given by the officer who superintends the vessel's discharge. Powers are conferred by Act of Parliament upon the Board of Customs, to require from the first two of these, such statements as may answer the desired end; the third, being its own servant, is necessarily amenable to such orders as it may issue. The master of every vessel is bound within twenty-four hours of his arrival, and before breaking bulk, to report to the Collector of Customs for the port at which he may arrive, the place from whence he comes, with the number and description of all the packages or parcels of goods comprised in his cargo. Then the importer or owner is bound, before he can obtain permission to have his goods landed, to make an entry setting forth the ship in which, and the country from which brought, the number of his packages, and description of his goods, with their quantity by weight, tale, or measurement, as well as their value. In the comparison of these two statements we have the means of discovering whether one or both have duly brought to the knowledge of the authorities the fact of such importation, pecuniary penalties being attached to negligence or inaccuracy in these respects. The master has a general knowledge of the nature of the goods he is bringing, but of their precise description or quantity, and still less of their value, he can have no means of forming a correct opinion. These particulars, however, must be (more or less) known to the parties to whom they are consigned, and this knowledge the Crown demands that they shall impart to its officers, not from any inquisitorial desire to know the secrets of each individual's trade, but for the security of the revenue, and the acquisition of statistical information from those best qualified to afford it.

The importer's entries are of three kinds, first, those in which the goods being liable to import duty, he tenders payment of the amount due upon them; secondly, those on which duty being chargeable, he wishes to place them in bond until such time as he is ready to pay the duty, or to re-export the goods without such payment; and thirdly, those on which no duty being due to the Crown, the goods come into his possession so soon as landed. There is also a fourth kind of entry, when the duty is paid upon goods to be taken out of the warehouse. The first and second together include all the dutiable goods imported ; the first and fourth the portion of the same delivered for home consumption.

These entries are passed in duplicate, the originals, when completed, becoming the warrants, by virtue of which the goods they represent are delivered from the ship or warehouse ; and the copies, technically termed bills, the foundation for the statistical accounts; for which purpose they are forwarded daily from every port in the kingdom to the central office in London. Those for articles on which duty is being paid, must give correct quantities, otherwise the goods are detained until the error is rectified. They have for many years past been recorded daily in the office registers; but those on which no duty is taken, have not, till since the general revision of last year, been so dealt with ; the records being raised from separate accounts furnished by the officers so soon after the discharge of the vessel as they can be made up. Thus two systems prevailed, goods paying duty being deemed an importation or delivery of the day on which the entry was passed; whilst others only dated from the completion of the landing account, often weeks or months after their actual arrival; and the weekly or monthly return which ought to have shown the full imports for the period, really only included those which were finally examined, and the accounts respecting them made up. This has now been altered, and since the commencement of last year every entry is recorded at once. It therefore becomes of importance that the particulars they contain should be correctly given, and means taken to detect and rectify any errors which may creep in. This being done, it only remains for the department faithfully to perform its functions, and correct statistics must be the result.

2. *Particulars required.*

The points on which it is essential that accurate statements should be made in these entries are four, relating, first, to the country from which the goods are brought; secondly, the description of each article; thirdly, its quantity; and, lastly, its value.

A. *Country of Origin.*

For the guidance of the officers and all persons concerned in the passing of entries, there is issued an authorized " List of countries and divisions of countries as they are henceforward to be distinguished on the statistical records of the commerce and navigation of the United Kingdom." This list formerly enumerated 178 countries or parts of countries, many of them being subdivided according to certain arbitrary boundaries, as, for instance, France and Spain, as within and without the Mediterranean; the United States, whether north or south. Many of these distinctions it was found impossible satisfactorily to maintain, and others appeared to be useless. They were, therefore, swept away, and a new list issued with only 112 distinct headings. The result of this condensation will be that certain countries, which have hitherto been specified, will no longer have a separate place, but be included with others in larger divisions. Thus the West Indies are now divided solely according to nationality; all those belonging to Great Britain are included together, and the trade of Jamaica, Barbadoes, &c., will be found merged with the smaller islands under British West Indies. The presidencies of India and the divisions of Australia are still separately retained.

A complicated question, however, here arises, as to the way in which goods passing through other countries in transit to or from this should be dealt with; whether as imports or exports from or to the original country, or from that to which they are shipped to this country or landed abroad. A ship takes goods from London to Portland in America, to be thence forwarded to Quebec; shall these be deemed as exported to the States or to Canada? Another brings goods from Boulogne, which have been brought by rail from Marseilles, which place they reached from Naples. Are these to be importations from France or Italy? In former times, when railway transit and forwarding companies were unknown, a very simple rule sufficed; goods taken on board at any port were deemed to be an importation from that port; and goods sent to any place were deemed to be exported to the port at which the ship in which they were sent was to unload her cargo. An adherence to this rule leads now to the most anomalous results; very large quantities of goods are received or taken from here, on " through rates," which means that the journey is performed in many stages, and with many changes of conveyance, and yet it can be of little consequence how they are carried to or from their ultimate destination or place of origin. It is often mere matter of accident by which route they are conveyed; yet it makes a vast difference to the trade accounts whether they are assigned to one or the other, and may destroy altogether the comparison of one year with the other. This will be made plain by referring to the trade with British India, or with the countries on the Pacific shores of America. Goods shipped in Calcutta, by a vessel coming round the Cape of Good Hope or through the Suez Canal, will be taken as arriving from Bengal; but should they break their voyage by a railway transit across the Isthmus, and be re-shipped at Alexandria, they will be entered as if from Egypt. Again, a Liverpool company is engaged in carrying goods to and from Chili, Peru, and other countries in the Pacific, as well as to Mexico, Cuba, the West India Islands, China, Japan, &c. All those for places this side of the Isthmus of Panama are rightly assigned to their respective countries, because the Liverpool vessel receives or discharges them there ; but all which are sent across the isthmus and there delivered by the railway, or carried further by the ships of the same or an allied company, are considered as from or to Colon in New Granada, where the first vessel commences or ends her voyage. Nor is this evil one that can be easily remedied ; and, in the absence of a remedy, the old rule still prevails in some instances, and in others the simpler plan is adopted of disregarding the changes or breaks in conveyance, provided only the journey be continuous. Until this is universally acknowledged, any attempt to ascertain the extent of our trade with such countries as have indirect as well as direct channels for the passage of their goods, or to compare the results of different years, must be utterly fallacious. In all cases the parties entering their goods at the Custom houses here, must know from whence they are receiving or whither they are sending them, and it is quite as easy, indeed more so, to declare the final rather than the intermediate port. The only principle upon which it is safe to act, seems to be that of considering the terminal points in the journey the goods perform, as those of departure and arrival. [The principle here contended for is now adopted, and since it is the practice to carry all imports to the country of origin, and exports to that of ultimate destination, so far as these are known, and are disclosed in the documents prepared by the traders. It is probable, however, that some of these escape being so noticed, and hence that the trade conducted with countries reached by circuitous routes and inland communication fails to be fully shown, whilst that with countries having transit ports, is, to some extent, unduly magnified.]

Yet this will fail to be precise when they change hands between these points, and is at best insufficient to deal with those which are re-packed or arranged for further transit. Jamaica at one time owed its commercial importance to being the depôt for goods afterwards sold to the traders with South America. St. Thomas and Nassau are still places of considerable trade, but of small consumption. There are some countries, such as Switzerland (from her having no ports), with which we appear to have no trade; and many, Austria for instance, which show but little, because the greater part passes through others; although our relations with both these may in reality be as direct as it is in cases where it is more clearly manifest. It is very desirable that attention should be directed to all these points, as showing that many of the results at which we arrive cannot be taken without some limitation, and also for the purpose of eliciting opinions which may aid in the acquisition of perfectly accurate statistical knowledge.

B. *Descriptions of Goods.*

The next essential point is that which determines the precise description of the articles imported. This, like the country of origin, is regulated by a " List of articles of merchandise, imported into the United Kingdom, showing the designations by which they are to be distinguished," enumerating 389 distinct articles, and having an appendix for " certain articles which are not specifically enumerated in the import list, showing the revised denominations under which they are to be distinguished in the entries," in which 417 other articles are mentioned. The lists under which the articles were kept in the accounts prior to last year were extended to 886 heads, embracing numerous subdivisions now omitted, because it had been found that the attempt to keep them up only tended to produce errors. In the case of articles of large import and distinctive character, there is no difficulty in determining to what denomination they belong.

Wheat, cotton, tea, wine, at once assume their proper position, but with many articles, manufactured ones especially, the class in which they should be placed is very doubtful. A clock, for instance, would seem to be a clear title under which to include every description, but in many of those imported, the timepiece is the least valuable part; for the case and stand may be works of art, of metal, porcelain, wood, or other material, and would then properly fall under one of these heads. The list at present in use has been prepared with much care, with a desire to give a distinct place to every article of commercial importance, and to exclude those of limited or unfrequent importation; yet many are excluded or grouped together, which the importers or producers of the article would wish to see specially distinguished. It is to be feared that in the condensation which has taken place, information which for many reasons would be very valuable has ceased to be noted. Those who consult these accounts from time to time discover omissions which they regret, and endeavour to have them repaired; but there is this great difficulty, that any alteration not only increases labour, but destroys comparison with the accounts already published under a different regulation.

c. *Quantities.*

The third point has reference to the quantities of the article. With those that are liable to duty there is not so much difficulty, since sooner or later they will be weighed or measured for the assessment of duty; but for those which yield no revenue this would be impracticable. Besides the expense, it would involve such a delay in dealing with the goods as to seriously impede the operations of trade; and in very many cases goods are so packed as to make it troublesome and destructive to ascertain the contents of the packages in which they are contained. Until recently, the importer's entry for free goods, although stating the number, weight, or measurement, as the case might be, was not

taken as correct until endorsed by an officer who, without
actually examining the goods, exercised such a supervision
over their landing as would, it was thought, enable him to
detect any serious error. With dutiable goods going into bond,
no weight, &c., at all was stated by the importer, and none
could therefore be taken to account until the necessary examination of the goods discovered the exact quantity. It
was proposed many years ago, that the importers should
render an account of the contents of their several packages,
but a fear lest they should not be able to do so with sufficient
accuracy prevented this plan being adopted until recently.
The extreme importance, however, of obtaining information
on this point at an early period, and the consideration that
in dealing with large numbers of entries, minor errors would
balance each other so as to leave the ultimate results substantially accurate, induced a change of system. Now the
first records are made from the importer's entries. Most
articles are brought here in packages of certain recognized
sizes, the usual weight or measurement of which become
known to those through whose hands they pass, and even in
the absence of any invoice or other statement, the exercise of
ordinary care in computing the quantity a number of packages will contain, is certain to give a very near approach to
accuracy.

As before stated, in the case of goods liable to duty on
consumption in the United Kingdom, it becomes necessary
for revenue purposes to ascertain the exact quantities, and
therefore the statement in the entry is only provisional. It
may and does serve a temporary purpose, but the permanent
records are corrected so soon as the landing accounts are
made up. The same means of correction do not exist with
respect to goods that are free of duty. These are subjected
only to a cursory inspection by the examining officers, who
are directed to satisfy themselves by examination of the
goods or the wharfinger's landing accounts, that the variation
is not excessive. If the error be beyond 10 per cent., either
more or less, a correction is made, but those of a lesser

degree are thought to balance each other, on the principle
that where the basis on which the calculation rests is sound,
the average result may be safely taken. Given the usual
weight of a cask of tallow, or the contents of a pipe of wine,
and it is very improbable that the sum of a thousand estimates will be very far from the truth.

D. *Values.*

There remains then but one point in which the accuracy
of the statistics depends upon that of the information derived
from the importer's entry, namely, the value, and this is
one of great difficulty, the results hitherto obtained being
far less satisfactory than they have been in other respects.
So far as regards any particular article, and comparison in it
of one year with another, quantity is a far better test than
value, the one being a fixed, the other a fluctuating standard; but for the purpose of bringing together the various
articles which each country sends us, or of ascertaining the
extent of our trade with the whole world, no other means
exists but the reducing of all to one common equivalent.
The asking of these values from the importer is quite an
innovation on previous methods of acquiring this knowledge.
Previous to 1871, the real values of all articles that could be
entered either by tale, weight, or measurement, was computed, not declared; the basis of computation being obtained from special lists of prices furnished by appointed
agents, an examination of the ordinary prices current, and
any other available source which could guide the judgment
of those by whom they were estimated. This system had
the defect that it could take but little account of the special
qualities of the parcels of goods at any time imported, but
only the average market price of each month, excepting in
so far as the agent employed had knowledge of the class of
goods then coming forward. For some articles, this average was very accurately ascertained; of these, tea may be
cited as an example, but then almost all of it is brought to

the port of London, and is there disposed of by public sale, or through the instrumentality of a few brokers to whom the actual quality of each month's arrival is well known. But in others, say wine, the quality, and therefore the value, could scarcely be ascertained; yet even in it a tolerably correct average could be struck by those who had the opportunity of consulting the various importers. The present system has great disadvantages, arising from the want of knowledge on the part of the importers, the indifference of many who pass the entries, and the impossibility of the department exercising a valid check. It is well known that a very large proportion of the goods sent to this country are on consignment, and not on purchase, in which case there is no invoice or statement of prices. In these cases the consignee is very much in ignorance of their quality or price, and therefore unable to fix a proper value until they have been examined and sampled. Where, again, as is very frequently done, the entry is made by a mere agent, who may gather the description of the goods from the ship's report, and estimate the weight from the nature of the packages; there is no guide at all to the value. In other instances there is great indisposition to let the true value be known. Supposing, as is constantly the case, wine to be brought from Hamburg in casks, branded with the mark of the best Spanish vintages, it is very improbable that, however vile the stuff may be, it will be valued at less than the price of good sherry. The greatest vigilance, therefore, is necessary to guard against the most erroneous values, but the department can only interfere in extreme cases, for it is unable to discover or question any but very extravagant departures from the average. The law has given it the power of calling for invoices or other proof, which is frequently done, and fines are often inflicted for wilful or careless departures from the truth. The only real security, however, is in exciting an interest amongst those who have to declare the value. When once it is understood that these and other particulars are of real importance, there is, in importers generally, too much good feeling and desire to do what is right, to permit of other than the best information it is in their power to give being placed at the disposal of the authorities. There seems, however, no way of providing for the very numerous cases in which the consignee is ignorant of the value, or the agent who puts in the entry is without instructions to guide him. At present, the change of system produces, in many articles of import, an apparently great divergence between the values of this and former years. Had the old plan, as was done in 1854, been maintained for one or two years, in conjunction with the new, it would have served as a basis of comparison, and have shown whether the present method is of sufficient accuracy to compensate for the labour and cost its adoption entails.

In the earlier stages of the system established on the formation of the Inspector-General's office, the value was taken from fixed official rates, founded on the ascertained prices which all known articles bore in the year 1694; with the addition of such new articles as afterwards sprung up, at the prices they each bore in the first year of their introduction. These values remained unaltered, and were used down to 1870, for the computation of the "official value" now altogether abandoned. It was supposed that by a continuous computation of the value at the same rate year after year, a comparative statement would be arrived at of the true progress of trade; and that by applying the same price on all occasions, the total value would furnish a measure of quantity. This was strictly true as regarded the articles singly, and would also be true of them collectively, so long as the relative quantities of each bore the same proportion to that of others and to the whole. Thus France sends us both wheat and wine; if in any one year the quantities were equal, but in another year the quantity of the one be reduced, and that of the other increased, each by one half, the "official value" of the whole, to be a measure of quantity, ought to be the same; but inasmuch as the rate of the two articles would differ, the calculated result would differ also.

c

Again, this country is a large importer of agricultural produce and raw material, many articles of which, from increased
demand and diminished supplies, have greatly risen in
value; and is a large exporter of manufactured goods,
which, from improvements in machinery and extended employment of capital, have fallen in the cost of production.
Last year we imported, principally from France, 3,351,106
great hundred of eggs, valued at £1,265,484, and exported
to France 87,969,530 yards of cotton, at a value of
£1,688,094, leaving us creditors of that country, so far as
these two articles are concerned, for nearly half a million of
money. The actual value of the eggs was about 6s. per
great hundred, and of cotton 4½d. per yard, but the "official"
rates were 9d. and 1s. 6d. respectively. Calculating the
values at these, the eggs would be worth but £125,666, and
the cottons £6,597,700, showing a balance in our favour of
nearly six and a half millions, instead of only a half million.
This is doubtless an extreme case, but some such process of
change has been going on in most of the articles and
countries with which we have trading relations. It is
clear, therefore, that any reliance upon the "official values"
could only lead to mistaken opinions and fallacious results.
It was considerations of this kind that led to the substitution of a declared value for exports in 1798, and a computed value for imports in 1854, this latter being again
changed last year to a declared value like that given for the
exports.

III.—*Exports.*

An analogous process to that thus described for the imports is pursued with the exports of British produce and
manufacture. The countries are kept under the same headings, and a similar list enumerates 211 articles of which a
separate account is kept, in lieu of 446 which the former one
contained, whilst an appendix describes the proper places to
which 120 others are to be carried. The law imposes on every

shipper the duty of putting in a "specification" for each, shipment, stating the vessel and country to which she is proceeding, and the number of packages, with their contents in quantity and value. This document must be filed within six days after the sailing of the vessel, by which time also her master or owner is bound to deliver a manifest setting forth the whole contents of her outward cargo. The specification and the manifest being compared together, show that every article has been properly entered, and the same provisions which secure a correct statement of the various particulars on importation also rule with exporters. These have for many years past furnished all the information procured respecting British goods, and with much greater assurance that the weight and value can be correctly given than in the case of imports; since these particulars must in all cases be within the knowledge of those by whom the goods are shipped. It is feared, however, that with regard to both, there is less attention paid than there ought to be to full and accurate information being given; and if it seems that in these observations too much space has been given to these small matters, it has been from the conviction that it cannot be too widely known how utterly impossible it is for the department to prepare or furnish correct accounts, if the materials put into its hands for that purpose are not substantially accurate. There has been too much disposition to consider the passing of Customs entries as a mere formality, imposing an impediment to the prompt transaction of commercial business, a disagreeable duty to be got through or slurred over with the greatest ease and rapidity. In many cases, too, there is reason to think that there is an indisposition to make known the full particulars, from a fear that in so doing the nature of operations which it is not desirable to divulge may thereby become known to others who are probably rivals in trade. It is to be hoped, however, that a more enlightened spirit will prevail, and that in proportion as the benefits of full information on all points of trade become felt, greater care will be exercised by all with whom it rests to make the trade accounts as perfect as possible. If what has been here said on the subject have any effect in helping on so desirable a result, the time and attention given to it will not have been in vain.

[In republishing these observations as they were written, it is necessary to express regret that they should have been unfortunately open to the construction that they were intended to throw discredit upon the method adopted, whereas the object held in view in thus pointing out the dangers which existed, and the difficulties which might arise, was to incite those by whom the original entries were prepared to greater diligence in ascertaining and furnishing the correct particulars. That much trouble did arise from this source is well known to all who transact this business; also that, even after years of experience and exercise of the greatest care, there is room for much improvement in this respect on the part of those who appraise and declare the values of their goods.]

IV.—*Nature of Records and Publications.*

If the foregoing remarks have, as it is hoped, fully explained the sources from which statistical information is obtained, they will also have shown the nature of the records kept in the Statistical Department. Receiving the bills each day, they are at once entered into appropriate registers, which show in detail the trade carried on, both inwards and outwards, at each port in the United Kingdom; these are ranged under Articles and Countries, and specify in each case the quantity in its appropriate denomination, and the value as declared by the parties passing the several entries. By the addition together of the several items and tabulating the totals in proper forms, every description of information within the range supplied by the first entries can be obtained at pleasure. Their stated use is to supply the periodical returns to be laid before Parliament, or published in the " Gazette " for public information, but they are also drawn upon to no small extent for special accounts moved for by members of Parliament, and supplied to the Government, or, by its direction, to various individuals or public bodies making application for them. Records of this nature, more or less fully compiled, are in existence from the year 1696, and every successive year adds to the sum of the knowledge we possess of the history and progress of our national industry and commerce.

The magnitude of this work will appear from the number of documents which have to be dealt with. Those for goods paying duty on arrival or going into the warehouse, many of which contain more than one article, exceed 120,000 annually; those for free goods, 230,000; for delivery from the warehouses on payment of duty, 1,300,000: for the exports there are close on 100,000 for dutiable articles, many of them containing six to ten items, and for British goods more than 500,000, averaging five or six articles in each. These have to be distributed over the 135 ports in the United Kingdom, subdivided into the 600 articles contained in the two lists, and the 112 countries.

The regular publications for which the department is responsible are, 1st, a weekly account of corn, inserted in each Tuesday's "London Gazette," containing a statement of all that has been imported or exported up to the preceding Saturday; 2nd, the Monthly returns of trade printed for the House of Commons, and issued on the 7th of each month, containing condensed accounts of the principal articles of imports and exports during the preceding month, and a cumulative account for so many months as have elapsed in the same year, compared with similar periods in two preceding years; 3rd, Quarterly accounts of the value of merchandise imported, and the British produce and manufactures exported to each foreign country and British possession in the past quarter, and six, nine, or twelve months in each of the three years; and, 4th, an Annual Statement of a much more elaborate character, which makes its appearance in the shape of a large quarto volume, after the preceding accounts have been subject to revision and correction.

A variety of tables are also published in the " Statistical Abstract for Fifteen Years," issued annually by the Board of Trade; and much valuable information is given in the Annual Report presented by the Commissioners of Customs.

In using these accounts, it is needful to bear in mind that, for reasons to be presently explained, those for the weekly, monthly, and quarterly periods are all prepared from the importers' entries, and therefore liable to correction; but that the Annual Statement has bestowed upon it all the care which it is possible to give, and is, before publication, made as correct in all particulars as it is in the power of the office to make it.

V.—*Alterations in System.*

In the system on which these accounts are prepared, as well as in the form in which they are issued, very great alterations took place at the beginning of last year. Numerous complaints having been made both in Parliament and the public prints, that they were delayed so long as to be practically useless, and that they seldom agreed with the statements put forth by other parties, a Treasury committee was appointed, by whom the whole subject was thoroughly investigated, and on whose recommendation the changes took place. The delay in the production of the monthly account was found to arise from an endeavour to compile it from the landing accounts, which often take six weeks or two months in completion ; and the differences between the official and private statements, from the fact that all these landing accounts could not be got in for the proper month, and, therefore, some of them had to stand over till the following one. In reality, the official account was not, nor did it pretend to be, an accurate one for the specific month, but only so far as the examination of the goods had been completed in time for them to be included. The assumption that

so much as was left out at one time would be compensated
by an equal quantity on the next occasion, proved utterly
fallacious, as was thus represented to the committee:—" If
.this information [the landing officer's account] could in all
cases be obtained prior to the preparation of the account, it
would be, in every respect, the most satisfactory source from
whence it could be supplied, but weeks and months often
elapse before it is received. In one bundle of bills acciden-
tally taken for inspection, all of which were going into the
October account, only eight properly belonged to that
month, whilst there were eight, eight, and ten, belonging to
June, July, and September respectively. It thus happens
that the monthly account, as published about the 25th of the
succeeding month, contains only a portion of the month's
imports, with a large remanet from the preceding month,
and smaller quantities of two, three, and four months further
back. The weekly account of corn is probably two or three
weeks out of date. It is true the average may be correct,
but so great are the fluctuations in the arrivals, that, as at
present given, the accounts afford no sort of reliable information for the specific period they profess to represent. So
serious is the divergence from the truth, in the article of tea
for instance, that the account would often be many millions
of pounds out, but that a plan has recently been adopted of
adding an estimate of the quantity arrived but not weighed,
thus altogether departing from the principle of using only
such landing accounts as are made up. In tobacco, wine,
brandy, and sugar, it is known that the deficiencies must be
quite as large, but no means exist of obtaining estimates."
" Would it not be well that these statistics should be divided
into two classes ? The one possessed of transitory interest,
as the guide for present commercial and financial purposes,
the other of lasting value as the permanent record of the
national trade and progress. For the one (embracing weekly
and monthly accounts), early publication is essential, whilst
only a proximate accuracy and fulness is required. For the
other, that they should be strictly correct and full in detail,

whilst sufficient time may be taken in their preparation to ensure these important requisites. What is wanted in the first case, is not a statement of such goods as are actually landed and accounted for, but of such as are really in the country, available for consumption, the subject of bargain and sale, and capable of influencing calculations as to future operations. This information the mercantile world have at present no means of obtaining, except from the circulars of the brokers or others engaged in particular branches of trade, which are only to be relied upon to the extent of the knowledge within reach of their several compilers. To give effect to this view it is proposed that in the first instance the importer's account of weights, &c., should be taken at once instead of waiting for the landing officer's return. That from these the records in the registers should be made, reserving an additional column or spare line in which to insert the true quantity when ascertained. These entries would be made from day to day, and at the close of the month adopted for the transitory account. So soon as accurate information can be obtained, a correct total should be made for the annual and permanent one. In this mode the one might be ready in three to five days after the month ends, instead of the 20th or 25th as at present; and for the other we should obtain that which now we *never get*, a really true record of the imports of each respective month." These representations and suggestions met with approval, and have been carried out since 1st January, 1871. How far the anticipation of approximate accuracy for the prompt account, and of real results for the permanent one, have been realized, will appear from the following table of the weights as given by the importers' entries, and the actual quantities of the principal dutiable goods imported within the year.

	Importers' Entries.	Actual Quantities.	Percentage of Error.
Cocoa............	17,096,729	17,132,236	− 0·21
Coffee............	189,977,648	191,907,645	− 1·01
Currants.........	1,040,619	1,024,946	+ 1·53
Spirits...........	13,984,412	14,607,514	− 4·27
Sugar	11,086,362	11,232,284	− 1·30
Tea..............	171,094,275	169,776,576	+ 0·77
Tobacco..........	72,231,263	76,592,930	− 5·70
Wine.............	16,605,774	16,821,645	− 1·30
All dutiable articles together.	492,431,233	499,905,922	− 1·50

These articles are selected because, for revenue purposes, they are actually weighed or measured; and there can be no reason for supposing that in those which are not so tested, the importers' entries need be less correct. This change is the basis of the present system, rendering it possible to produce the monthly account sufficiently early to be of material use, and making it a substantially accurate statement of the transactions of the period which it professes to represent.

The other great feature in the altered accounts, which has before been entered upon so fully, is that of substituting a declared for a computed value. There are no means of testing the results of this in the same manner as there are with the weights, and as yet (1872) it has not been in operation long enough to affirm with certainty that it may not secure as correct returns as were formerly obtained, although the tendency of many observations is to point in a contrary direction.

Allusion has before been made to the fusion of the two statistical offices into the one present department, and the direct publication of the returns which emanate from it as the means whereby much economy of time and uniformity in practice has been promoted. In addition to this, the practice has been introduced of prolonging the official labours for the three or four first days of the month, to a late hour in the evening, according to a plan for expediting the preparation of the accounts proposed in 1857, but only now carried out. Without this it would be impossible to collect together the innumerable items, the totals of which fill two columns in every one of the fifty or sixty pages which make up the monthly issue ; and thus secure its early production, without at all interfering with the current work.

Although not exactly appertaining to the object with which this paper has been written, it may be satisfactory shortly to state that these several alterations and improvements have been conjoined with a considerable reduction of the amount formerly expended in the production of statistics. It is very difficult to estimate how much of the charges for the Customs establishment must be set down to the collection of the revenue, or how much to the multifarious duties, unconnected with the receipt of money, which it has to perform ; but an examination of the Estimates for last year, as well as this, in comparison with those for 1870, will show a saving in the Statistical offices alone of some £18,000 per annum, being from a-third to one-half of the previous annual expenditure.

VI.—*Bill of Entry.*

Notwithstanding the length to which this paper has extended, the subject would be left incomplete were no mention made of another branch of statistics relating to trade, which, though springing from an unofficial source, are often confounded with those of official origin, namely, the publications of the Bill of Entry in London, and many of the larger ports. These comprise daily lists of ships arriving and sailing, with accounts of their cargoes and other particulars of considerable interest to the trading community, as is evidenced by the large sale of these printed lists. In addition to these, manuscript accounts are rendered on special application. It is not perhaps so generally known as it might be, that for a moderate charge any kind of information that can be gleaned from the Customs records is supplied by this office, and, though not possessing any official authority, it may be relied on as obtained from official sources. The office from which these are issued, though having a local habitation in the Custom House at London, and more or less intimately connected with those at other ports, is not at all under the authority of the Customs Department; it is a singular remnant of the old times, when peculiar privileges were conferred on favoured individuals for their pecuniary advantage. One of these acquired, in the year 1660, by letters patent, the exclusive right of access to all official documents connected with the Customs reports and entries, and of obtaining and publishing any portion of the information they contain. This patent has some years yet to run, having been renewed upon satisfactory evidence having been adduced that the work it performs is of public utility, and such as no other machinery is in existence to carry on. It has been proposed for the Government to take over the duties of this office, and to merge them in those of the Statistical Department; but it is at least questionable whether the kind of business it transacts is one which could be managed with the same profit as by private parties, or whether much of it could be efficiently regulated under the system of management necessary for a public office. It is certainly not that which ought to be performed at the public cost, but should, as it is, be paid for by those for whom it is done. An additional reason for maintaining it on the present footing is to be found in the circumstance that the patent is held by the trustees of the Customs' Benevolent Fund, which is conducted on the principles of a life assurance society for the benefit of the widows and children of Customs officers. All the profits acquired by the Bill of Entry business go in aid of the premiums paid on life assurance and annuity policies taken up exclusively by members of the Customs Department, of whom it cannot be said that they are an overpaid portion of the public service. [Since this paragraph was written the patent has expired, but, pending permanent arrangements, those already in existence remain in operation.]

VII.—*Conclusion.*

In gathering up the substance of the foregoing some-what discursive statement, it may be repeated,—

That the object of our system of trade statistics is to keep an accurate record of the trade carried on by each port in the United Kingdom, in every article of import and export; distinguishing that with each foreign country or British possession; and showing the quantity and value of the several goods. To collect their several items into weekly, monthly, quarterly, and yearly totals, tabulated in conve-nient forms; and to publish these at the respective periods.

That the Board of Trade prescribes the nature and extent of the returns so given, which, under the authority and direction of the Treasury and Board of Customs, are prepared and published. That these returns are condensed and sim-plified in the number of countries or divisions of countries shown, and in the number of articles specified; it being de-sired to show distinctly each article of importance by itself, and those not sufficiently important in groups or classes.

That this preparation and publication devolves upon the Statistical Department, which receives, with some few ex-ceptions, daily from every port in the United Kingdom, in original when they can be spared for the purpose, or other-wise in duplicate, the several documents by which the owners of the goods enter and clear them; and from these compiles the records and publishes the returns.

That the several importers and exporters are required, under penalty imposed by Act of Parliament, to supply all the information required in the several particulars of country, goods, quantity, and value.

That the Statistical Department possesses checks for the countries, and, to some extent, the goods, in the masters' reports of cargo; upon the quantities or the weights, &c., so far as dutiable goods are concerned, and in a cursory inspection over goods free of duty, taken and exercised by the Customs officers, upon whom the safety of the revenue rests. But that for the value, it has no means of ascertaining whether it is correct or not, excepting by a demand for the invoices or other proof, whenever a wide departure from the usual average justifies a call for these documents ; and that unless the information furnished as to value be in all, or nearly all, cases so much more precise than could be obtained by any estimate or calculation, all the labour of this method will be entirely lost.

That through the alterations recently made in the Statistical offices by the union of the two into one, by the simplification of the particulars given and distinctions preserved, by the extension at certain seasons of the hours of attendance for the various employés, and by the direct action of the department, the monthly account has been diminished in bulk, and is now issued on the 7th instead of the 25th of each month, containing all the transactions of the month to which it relates; and that the publication of the Annual Statement can be much expedited.

That by these alterations the charge upon the estimates for statistical work is reduced to between two-thirds and one-half of what it formerly was.

From all that has been said, it will be apparent that, with honesty and accuracy on the part of those who provide the information, and fidelity and industry on the part of the Statistical Department, the means exist of supplying full, trustworthy, and complete intelligence of the country's progress in its commercial intercourse with the whole world.

In conclusion, allow me to repeat, that in thus bringing these several points to your notice, my object has been two-fold ; to explain and assist the use of the several statistical publications which are prepared at the expense of the country, and to bring all the influence which it is possible to obtain, to bear upon the accuracy and fulness of the information on which they are founded. If, in so doing, I have failed to collect or impart the statistical facts or results which might have been expected from this paper, the Society may command my services to repair the omission in any way it sees fit to prescribe.   If, in entering upon so many details, I may be thought to have attached undue value to matters of minor importance, I trust they will not therefore be deemed to be of but little moment. And if, in dealing with the subject, I have prolonged these observations to a wearisome length, I trust you will set it down to the enthusiasm of one who has spent the best part of an official life, now long past its meridian, in constant efforts to increase the value, lessen the cost, and improve the character of the various records and publications which make up the sum of our trade statistics.

II.

The Progress of our Foreign Trade, Imports and Exports, during Twenty Years, 1854-74.[1]

THERE are two purposes for which statisticians exist; two objects to be kept steadily in view by every collector of statistical information. The first is that of carefully gathering together facts and figures on every subject " calculated to illustrate the position and prospects of society," and so storing them up as to be accessible to all who may need the information they afford. The second, that of from time to time selecting from the stores so accumulated such particulars as should command attention, whether from their intrinsic importance or their relation to the subjects occupying the thoughts of those who may not have time or opportunity for the task of personal research—thus giving a present value to past labour, and in effect materially influencing the course of human thought and action in all that relates to the property of the nation or the welfare of its members. It is the latter of these purposes which is attempted to be served by the present paper.

There can be little question as to the importance of the subject, or the interest which is taken in it, by those who are inhabitants of a country so essentially dependent for its prosperity upon the continued progress of the trade and manufactures to which it owes its present greatness; and a belief that some light may be thrown upon our present condition

[1] Read before the Statistical Society, 18th May, 1875. Vol. xxxviii.

and our future advancement, by a careful consideration of the history of the past, must be the excuse, if such be needed, for this endeavour to place its more prominent features before the Fellows of this Society.

In thus tracing back for some years the course which our foreign and colonial commerce has taken, recourse has been had to the successive volumes of the " Annual Statement of Trade and Navigation" issued by the Statistical Department of the Board of Trade, from 1833 to 1870, and since then by the Statistical Department of the Customs. The whole of the figures used are taken from these publications, and therefore rest upon official authority, although for their collection into the tables appended to this paper and the calculations or conclusions founded upon them, the writer is individually responsible. The period of twenty years has been chosen not alone as a convenient one for which to exhibit the comparative results of our trading operations, but likewise from the circumstance that in 1854 a change took place in the method by which the import values and those for the exports of foreign goods were ascertained, which renders any accurate comparison with former years quite impossible. Prior to that year the values given were "official;" since that time " real;" "computed " up to and including 1870, and then " declared." By " official " is meant a calculation from the quantities "according to rates of value fixed so long back as 1694." [1] By "computed real" is to be understood the average market value, " including all the charges of freight and landing, but exclusive of duties." [2] The " declared " values should represent "the actual value of the goods at the time of importation," [3] derived from a declaration required from the importers on the first entries passed by them for their goods. The " computed" and " declared " values should in the aggregate be alike, and may therefore be fairly compared with each other. Not so, however, with the " official," as was shown by a comparison of the two for

[1] " Preface to Annual Statement," 1854.   [2] Ibid.
[3] "Monthly Account of Trade and Navigation," July, 1871.

the year 1854, in which they were prepared upon both
systems, when—

£

The old official value of imports amounted to[1]... 124,338,478
New computed real value........................... 152,591,813

Showing an excess of real value of 22¼ per cent.= 28,253.335

At the same time the exports of foreign and colonial produce were—

£

Old official value 29,821,656
New real value.. 18,648.978

The old value being in excess 38 per cent.= 11,172.678

Two or three instances, taken from the same source, will
still further illustrate the fallacy of this system, and show the
impossibility of comparing the results attained under it with
those under the present plan :—

1854.	New Real Value.	Old Official Value.
	£	£
Wood	11,064.094	1,812,690
Corn	21,760.283	10,138.778
Cotton, raw..................	20,175,395	28,656,756
Tea	5,540,735	8,579,204

These examples are worthy of note, because it so often
happens that ignorance of the change of system leads to the
quotation of figures for values prior to 1854, as if they were
of equal worth to those from that date forward.   The same
difficulty does not exist with regard to the export of British
goods, the declared value for them having been adopted as
far back as 1798.

Being thus restricted in the date to which we can go back
for import values, the series commences with 1854.   Another
year would have been more satisfactory, since the Russian

[1] " Annual Statement for 1854."

War, which then broke out, may be deemed to have affected the trade of that and the following year; but not to so great an extent, however, as might be supposed, as will appear from the *official* values for it, and the few preceding years wherein there is much the same sequence, as is manifested by the real values of Table I. for succeeding years.

	Imports.	British Exports.
	£	£
1849	105,884.263	63,596,025
'50	100,469,067	71,367,885
'51	110,484,997	74,448,722
'52	109,331,158	78,076,854
'53	123,099,313	98,933.781
'54	124,338,478	97.184,726

There are two aspects in which the commerce of the kingdom may be viewed : the one embracing all goods imported and exported, including those brought to it for a market and again carried abroad; the other excluding these and showing only the foreign and colonial goods retained, and the British goods exported. The first may be deemed the merchant's view, since to him it matters not whether the goods he sells are for home or foreign use, of home or foreign production. The latter, however, is the more important view to the political economist, since the general condition of the country is evidenced and influenced by its ability on the one hand to pay for the goods it consumes, and, on the other, by its power to produce and sell the articles on which the employment of so large a portion of its population depends.

The several tables [1] have been drawn out with the design of clearly showing :—

---

[1] Several of the tables to which reference is made have not been inserted; and the same omission has been followed in those appertaining to subsequent papers. Their bulk would have unduly swelled the volume, and possibly have given it a forbidding appearance. The

1st. The gradual yearly progress of our commerce under the three heads of original imports, re-exports, and retentions for home consumption or manufacture, with the percentage of increase or decrease upon its immediate predecessor in each year, and upon 1854, the first year of the series. Also, in like manner, the total exports, divided into those of foreign or colonial origin, and those of home produce or manufacture; but it must be borne in mind that the exports of foreign and colonial articles thus shown are only those which leave our hands in an unaltered condition, for if subject to any manufacturing process or change of character, they become classified as of British manufacture, and are included as such in the columns devoted to that class.

2nd. The proportion of trade carried on both inwards and outwards with the principal countries of whom we are customers, and to whose markets we send our productions. These figures, on account of the space which would be occupied by a statement of each year's traffic, are only shown for every fifth year, and the percentage of increase as before upon the figures of 1854. A very imperfect idea, however, will be given of the extent to which we trade with many countries, from the indirect routes by which much of the transport is effected, and the varying channels through which this takes place. With some countries there is little but direct trade. Russia, for instance, neither receives nor sends us much but in vessels from or to her own ports and ours; but Germany obtains a large portion of her supplies—and forwards hers to us—through the ports of Holland, and even by railway through France. The goods which in ordinary seasons are shipped from Hamburg, when that port is closed by the ice come to us viâ Altona, and then get credited to Denmark. A line of steamers in connection with the French steamers to the East, periodically takes large

special points of interest are in general incorporated with the text, or are contained in other papers, and references are given to the original volumes in which they may be found by those who desire a more intimate acquaintance with their details.

cargoes to Marseilles, for transmission to China, Hong Kong, Japan, and other places; and on their return voyages they bring back cargoes from those countries transhipped at the French port. Before the Suez Canal was made, the ships of the Peninsular and Oriental Company which now go through the canal cleared out in this country for Egypt, to which country the goods they carried were deemed to be exported; and in like manner goods brought through the Red Sea and overland to Alexandria, were treated as imports from that place. The same thing happens in the winter season with goods to and from Canada *viâ* Portland in the United States. This evil is, as stated in the "Monthly Return" for January of the present year, in process of correction, and so far as the ultimate destination is known, the exports are now credited to the countries to which they properly belong. Too much reliance must not, therefore, be placed on the relative extent of our trade with the various countries specified in the tables, since for this reason there is in many cases much intermingling of one with the other. Neither is it always right to judge of the growth or decline from year to year of the trade with any particular country, since with the starting of new lines of communication material changes in this respect may and do arise.

3rd. The principal articles of which our imports and exports consist are separated for each fifth year in the same manner as the countries are.

In all these tables we are dealing with the values—necessarily so for the first and second purposes—since the totals can only be obtained by reducing the denominations of weight, measure, &c., in which the goods are taken to account to the common measure of value in pounds sterling; and this being done for the grand total as well as for the amounts to and from the different countries, it is well to show the different articles in the same form. These sums, however, fail fully to show the variations from year to year, because, being founded upon the market prices existing at the time, which are constantly shifting, it is necessary to take such fluctuations into consideration in arriving at a correct judgment as to the real increase or decrease which is taking place. To assist in arriving at right conclusions on this point, there have been added tables, showing the quantities of some of the articles of greatest magnitude, with the percentage of increase for last year over that of the year with which we commence. A comparison of the rates of increase in the value and the quantity of each article will show whether the additional value is due to greater bulk or to higher price.

It should be noticed that one portion of the goods brought to and taken from this country is not included in any of the tables, namely, those which are merely sent hither to find a vessel going to the place for which they are destined, and are transhipped from one ship to another without being landed here. A somewhat rough account is taken of their value (and in many cases the quantities of the articles). This is of some importance, because thus passing into and out of our waters they furnish employment for our ships and men, and its increase is an element of additional mercantile or maritime prosperity.

The whole value of these transhipments during the past twenty years is as follows:[1] —

[In million £'s to two decimals.]

	£		£
1854	5·05	1865	6·47
'55	3·58	'66	7·72
'56	4·58	'67	6·66
'57	4·51	'68	7·28
'58	4·49	'69	8·12
'59	6·65	'70	10·94
'60	5·14	'71	11·36
'61	4·42	'72	13·90
'62	4·71	'73	13·76
'63	5·33	'74	11·42
'64	5·99		

[1] It would have disturbed the whole course of the argument to have carried on the several figures to last year, when trade had again become depressed. The figures therefore for the five years which have

Before speaking of the general results, it may be expedient to take the several tables in which these are shown, and point out the nature and peculiarities of each, bearing in mind that the great object of this paper is to draw attention to the disparity between the transactions in the first and the last years of the series selected.

In Table 1. we find that a total import, valued in 1854 at £152,300,000, had grown by 1874 to one of £370,000,000, an increase of 143 per cent., or at the rate of rather more than 7 per cent. per annum; not, indeed, by regular advances, for there are many fluctuations in the rate of progress, the years of greatest increase being 1856, 1860, 1863-64, 1866, 1871, and 1872, those of retrogression being 1855, 1858, 1865, 1867, and 1874. The second column of the table shows the extent to which the goods thus imported were again taken away to other countries, the whole importations during the twenty-one years amounting to 5,340 millions of pounds sterling, and the re-exportations to 860 millions, or about one-sixth part. The increase in this branch of trade has been proportionally greater than that of the imports, namely, 209 per cent., or at the rate of 10½ per cent. per annum, and is somewhat more equally distributed; the years in which it has receded being 1858, 1866-67, 1869-70, 1872-73. In 1861 and 1862 there were great steps upwards, and again in 1871, in which the highest point was attained, namely, an advance on its predecessor of 36 and on 1854 of 225 per cent., since when there has been a continuous fall. Deducting the re-exports from the original imports, we should arrive at the value of the goods retained in the country. And here the increase is not so

elapsed since this paper was written, are in this and subsequent places inserted for reference, in a foot-note only.

	£
1875	12·14
'76	10·82
'77	12·18
'78	11·16
'79	10·98

great as that of the first receipts, being but 134 per cent. This gives an annual rate of 6⅞ per cent., fluctuating from an increase in 1856 of 21·7 to a decrease in 1858 of 13·6 per cent. on the years immediately preceding. Those in which the greatest rise took place were 1856, 1860, 1864, 1866, and 1872; those of falling off 1855, 1858, 1865, 1867, and 1874.

Table II. exhibits similar statements for the exports. The second column, that which shows the foreign and colonial re-exports, being necessarily identical with the same column in Table I. The total increase here has been from 116 millions in 1854 to 297 in 1874, or 156 per cent., giving an average rate of nearly 8 per cent.—a more regular one than in the imports—the greatest range being from an increase in 1863 of 18·5 to a decrease in 1867 of 5·5 per cent. The years of greatest increase were 1856, 1859, 1863-64, 1866, and 1871-72, those of decrease 1858, 1861, 1867, and 1873-74. The whole exports of the twenty-one years amounted to £4,300,000,000, of which 860, or about one-fifth, were re-exportations, leaving £3,400,000,000 as British produce or manufacture. Of these latter the growth has been from £97,000,000 in 1854 to £240,000,000 in 1874, or an average rate of 7⅛ per cent. increase, the irregularities being as great as in the other cases, namely, from a decrease in 1861 from its predecessor of 7·9 to an increase in 1863 of 18·2 per cent., the years of largest growth being 1856, 1859, 1863-64, 1866, 1871-2; those of recedence 1855, 1858, 1861-2, 1867-68, and 1874.

In Table III.[1] the total value of the imports for every fifth year is divided into that from our Colonial possessions, and from Foreign countries; and again, between the principal possessions and countries, with the object of showing from whence we draw our supplies, and the variations in our relations with each. To have done this for every year would have taken up too much space, therefore only the percent-

[1] For Tables III. to IX., see "Journal of Statistical Society." June, 1875.

age of increase in 1874 upon 1854 has been drawn out in the
last column. From this table it will appear that the proportion of receipts from our own possessions at present is
between one-third and one-fourth of the whole ; and that of
these India is by far the most liberal contributor to our wants,
four-ninths of our colonial supplies being drawn from thence.
Australia stands next, with rather more than two-ninths,
bidding fair by the rapidity of its increase to distance its
elder sister ; the one having in the twenty years advanced
from £4,300,000 to £18,500,000, or 330 per cent. ; the
other from £13,000,000 to £37,500,000, or 189 per cent.
Mauritius and South Africa have advanced by 125 per
cent., and our North American possessions by half as much,
whilst the West Indies remain almost stationary, the increase
being but 4 per cent. Of foreign countries by far the
greatest sender, at this time, is the United States, from
whom we last year drew to the value of £74,000,000 out
of £289,000,000, or more than one-fourth of the whole.
Next to the States comes France with £47,000,000 or one-
sixth, then Russia with £21,000,000, and Germany with
£20,000,000. It must be observed, however, that for the
reason before alluded to these figures do not altogether
accurately represent the relative trade of the different countries—France being credited with the goods from the East
which pass through her ports in transit ; the United States
with some which come from Canada ; Holland and Belgium
probably with that of Germany. The bulk of that from
Egypt is brought from the East, and the imports which used
to be landed on one side of the Isthmus and re-shipped on
the other now pass in increasing quantities through the Suez
Canal.

Table IV. serves the same purpose for the exports from
the United Kingdom, and here we find a not very different
proportion in the relative trade to British and foreign
places, from that which we observed in the imports, a total
of £297,000,000, giving £77,000,000 to our colonies.
The same countries, too, seem to be our largest purchasers,

though not in the same relative degree. India takes
£29,000,000 out of the £77,000,000, and Australia
£21,000,000; but the latter does not advance with anything like the same rapidity as the former, the respective
increases in 1874 over 1854 being 56 and 173 per cent. Of
the foreign countries, the United States is again one of the
largest dealers, £32,000,000; but Germany outstrips her
by more than £2,000,000, standing at the head of all with
£34,500,000. France comes next with £29,000,000, and
Holland with £23,000,000; all these being portions of the
£220,000,000 sent to foreign countries in 1874. The
total growth since 1854 has been from £116,000,000 to
£297,000,000, or 156 per cent.; British possessions have
risen from £36,000,000 to £77,000,000, and foreign
countries from £79,000,000 to £220,000,000, or 113 and
177 per cent. respectively. The same remark as to the effect
of the transit trade applies to these figures as it did to those
of the import.

Table V. deals with the values of the principal articles
for the same years for which the previous table did with the
several countries, and in the same manner shows the increase in the last year over the first. An attempt has been
made to divide the articles into classes, so as to show the
different rates of increase; but this is somewhat imperfectly
done, from the difficulty of strictly defining to which class
certain goods properly belong.[1] First in order stand those
which undeniably belong to articles of food, beginning with
grain and farinaceous substances, going on to living animals,
next to animal products, then to vegetable substances for
food and drink, supplemented by the addition of alcoholic
liquids and tobacco. It is here that the greatest increase
has taken place, for whilst that of the whole imports has
been but 143, this has been 165, or including spirits, wine,
and tobacco, 151 per cent.; nor does this fully represent
the growth in our consumption; for if wheat, which appears

---

[1] Food tables will be found in Papers IV. and V., " On Foreign Food
Supplies."

to have been exceptionally large in 1854, be left out, the other articles of food will show an excess of fully 200 per cent., or a treble quantity in twenty years. In some the additional receipts are really enormous: thus potatoes are multiplied sixty-fold, eggs eleven, bacon and hams seven, butter and cheese four and five-fold. Tea has more than doubled, and in most of these by far the greatest gain has taken place in the last quinquennial period. Live animals are four times greater than in 1854, but do not keep pace with other articles, for there has been a slight falling off since 1869. Spirits show an actual decline of 6 per cent., being the only article in this class which is less than in 1854; but wine has increased 90 and tobacco 187 per cent.

Next in order are placed the raw materials, which form the staple of our textile fabrics, and, by way of contrast, the manufactures from these materials, which are imported in their finished state; the former have increased 130, the latter 250 per cent. The most remarkable growth in the raw material is in jute, an article which may be said to have sprung into existence as one of import at the time of the Russian war, and during the cotton famine to have taken such a hold on our markets as to have increased 540 per cent. On the other hand, silk has during the same period declined 14 per cent. in the raw, but increased 298 per cent. in the manufactured article. Wool likewise has increased, both raw and manufactured, and in each at almost exactly the same rate—248 and 243 per cent. There is this difference, however, that the amount of the raw products is considerable, namely, in 1874, £90,000,000, but in the manufactured only £15,000,000, the one being nearly a fourth, the other only a twenty-fifth part of our total imports. In neither does there seem to be any great growth going on, since the imports of both in 1869 were very nearly the same as those of 1874.

The metals, which form a not inconsiderable item of import, viz., £11,000,000 last year, have increased 211 per cent.; lead standing first and iron next. In wood there

appears to have been but little alteration in the first four
periods, whilst in 1874 it is nearly double that of 1869, the
whole increase upon 1854 being 84 per cent. A few other
miscellaneous articles are included, in which hides show a
growth of 259, and oils a decrease of 4 per cent.

Although numerically these specified articles do not form
a large proportion of our total imports, in value they embrace nearly five-sixths; and may therefore be taken as a
fair evidence of the general progress. It is probable that
in some points the comparisons may not be strictly accurate,
owing to minor alterations in the classification of different
descriptions of the same goods, by which the totals given
may not always include the same subdivisions. This remark
applies more to the arrangement under quantities, which will
be found in Tables VIII., IX., and X.

In Table VI. the same particulars are given for some of
the articles of which the exports form an important consideration. By deducting the values here given from those of
the preceding table we may arrive at the amount retained
in the country, and shall find that in some articles this is
but a small proportion of the quantity brought here for a
market in 1874. As examples of this, coffee was imported
to the value of rather more than £7,000,000, of which
£5,000,000 were again taken away; rice brought in is
valued at £3,600,000, and taken away to the extent of
£2,500,000; tea came in £11,500,000 and went out
£2,500,000, a much smaller proportion. On the other hand,
of nearly £31,000,000 worth of wheat we parted with
barely £600,000; of sugar, to £20,000,000, we parted with
but £700,000; and of cotton, out of £51,000,000 worth,
less than £7,000,000 left us.

Table VII. is the counterpart of Table V., but dealing with
the exports of British produce and manufacture. The
articles enumerated are fewer than those of the imports were,
although they represent about the same proportion, viz., for
1874 five-sixths, or £203,000,000, out of £240,000,000,
quite sufficient to indicate the general course which the

trade has taken.   Of these cotton manufactures and yarn
together show for £74,000,000, or about three-eighths of
the whole.   The increase on these has been to the extent of
134 per cent.   Iron and steel come next with £31,000,000,
an increase of 146 per cent., and then woollen manufactures
and yarn £28,000,000 ; these three branches of manufacture alone furnishing more than half of all our exports, and
manifesting an increase of 142 per cent.   Coals afford
£12,000,000, linen manufactures £11,000,000, and silk
£3,000,000 towards the total exports of 1874—an increase
on 1854 of 460, 113, and 85 per cent. respectively.   A remarkable instance of the varied character of our trade is
shown in what might have been thought a trivial article of
manufacture, namely, empty bags and sacks for packing
goods, of which we exported to the value of a quarter of a
million pounds in 1854, and one million and three-quarters
in 1874.

In all the foregoing tables we have been treating of values
alone, and not at all of quantities.   This, as before explained,
is necessary for the general purposes of comparing one
year's transactions, one country's trade, or the dealings in
one article as compared with others ; but for ascertaining
with anything like precision the advance or otherwise of the
several articles through a series of years, it is indispensable
that we should consider quantities as well.   Indeed, this is
the more important of the two, for fluctuations of price
whilst very important in regard to questions of profit and
loss, whether to the manufacturer, the trader, or the nation,
will be misleading in attempts to form estimates of the increased production, sale, or consumption of the various
articles, whether foreign or British, in which we trade.
Three tables have, therefore, been prepared, in which the
quantities of the same articles for the same periods, with the
like increase of one year over another are displayed, so far
as is possible.   In many cases it would be impracticable
to do so, because the values alone are capable of being re-
gistered.   This happens also with some articles of which

the values are given, as woollen manufactures, which heading includes a number of subdivisions, all capable of being grouped together for a joint value, but not so for a common quantity, because the separate quantities, such as weights and measurements, pieces, or pounds and yards are not capable of being added together. Neither must it be taken that in all cases the values shown for any article are for identically the same parcels of goods as are shown under quantities, as for instance, wood, where the value includes staves, firewood, and furniture woods, the quantities only those of hewn and sawn; but with such an article as tea, where the value and the quantity are for the same amount of goods, the division of one by the other would give the actual average price per pound in each year.

Table VIII. is for the principal articles of import, and they, though much fewer in number, are ranged in the same order as in Table V.

Table IX. contains the same details for portions of the foreign and colonial produce re-exported, and Table X. for the exports of British goods. In many of these latter the disparity of increase is so great that it may be well to range them side by side, thus :—

	Increase in.	
	Value.	Quantity.
	Per cent.	Per cent.
Alkali......................	462	356
Bags empty.................	562	1·043
Beer and Ale..............	86	40
Coals	462	223
Cotton yarn...............	117	49
Sugar, refined.............	463	644
Woollen yarn..............	257	123

Such are a few of the more noticeable points brought out by an inspection of the several tables, and having, it is hoped, thus far kept within the strict bounds of a statistical

paper, I would trespass somewhat upon the time and indulgence of my hearers or readers—trenching in some measure
upon the province of the political economist—to pass in review some of the conclusions at which their consideration
may enable us to arrive.

Perhaps the most important feature in the whole is to be
found in the enormous increase in the quantities and values
of the food, other than that produced in our own country,
which we are able to purchase and consume—an increase
totally out of keeping with that which has taken place in the
population.   The estimated number of inhabitants to be fed
in 1854 was 27,800,000; in 1874, 32,400,000—a difference of 4,600,000, or 16 per cent. ; whereas the supplies
of food from abroad, after making due allowance for those
re-exported, cannot be taken at less than 150 per cent.
more than they were twenty years ago. The reason for this
disproportion is two-fold : first, that the production of food
at home does not keep pace with the growth of our population ; and next, that with increasing means of purchasing
food, the quantity consumed by the mass of the people is
greater, if not in bulk, yet in value. From the official tables
—first, I believe, compiled in 1867—we find that the acreage of land under cultivation for corn and green crops in
that year was 16,384,000, and in 1873 almost exactly the
same, viz., 16,394,000 acres. At the same periods we had
of live stock—

	In 1867.	In 1873.
Cattle	8,731.000	10.154,000
Sheep	33.818,000	33,982,000
Pigs	4,221.100	3.564.000
The population having been	30.335,000	32.125,000

Except, therefore, to the extent to which improved
methods of cultivation had increased the productiveness of

the soil, it does not appear that in these six years there had been any substantial addition to the quantity of food grown at home. If this be so, the supplies needed for the additional mouths must have been chiefly drawn from abroad. This might probably account for a large portion of the increased value within that period, but not for the 30 to 35 millions, which have since 1869 been added to our annual payments for food; and hence it is evident, as indeed other circumstances prove, that there must be greater purchasing power in some or every portion of the community. That both the causes alluded to are in operation is also manifest from the unequal rate at which, in proportion to the population, the increase of consumption goes on in articles of which part is produced at home and part obtained from abroad, and in those derived from the latter source. Wheat, bacon, butter, cheese, eggs, have all risen with far greater rapidity than sugar, tea, tobacco, and wine. What we have to provide by foreign importations of the first class, is the excess over previous consumption of both home and foreign produce. Of the latter, over foreign alone, and the percentage of increase should for the former class be calculated not upon the importations of 1854, but upon these added to the quantities raised at home.

The contrast between the variations of price in different classes of food is very marked. Take potatoes for one : the increase in value is sixty-fold, in quantity but thirty-three-fold, showing that the price we now pay for the same weight is nearly double what it was twenty years back—in 1854 barely 3s. per cwt., in 1874 more than 5s. per cwt. Wheat, however, which has increased 158 per cent. in quantity, is only 97 per cent. greater in value. So with rice : 421 in weight only makes 268 in value. On the other hand, butter, cheese, bacon, eggs, lard, are all dearer than they were in 1854 ; in eggs, especially, we see that whilst the number is eight times, the value is eleven times as great ; all tending to show that though grain—which is the produce of countries in all parts of the world—is cheaper, meat, dairy produce, and those articles for which we are limited to places near at hand, have risen so much in cost, that practically the necessaries of life are dearer than they were in the year with which our observations commence.

A very satisfactory indication is furnished by the growing addition to our employment of the raw materials which form the staple of our textile manufactures, and in the metals which are so largely worked up and sent away as British manufactures, as well as in wood, hides, seeds, &c. Turning to the Exports of British manufactures, we find the same results, the increase being very general; cotton, linen, and woollen manufactures having all more than doubled both in value and quantity, keeping pace with the larger importations of the raw materials from which they are produced. Here again the increase is more than commensurate with that of the population, showing that if the average consuming power is raised, so also is that of producing and manufacturing. Must not this be due to the extended employment and the superior character of our machinery, through which a far larger amount of material is worked up by each hand? otherwise such an extension of our manufactures could not possibly have taken place.

There are several points of great interest connected with the different countries with which we have the largest trading relations and the progressive growth of these. We must leave Russia out of the question in comparing the two years we have chosen, because of the Crimean War in 1854; but the fact of her now sending us nearly twice as much as she takes from us, shows the extent to which she has served as a granary for the United Kingdom. The same cause produces the same result with regard to France, and in some degree the United States. On the other hand, Germany and Holland are both better customers to us than we are to them. The disproportion between the imports from, and the exports to several countries are so remarkable, that they deserve to be placed in contrast. First, those in which our imports are now in excess.

[In million £'s to two decimals.]

	1874.		1879.	
	Imports.	Exports.	Imports.	Exports.
	£	£	£	£
Russia........................	21·40	11·30	15·88	10·61
Sweden and Norway........	10·97	7·30	8·39	3·94
Belgium......................	14·93	12·90	10·73	11·89
France........................	46·69	29·40	38·46	26·56
Spain.........................	12·85	7·70	8·40	3·76
United States...............	74·10	32·30	91·82	25·52

Then those in which the exports are greater:—

[In million £'s to two decimals.]

	1874.		1879.	
	Imports.	Exports.	Imports.	Exports.
	£	£	£	£
Germany......................	19·97	34·50	21·60	29·62
Holland.......................	15·81	22·60	21·96	15·45

On the whole it will be seen that our imports are now
£370,000,000 against exports of £297,000,000. In olden
times this would have been thought a serious evil. It was
at one time considered that the country which received
goods to a greater value than ·it returned must inevitably
become impoverished. A different theory then arose. It
was thought that no country (not being one in which the
precious metals existed,) could go on paying in goods more
than it got back, and therefore it must be taken that in
some way or other the exports, though smaller in amount,
did in fact meet the claims upon us for the larger imports.
That consequently the disparity between the two was a
source of congratulation, since the excess of value in the one
over the other was really so much wealth accruing to us
as the balance of our trading operations. To a certain
—perhaps a considerable—extent this was true. The ex-

port values being fixed at the time of shipment, did not
represent the charges of transit or the profits to those who
shipped them; whilst the import values being those at
the time of arrival, did include the expense of bringing them
and the profit on their sale by the first importers, most or all
of which accrued to this country as being the greatest
carrier both out and home, as well as the depôt in which
they were sold. Such an explanation, however, cannot serve
to account for so large a difference as now exists. This to
the minds of many can only be accounted for in one of two
ways: either that there is some error in the method by
which the values are ascertained, or that we are really
doing a business which is alarming in its tendency towards
ultimate bankruptcy. But surmises and fears like these
may well be dismissed, and the belief that the difference
is really an accession to the accumulated wealth of the
country fully entertained.[1]

It is obvious that for years past there has been an annual
increase, not only in the capital devoted to reproductive
expenditure, which, when it is judiciously devoted to this
purpose, goes on increasing in the way of compound interest; but also in that which seeks investment abroad.
That a large amount of capital thus supports foreign loans,
makes railways, and likewise maintains gas, water, harbour,
and other companies is well understood; but it is almost
impossible to form an estimate of the annual return it makes
in the shape of interest or dividends. Beyond this, however, there is reason to believe that considerable sums are
invested in private agricultural and manufacturing undertakings, as well as employed in trading pursuits. What
more likely than that the manufacturer at home, who finds
the demands of labour interfere with his ability to gain an
adequate return for his capital here, should carry some of it
to like uses abroad? Or that the merchant who desires to

---

[1] It will be seen in the subsequent paper, " On the Preponderance
of Imports," that this view is much modified by the progress of trade
since the year when this was written.

draw consignments of foreign or colonial produce to his establishments at home, should advance the money which pays for the cultivation of the soil and the gathering in of the produce; should build or charter the ships, not only those which are employed in the direct trade, but in the coast or international carrying in distant countries? It is well known that on this system the cultivation of our West Indian colonies was carried on so largely when slavery existed there; that in this way the Northern States of the Union in America reaped the profits of slavery in the Southern; and there is no doubt that scarcely a country exists, or cultivation or manufactures carried on in any part of the world, in which British capital or British skill, paid for in money value beyond the cost of its maintenance, has not its share. Now, all this is in reality carried on more by credit than the actual transmission of money, but it nevertheless brings in large profits which in one shape or another must be remitted to this country. And why not in goods for which no equivalent exportation is made? This will go on in an accelerated ratio, so that it is not absolutely impossible to conceive that the time may come when the imports we receive will not do more than represent the returns made for the use of British capital and credit. The recipients of these returns have but to consume the produce of our home growth and labour, in reality paying for them with the goods drawn from abroad; and thus manufactures might flourish and prosperity exist without a single article of export ever being made. The true interest of the capitalist at home, who finds that either there is a superabundance of that which he has to employ, or that the conditions of the labour market here prevent his obtaining an adequate return, seems to be, to seek to stimulate production elsewhere, or to encourage trade in distant places; himself directing from hence their proper developments, and enjoying here the fruits of his means and his talents.

Still the question arises on the face of these figures, whether in truth the trade of the kingdom has not received

a decided check.   It will be seen that 1871-72-73 were the
years in which it seemed to have reached its highest point,
and that 1874 contrasts unfavourably in every particular.
The percentages of increase which in the former years had
reached, for retained imports 136, for exports of foreign
goods 225, and of British 164 per cent., have in the last
receded to 156,209, and 146 respectively. The four months [1]
of the present year manifest a considerable decline upon the
corresponding period of last year, and would thus evidence that the diminishing process is still going on.   Time
alone will show whether this is one of those cycles of
comparative stagnation from which we have often before
recovered, or whether the conditions which regulate the relations of capital and labour to each other have not really so
changed that we are transferring our superiority to other
lands.   Enough, however, has been said to show the enormous strides which British commerce and manufacture has
made within the last twenty years.   We may yet indulge
the hope that our prosperity, not having reached its climax,
will shortly manifest as great a revival as we have often
witnessed before; and will in future years attain still greater
magnitude, if not with quite as rapid a growth as hitherto
has rewarded our national enterprise, wealth, and skill.

[1] Imports in 1874, £123,915,925 ; in 1875, £119,549,154.   Exports (British) in 1874, £77,234,354 ; in 1875, £73,282,069.   Full
tables of imports and exports for subsequent years are given at pp. 61,
66, et seq.

APPENDIX.

TABLE I.—*Total Value of Goods Imported into the United Kingdom, and of those Re-Exported therefrom in each Year from 1854 to 1874, with the Increase or Decrease per Cent. in each on the previous Year, and also on 1854* [1875 to 1879 added at foot.]

[In million £'s to two decimals.]

Year.	Imported.			Re-Exported.			Retained for Home Consumption.		
		Increase or Decrease.			Increase or Decrease.			Increase or Decrease.	
	£	Pr.Year.	On 1854.	£	Pr.Year.	On 1854.	£	Pr.Year.	On 1854.
		Per cnt.	Per cnt.		Per cnt.	Per cnt.		Per cnt.	Per cnt.
1854	152·39	—	—	18·63	—	—	133·75	—	—
'55	143·54	− 5·7	− 5·7	21·00	+ 12·7	+ 12·7	122·54	− 8·4	− 8·4
'56	172·54	+ 20·2	+ 13·2	23·39	+ 11·4	+ 25·5	149·15	+ 21·7	+ 11·5
'57	187·84	+ 8·4	+ 23·3	24·11	+ 3·0	+ 29·4	163·73	+ 9·8	+ 22·4
'58	164·58	− 12·1	+ 7·9	23·17	− 3·9	+ 24·4	141·41	− 13·6	+ 5·7
'59	179·18	+ 8·8	+ 17·6	25·28	+ 9·1	+ 35·7	153·90	+ 8·8	+ 15·1
1860	210·53	+ 17·5	+ 38·1	28·63	+ 13·2	+ 51·7	181·90	+ 18·1	+ 36·0
'61	217·49	+ 3·3	+ 42·7	34·53	+ 20·6	+ 85·4	182·96	+ 0·6	+ 36·8
'62	225·72	+ 3·9	+ 43·1	47·18	+ 22·1	+ 126·5	183·54	+ 0·3	+ 37·2
'63	248·92	+ 10·0	+ 63·3	50·30	+ 19·2	+ 170·0	198·62	+ 8·2	+ 48·5
'64	274·95	+ 10·6	+ 80·4	52·14	+ 3·7	+ 180·0	222·81	+ 12·2	+ 66·6
1865	271·07	1·4	+ 77·9	53·00	+ 1·6	+ 184·7	218·08	− 2·1	+ 63·0
'66	295·29	+ 9·0	+ 93·8	49·99	+ 5·7	+ 163·0	245·30	+ 12·5	+ 83·4
'67	275·18	− 6·8	+ 80·6	44·84	10·3	+ 140·9	230·34	− 6·1	+ 72·2
'68	294·69	+ 7·1	+ 93·4	48·10	+ 7·3	+ 158·4	246·59	+ 7·5	+ 84·3
'69	295·46	+ 0·3	+ 93·9	47·06	− 2·2	+ 152·8	248·40	+ 0·8	+ 85·7
1870	303·26	+ 2·6	+ 99·0	44·49	− 5·5	+ 139·0	258·76	+ 4·2	+ 93·4
'71	331·02	+ 9·2	+ 117·2	60·51	+ 35·9	+ 225·1	270·51	+ 4·5	+ 102·2
'72	354·69	+ 7·2	+ 132·7	58·33	− 3·6	+ 213·4	296·36	+ 9·5	+ 121·6
'73	371·29	+ 4·7	+ 143·6	55·84	− 4·3	+ 200·0	315·45	+ 6·5	+ 135·8
'74	370·08	− 0·3	+ 142·9	58·09	+ 3·0	+ 211·6	311·99	− 0·9	+ 132·5
Total 21 years	5,339·71	—	—	863·61	—	—	4,476·10	—	—
Average	254·27	—	—	41·11	—	—	213·14	—	—
1875	373·94	+ 1·0	+ 145·4	58·15	+ 0·1	+ 211·9	315·79	+ 1·2	+ 136·1
'76	375·15	+ 0·3	+ 146·2	56·14	− 3·4	+ 201·2	319·01	+ 1·3	+ 139·3
'77	391·42	+ 5·1	+ 158·1	53·45	− 4·8	+ 166·7	349·97	+ 9·9	+ 154·9
'78	368·77	− 6·5	+ 142·0	52·63	− 1·6	+ 182·3	316·14	− 7·3	+ 136·4
'79	362·99	− 1·6	+ 138·2	57·25	+ 8·8	+ 207·1	305·74	− 3·3	+ 128·6

TABLE II.—*Value of Goods Exported from the United Kingdom, distinguishing those of Foreign and Colonial Produce, and those of British Manufacture, in each Year from 1854 to 1874, with the Increase or Decrease per Cent. in each Year, on that of its predecessor, and also on 1854.* [1875 to 1879 added.]

[In million £'s to two decimals.]

Year.	Exported.			Foreign and Colonial.			British.		
		Increase or Decrease.			Increase or Decrease.			Increase or Decrease.	
		Pr.Year.	On 1854.		Pr.Year.	On 1854.		Pr.Year.	On 1854.
	£	Per cnt.	Per cnt.	£	Per cnt.	Per cnt.	£	Per cnt.	Per cnt.
1854 ..	115·82	—	—	18·64	—	—	97·18	—	—
'55 ..	116·69	+ 0·7	+ 0·7	21·00	+ 12·7	+ 12·7	95·69	− 1·5	− 1·5
'56 ..	139·22	+ 19·0	+ 20·2	23·39	+ 11·4	+ 25·5	115·83	+ 21·0	+ 19·2
'57 ..	146·17	+ 5·0	+ 26·2	24·11	+ 3·0	+ 29·4	122·06	+ 5·4	+ 25·6
'58 ..	139·78	− 4·4	+ 20·2	23·17	− 3·9	+ 24·4	116·61	− 4·5	+ 20·0
'59 ..	155·69	+ 11·4	+ 34·4	25·28	+ 9·1	+ 35·7	130·41	+ 11·8	+ 34·2
1860 ..	164·52	+ 5·7	+ 42·1	28·63	+ 13·2	+ 53·7	135·89	+ 4·2	+ 40·0
'61 ..	159·63	− 3·0	+ 37·7	34·53	+ 20·6	+ 85·4	125·10	− 7·9	+ 28·7
'62 ..	166·17	+ 4·1	+ 43·5	42·18	+ 22·1	+ 126·5	123·99	− 0·9	+ 27·6
'63 ..	196·90	+ 18·5	+ 70·0	50·30	+ 19·2	+ 170·0	146·60	+ 18·2	+ 50·8
'64 ..	212·59	+ 7·9	+ 83·4	52·14	+ 3·7	+ 180·0	160·45	+ 9·4	+ 65·1
1865 ..	218·83	+ 2·9	+ 88·9	53·00	+ 1·6	+ 184·7	165·83	+ 3·4	+ 70·6
'66 ..	238·91	+ 9·1	+ 106·3	49·99	− 5·7	+ 168·0	188·92	+ 13·9	+ 94·3
'67 ..	225·80	− 5·5	+ 94·9	44·84	− 10·3	+ 140·9	180·96	− 4·2	+ 86·2
'68 ..	227·78	+ 0·9	+ 96·7	48·10	+ 7·3	+ 158·4	179·68	− 0·7	+ 84·9
'69 ..	237·02	+ 4·0	+ 104·7	47·06	− 2·2	+ 152·8	189·96	+ 5·7	+ 95·4
1870 ..	244·08	+ 3·0	+ 110·8	44·49	− 5·6	+ 139·0	199·59	+ 5·1	+ 105·3
'71 ..	283·58	+ 16·2	+ 144·9	60·51	+ 35·9	+ 225·1	223·07	+ 11·8	+ 129·5
'72 ..	314·59	+ 10·9	+ 171·6	58·33	− 3·6	+ 213·4	256·26	+ 14·9	+ 163·6
'73 ..	311·01	− 1·1	+ 168·6	55·84	− 4·3	+ 200·0	255·17	− 0·4	+ 162·5
'74 ..	297·65	− 4·5	+ 156·4	58·09	+ 3·0	+ 211·6	239·56	− 6·2	+ 146·3
Total 21 years	4,312·43	—	—	863·62	—	—	3,448·81	—	—
Average	205·36	—	—	41·12	—	—	164·23	—	—
1875 ..	281·61	− 0·5	+ 143·2	58·15	+ 0·1	+ 211·9	223·47	− 6·7	+ 129·9
'76 ..	256·78	− 8·8	+ 127·1	56·14	− 3·4	+ 201·2	200·64	− 10·1	+ 106·4
'77 ..	252·35	− 1·7	+ 117·1	53·45	− 4·8	+ 186·7	198·89	− 0·9	+ 104·6
'78 ..	245·48	− 2·7	+ 112·0	52·63	− 1·6	+ 182·3	192·85	− 3·0	+ 98·5
'79 ..	248·78	+ 1·3	+ 114·8	57·25	+ 8·8	+ 207·1	191·53	− 0·7	+ 97·1

III.

The Growing Preponderance of Imports over Exports in the Foreign and Colonial Trade of the United Kingdom.[1]

SINCE 1872 a marked alteration has taken place in the relative values of the imports and exports of the United Kingdom. Up to that date, and indeed until the middle of 1873, the general progress of our trade showed a steady increase in both branches; and if here and there special circumstances caused one year to fall short of its predecessor, the deficit was speedily more than restored. We had come to look upon continual growth as the normal condition of our commerce, and though for about half a century the balance had been in favour of imports, this excess arose from their continuous increase, not as now, partly from the decrease of the exports. For 1872 the difference between the two—the balance of trade as it is usually termed—was 40 millions, for the present year it is nearly three times as much, 118 millions. So decided and rapid a change demands more than a superficial inquiry into its causes and effects, and it is hoped that the figures now to be produced will at least aid investigations as deep and searching as the importance of the subject requires.

I.—Earlier Period of Trade, 1816-53.

Before considering the particulars furnished from official sources regarding the trade of more recent years, it would have been interesting and useful to have taken a survey of an earlier period, and in so doing to have glanced back-

[1] Read before the Statistical Society, 19th December, 1876. Vol. xl.

ward so far as we have any data on which reliance can be placed.

Having this object in view, it would have been possible to commence with the year 1699, when both imports and exports were each estimated as slightly under six millions. Unfortunately, however, the accounts were kept in what were termed "official values;" that is, a tariff of prices supposed to represent the values of the various articles—and really doing so at the time when each first became known to, or distinguished in the trade accounts—was employed for the purpose of representing quantities by money. Such a system had its use as a means of comparing the current year with its immediate predecessor, but as prices altered, and the relative quantities of goods changed, it would so far depart from accuracy as to be of little worth. Exporters were for other reasons called upon to declare the values of their respective shipments, and the collected amounts were recorded; but no such step was taken for the imports until much later on. The figures, therefore, in the following table must be taken with great limitation.

The year 1816, with which the table commences, may be deemed the opening one of a new era in our commercial operations. The long period of continental and other warfare, culminating in the events of 1815, must have so disturbed our trading relations as to render any comparison of prior with succeeding years very unsafe. From that year to 1853 there appears to have been a steady progress in both imports and exports, but not by any means in the same ratio. The figures are here reproduced as an interesting if not an absolutely necessary introduction to the more definite details of the subsequent period; and the "declared" as well as "official" values of the British exports shown for the purpose of correcting many erroneous estimates which have been formed of the worth of our export trade during those years.

In the two columns on the opposite sides of the next page

TABLE I.—*Value of Goods imported into, and Exported from, the United Kingdom, from 1816 to 1853, Computed at the Official Rates : showing also the Declared Value of the British Exports.*

[In million £'s to two decimals.]

Years.	Foreign and Colonial Merchandise. (Official Values.)			Produce and Manufacture of United Kingdom.		Total Exports. —
	Total Imports.	Exported from United Kingdom.	Retained for Home Use.	Official Value.	Declared Value.	Official Values.
	£	£	£	£	£	£
1816 ...	27·43	13·48	13·95	35·72	*41·65*	49·20
'17 ...	30·83	10·29	20·54	40·11	*41·82*	50·40
'18 ...	36·89	10·86	26·03	42·70	*46·47*	53·56
'19 ...	30·78	9·91	20·87	33·53	*35·21*	43·44
1820 ...	32·47	10·56	21·91	38·39	*36·42*	48·95
'21 ...	30·84	10·63	20·21	40·83	*36·66*	51·49
'22 ...	30·53	9·23	21·30	44·24	*36·97*	53·47
'23 ...	35·80	8·60	27·20	43·83	*35·36*	52·43
'24 ...	37·47	10·21	27·26	48·73	*38·42*	58·94
1825 ..	44·21	9·17	35·04	47·15	*38·87*	56·32
'26 ..	37·81	10·08	27·73	40·96	*31·54*	51·04
'27 ...	44·91	9·83	35·08	52·22	*37·18*	62·05
'28 ...	45·17	9·95	35·22	52·78	*36·81*	62·73
'29 ...	43·99	10·62	33·37	56·22	*35·84*	66·84
1830 ...	46·30	8·55	37·75	61·15	*38·27*	69·70
'31 ...	49·73	10·75	38·98	60·68	*37·16*	71·43
'32 ...	44·61	11·05	33·56	65·02	*36·45*	76·07
'33 ...	45·94	9·83	36·11	69·99	*39·67*	79·82
'34 ...	49·37	11·56	37·81	73·84	*41·65*	85·40
1835 ...	49·03	12·80	36·23	78·36	*47·37*	91·16
'36 ...	57·30	12·39	44·91	85·22	*53·29*	97·61
'37 ...	54·76	13·24	41·53	72·54	*42·07*	85·78
'38 ...	61·26	12·71	48·55	92·45	*50·06*	105·17
'39 ...	62·05	12·80	49·25	97·39	*53·23*	110·19
1840 ...	67·49	13·77	53·72	102·71	*51·41*	116·48
'41 ...	64·44	14·72	49·72	102·18	*51·64*	116·90
'42 ...	65·25	13·59	51·66	100·25	*47·38*	113·84
'43 ...	70·22	13·96	56·26	117·87	*52·28*	131·83
'44 ...	75·45	14·40	61·05	131·55	*58·58*	145·96
1845 ...	85·30	16·28	69·02	134·60	*60·11*	150·88
'46 ...	75·93	16·30	59·63	132·31	*57·79*	148·62
'47 ...	90·92	20·04	70·88	126·13	*58·84*	146·17
'48 ...	93·55	18·38	75·17	132·61	*52·85*	150·99
'49 ...	105·88	25·56	80·32	164·53	*65·60*	190·09
1850 ...	100·47	21·89	78·58	175·44	*71·37*	197·33
'51 ...	110·48	23·73	86·75	190·66	*74·45*	214·39
'52 ...	109·33	23·33	86·00	196·18	*78·08*	219·51
'53 ...	123·10	27·75	95·35	214·32	*98·93*	242·07
38 years	2·267·29	522·77	1·744·52	3·395·46	*1·845·75*	3·918·23

will be found the yearly total values of the imports and
exports as derived from official sources. The middle
column on the import side of the table sets forth the value
of imported articles exported to foreign countries, which, in
any comparison with British exports, should be deducted.
This is done in the next column, which shows the difference
between the two, or the value of the imports retained in
the country for home use. Adjoining this will be found
the value of goods of home produce and manufacture
exported, constituting what may be termed the credit side
of the account. The difference between the two, as also
that between the right and left-hand columns, will give the
nearest approach to the preponderance or otherwise of
imports or exports it is possible to abstract directly from
these records, for the years embraced in this table.

For the reasons above stated, prior to 1854, we have no
means of accurately ascertaining in what relation the values
of our imports stood to those of our exports, but by a
change of system in that year the real import values were
obtained; and from this we learn that whilst the market
prices of the exports were continually falling, the not
unnatural result of improvement and competition in manufacture, those of the imports were constantly rising; the
equally rational effect of demand overtaking supply, and
the growing wealth of those who were the purchasers. In
that year the actual value of 152 millions of imports stood
officially at 124, whilst the true value of 116 millions of
exports was represented officially as 243 : an official deficit
in the one case of 28, and an excess in the other of 127.
Reasoning from the official valuation, we should conclude
the balance in favour of exports to have been 120 millions,
whereas the true figures show it to have been 37 millions
in favour of imports. Such being the case with the figures
up to 1853, any attempt to deal with them as showing the
progressive preponderance either way would be hopeless.
An attempt has been made to convert " official " into
" actual " for the imports, but it soon became evident that

the labour of such an effort would be greatly beyond the worth of the results to be obtained, results too doubtful to support any argument or to guide any judgment. It is probable, however, that in assuming the official value of 14 millions for the imports retained in 1816 to have been really equal to 17, as against 41 of British exports, and the 95 millions in 1853 as really 130 against 99 of exports, we shall not be far wide of the mark. If these be correct estimates, the foreign goods consumed in this country had between 1816 and 1853 multiplied sevenfold in value, and the exports of British goods only doubled, thus altering the excess from one side of the account to the other. It is probable that the time when the imports overtook the exports was about the year 1825, since when there has been a growing preponderance in their favour.

II.—*Period from 1854 to the Present Time.*

From 1854 the import values, as published in the monthly and annual accounts of trade and navigation, assumed a new aspect. They still continued to be computed, but upon the basis of the current market values of the articles, and as the declared values of the exports were given by the merchants upon the same foundation, the two sets of figures may be fairly brought into comparison. As such they are given in Table II., which is continued in the same form as Table I., with two exceptions. The official value, although discarded from the Trade accounts, continued until 1870 to be published in the Finance accounts annually presented to Parliament. For information, therefore, and as illustrating the discrepancies between them and the real values, they are inserted in the table as a second line for each year. Another column, too, has been added, in which the exports having been deducted from the imports, the difference is shown as an excess of the latter, and the percentage of this excess upon the export value has been brought out. An average for the twenty-three years 1854-76 inclusive, is likewise shown :—

TABLE II.—*In continuation of Table I., from 1854 to 1876, showing the Computed Real Values of Imports up to 1870, the Declared Values of Imports from 1871, and of Exports for the whole Period; also the Official Values up to 1869.* [1877 to 1879 added.]

[In million £'s to two decimals.]

Years.	Foreign and Colonial Merchandise.			Exports.		Excess of Imports.	Per Cent. on Bh. Expts
	Total Imports.	Exported from United Kingdom.	Retained for Home Use.	Produce and Manufacture of United Kingdom.	Total.		
	£	£	£	£	£	£	
1854 {	152·39	18·64	133·75	97·18	115·82	36·57	38
	124·42	*29·82*		*214·07*	*243·89*		
'55 {	143·54	21·00	122·54	95·69	116·69	26·85	28
	117·40	*31·50*		*226·90*	*258·41*		
'56 {	172·54	23·39	149·15	115·83	139·22	33·32	29
	131·93	*33·42*		*258·50*	*291·92*		
'57 {	187·85	24·11	163·74	122·07	146·18	41·67	34
	136·21	*30·79*		*255·39*	*286·19*		
'58 {	164·58	23·17	141·41	116·61	139·78	24·80	21
	138·15	*33·88*		*271·65*	*305·54*		
'59 {	179·18	25·28	153·90	130·41	155·69	23·49	18
	146·64	*37·23*		*297·35*	*334·58*		
1860 {	210·53	28·63	181·90	135·89	164·52	46·01	34
	164·73	*43·53*		*315·71*	*359·24*		
'61 {	217·49	34·53	182·96	125·10	159·63	57·86	46
	171·21	*50·15*		*289·35*	*339·51*		
'62 {	225·72	42·18	183·54	123·99	166·17	59·55	48
	160·69	*50·95*		*240·72*	*291·67*		
'63 {	248·92	50·30	198·62	146·60	196·90	52·02	36
	171·91	*54·91*		*258·19*	*313·11*		
'64 {	274·95	52·14	222·81	160·45	212·59	62·36	39
	173·96	*54·95*		*267·15*	*322·10*		
'65 {	271·07	52·99	218·08	165·84	218·83	52·24	31
	181·80	*62·45*		*301·61*	*364·06*		
'66 {	295·29	49·99	245·30	188·92	238·91	56·38	30
	201·19	*64·37*		*348·47*	*412·84*		
'67 {	275·18	44·84	230·34	180·96	225·80	49·38	27
	201·12	*64·75*		*361·75*	*426·50*		
'68 {	294·69	48·10	246·59	179·68	227·78	66·91	37
	220·88	*69·47*		*381·12*	*450·60*		
'69 {	295·46	47·06	248·40	189·95	237·01	58·45	31
	224·32	*67·10*		*388·98*	*456·08*		
1870...	303·26	44·50	258·76	199·59	244·08	59·18	30
'71...	331·02	60·51	270·51	223·07	283·58	47·44	21
'72...	354·69	58·33	296·36	256·26	314·59	40·10	16
'73...	371·29	55·84	315·45	255·17	311·01	60·28	24
'74...	370·08	58·09	311·99	239·56	297·65	72·43	30
'75...	373·94	58·15	315·79	223·47	281·61	92·33	41
'76...	375·15	56·14	319·01	200·64	256·78	118·37	59
	6·088·00	977·00	5·111·00	3·872·00	4·849·00	1·239·00	—
Avrge.	265·00	43·00	222·00	168·00	211·00	54·00	—

Note.—Figures printed thus (152·39) are computed to 1870, declared to 1876, those in *italics* are official.

1877...	394·42	53·45	340·97	198·89	252·34	142·08	71
'78...	368·77	52·63	316·14	192·85	245·48	123·29	64
'79...	362·99	57·25	305·74	191·53	248·78	114·21	60

III.—*Alterations to be made in Relative Values.*

Beginning then with 1854, we leave a period in which arbitrary and antiquated prices were employed to convert quantities into value, and come to one in which the values being based upon existing prices and known market rates, the figures given may be taken as a fair valuation of the goods at the time when they arrive and leave the country. They thus afford satisfactory information of the amount of trade which is being transacted, and by comparison of successive years of its advance or decay ; but they are still insufficient for enabling us to determine the balance of trade, or as it may be better stated, the actual amount of money or money's worth which is necessary for the settlement of the balances between the nation and its customers. And for this reason amongst others : that it is essential for uniformity's sake to lay down a rigid rule as to the time and place at which the valuation is taken, whilst under the actual conditions of trade the selling and the purchasing prices admit of continually changing adjustments. The goods which are sent abroad increase or decrease in value before they are used in payment for those we receive; these again are seldom placed upon the market at home at the same price as that at which they change hands abroad, and it is easy to perceive that the pound of value assigned to the import is not necessarily or often equivalent to the pound of export. For statistical purposes the value required is, that which the articles bear at the time when the vessels in which they are conveyed arrive at, or depart from, the several ports in the kingdom ; that is, the sum of money which should be given in exchange for the bill of lading, which is the title for possession of the property. This includes the cost of bringing our imports hither, but excludes that of conveying the exports to their destination, and thus leaves a considerable margin to be deducted from the one total or added to the other before the true difference can be ascertained. Again, in the official totals no account is taken of the coin and bullion which passes to and fro, and as regards the exports there are goods other than what is ordinarily termed merchandise, which need to be brought into the account, with other circumstances, to all of which a consideration in detail must be given.

To take the imports first. There is a large amount of specie and precious metal continually passing backwards and forwards between the various countries as a circulating medium, or in adjustment of the exchanges at the different monetary centres. The same coin or ingots may be, and are, transferred from one place to another very many times in the year, and though a separate account is kept of these removals, and much care is bestowed to make this as correct as possible, the value is not included in the totals of either the imports or the exports. To add the whole would unduly swell both amounts, but the balance must clearly be placed to whichever side it belongs. This will consist of the floating stock which for the time being happens to be remaining in the country, together with such quantities as are absorbed in the arts and manufactures, or employed in the increase or renewal of the coinage.

It is a far more difficult task to ascertain what allowances should be made for the charges upon bringing the articles of import from the place of production or purchase, to that at which the value is assigned, but the extreme importance of obtaining a correct estimate has been made the occasion of a series of extended and minute calculations, by which it is hoped an approximation to the actual cost has at least been obtained ; and as no mere statement of the results would carry conviction to the minds of those who are conversant with trade, it may be well to briefly describe the method which has been pursued. With cotton—the greatest of all our importations—as an example, quotations have been obtained of the actual amounts paid for freight from each of the principal ports in America, for the last twenty years; regard has been paid to the quantities shipped from each of these ports, and the periods of the year, whether in the slack or busy season, at which these have been made. An average has thus been arrived at for each year, and applying this to the average price per pound at which the cotton stands for the same year, the charge per cent. on the value has been ascertained. Similar processes have been gone through with corn, tea, sugar, wine, timber, &c., &c., to such an extent as to justify the conclusion that the declared import value is from this cause enhanced by $8\frac{1}{2}$ to $12\frac{1}{2}$ per cent. On a consideration of the whole it would seem that 11 per cent. is a fair average, and at this ratio the freight has been worked out for each year since 1854.

The validity of this estimate may be tested in another way. We have now from $4\frac{1}{2}$ to 5 million tons of British shipping employed in the foreign carrying trade; assuming £6 per ton per annum as a fair estimate of gross earnings, of which one-fourth is chargeable to the export trade, we shall have say 22 millions; but perhaps one-third of the imported goods are brought in Foreign ships, and one-half of this sum must be added for the freight carried by these, giving thus a total of say 33 millions—not greatly below the 35 millions which has been assumed as the deduction for the present year. To corroborate these calculations, the ascertained import freight lists of several vessels for a series of years, actually give an average of 89s. per ton, which very nearly corresponds with four-fifths of the £6 above assumed.

On the export side, all the alteration will be in the shape of additions. In the first place, we build many vessels for foreigners, which, sailing away with cargoes, are not themselves deemed to be exports, but are just as much so as other goods taken from the country. Careful inquiries by an eminent shipbuilding firm as to the average contract price per ton in each year for sailing vessels and steamers, have furnished a sum to be added on this account. Another item is that of victualling supplies and stores, which, though never included in the exports, should be, inasmuch as they are so much goods sent away for profit in the shape of freight to be earned on both outward and homeward voyages. It has been estimated, from a comparison of actual outlays obtained from various firms, that these will amount to 20s. a ton per annum for sailing vessels, and 30s. for steamers, and at these rates the calculation has been made. A further addition must be made for the quantity of coals shipped for the use of steamers. No record of this was kept until within the last two years, but dividing these quantities by the tonnage of the vessels to which they were supplied, and assuming a similar rate of consumption for previous years, it is not difficult to find a value for each year according to the prices given for cargoes exported at the same times.

It has been necessary to specify at some length the various methods by which these estimates—for they are not positive facts—have been obtained, in order that those conversant with the various branches of business may form some ideas as to their probable accuracy. Conjectural amounts may not be very safe to rely upon, but these have all been very carefully made upon data collected from numerous authentic sources, and have been subjected to most exhaustive computations, involving a mass of figures and a large expenditure of time, in order that the result might be deemed to have real worth. The several details are displayed in the following table :—

Table III.—*Showing the Corrections of Excess of Imports (Table II.) by Addition of Balance of Bullion and Deduction for Freight; and by Additions to Exports for Ships Built for Foreigners, Victualling, and Ships' Stores, and Coals for use of Steamers.* [1877-9 added.]

[In million £'s to two decimals.]

Years.	Apparent Excess of Imports.	Imports. Add — Bullion.	Imports. Deduct Freight.	Exports. Add Ships for Foreigners.	Exports. Add Victualling and Stores.	Exports. Add Coals for Steamers.	Assumed Balance to be Provided for.
	£	£	£	£	£	£	£
1854...	36·6	not ascertained	14·7	not recorded	2·8	·2	—
'55...	26·9	,,	13·5	·9	3·1	·2	—
'56...	33·3	,,	16·4	1·2	3·3	·2	—
'57...	41·7	,,	18·0	1·2	3·3	·3	—
1858...	24·8	9·9	15·5	1·0	3·4	·3	14·5
'59...	23·5	1·4	16·9	·9	3·4	·3	3·4
1860...	46·0	— 2·6	20·0	·5	3·2	·3	19·4
'61...	57·9	— 2·1	20·1	·3	3·3	·3	31·8
'62...	59·5	2·3	20·2	·7	3·5	·3	37·1
'63...	52·0	3·5	21·8	·6	3·8	·4	28·9
'64...	62·4	4·6	24·5	·9	4·2	·4	37·0
1865...	52·2	6·4	24·0	1·1	4·4	·5	28·6
'66...	56·4	12·6	27·0	1·2	4·4	·6	35·8
'67...	49·4	9·5	25·3	1·1	4·6	·8	27·1
'68...	66·9	4·6	27·1	1·4	4·6	·8	37·6
'69...	58·4	4·1	27·3	·9	4·6	·8	28·9
1870...	59·2	10·5	28·5	1·7	4·6	·9	34·0
'71...	47·4	4·4	29·8	1·4	4·7	1·0	14·9
'72...	40·1	— ·7	32·6	3·3	5·0	2·1	— 3·6
'73...	60·3	4·7	34·7	4·0	5·2	2·6	18·5
'74...	72·4	1·5	34·3	3·3	5·4	2·4	28·5
1875...	92·3	5·6	34·7	1·8	5·3	1·9	54·2
'76...	118·4	7·6	35·0	·6	5·5	2·0	82·9
19 yrs.	1100·0	88·0	499·0	28·0	83·0	19·0	559·0
Avrge.	58·0	5·0	26·0	1·5	5·0	1·0	30·0
1877...	142·1	— 2·7	37·5	·6	5·7	1·8	93·8
'78...	123·3	5·1	34·8	1·5	5·9	1·9	84·3
'79...	114·2	— 4·4	33·6	1·8	6·1	1·8	66·5

On the assumption, then, that the foregoing table has been correctly constructed from sufficiently accurate data, the figures in its final column should show the balances for each year since 1857, which England, in its trading relations

with the whole world, has had to provide for or to adjust.
They are, in fact, the money values of the goods she has
from time to time bought, over and above those she has
sold; and for them, in some shape or other, value has to be
given. Owing to various causes which affect the traffic of
particular seasons, the years do not present such regularity
as would justify a separate treatment. It will be best,
therefore, to consider generally the average for the whole
period, and then particularly the balances since 1872, when,
as will be seen, a marked change commenced.

IV.—*Excess of Imports during the Past Twenty Years.*

Taking the official figures as shown in Table II., we shall
find that during the twenty years ending in 1876 we had in
round numbers :—

	£
Imported foreign and colonial merchandise to the value of..	5,600,000,000
Exported foreign and colonial merchandise to the value of..	900,000,000
Retained in the country..................	4,700,000,000
Exported of British produce and manufacture	3,500,000,000
Leaving an excess of.....................	1,200,000,000
Equal to an annual average of..........	60,000,000

But taking into account the additions and deductions set
forth in Table III., this will be reduced to one-half, leaving
the true average or balance to be dealt with not far from
£30,000,000.

Two things are quite evident: first, that the country
cannot have suffered to this extent by any drain upon its
stock of precious metals; for we have taken into account
the ebb and flow of the coin and bullion, and with the additions to our circulating medium and the gold and silver
absorbed in the arts and manufactures, there must be more

of these with us than there ever was before ; to say nothing of the present accumulation in the Bank coffers. Secondly, that we have not become debtors to other nations, for we have proof in the large loans they have contracted here and the heavy investments we have made abroad, that as capitalists we have increased rather than diminished our holdings. Nor is there any difficulty in seeing in what manner the settlement has been effected.

In the first place, the investments of which we speak produce an annual income which has either to be remitted here or placed to our credit with those from whom we purchase. Mr. Seyd, in a paper read before the Society of Arts in March last, estimates the indebtedness of other countries to this at from 1,000 to 1,100 millions of money, yielding an annual interest of from 40 to 50 millions. Professor Levi, in a paper published in the Society's " Journal " for June, 1874, thus quotes from a Parliamentary paper the sums assessed to the income-tax as derived from foreign securities: Indian, £7,032,000; colonial, £2,840,000; foreign, £9,341,000; together, £19,213,000. Since that year, notwithstanding that several of our creditors have proved to be defaulters, the amount must have become much larger, and the exact sum not being important to the present question, it may serve to take the mean of the two estimates. This will be about £30,000,000 at this time, but cannot have averaged more than one-half or two-thirds as much for the twenty years.

We have next to take into account the drawings by the Government here on its Indian revenues, amounting to some 15 millions per annum. This also has been growing, or has been almost entirely created since 1854, and cannot therefore have gone very far in the past, although it is a most important item at the present, and will probably be still more so in the future.

Possibly these two sources of income have furnished nearly if not quite enough to pay for the excess of imports, and if so, the adjustment is complete. But further than this,

we have the profits of trading in the goods which go to form
the large amount of imports and exports, together making
a total of 10,000 millions for the twenty years, or an average
of 500 millions, which should have yielded a profit of some
20 to 30 millions per annum.

Another item in favour of this country will arise from the
earnings of her ships in the transport of goods to and
between foreign ports, the net proceeds of which having
to be remitted to the owners, will form a set-off against the
goods purchased abroad for importation at home. Any
estimate of its amount must be very doubtful, and may
range from 5 to 10 millions annually, subject, however, to
a deduction of such portions of both it and the home freights
as are payable to colonial shipowners. The freight on im-
·ports, being settled at home, cannot in any way enter into
the account.

In addition to all these, there must be a large return for
trade carried on abroad by our countrymen, who remit the
profits here to be spent or invested in this country; and
there are also the entirely unknown proceeds from capital
invested in private manufacturing and agricultural pursuits
by those who, remaining at home, expend the income
here.

From these facts we may safely draw the conclusion that
the surplus value of the imports must until recently have
been far from sufficient to meet all the claims this country
has upon others; and that the difference, whatever it may
be, must have remained abroad, swelling the indebtedness
of other nations to us, increasing the English capital employed
in foreign undertakings.

In itself, therefore, there is no reason why either the
excess of past years, the greater surplus of the present, or
she still larger sums we may conceive of for the future,
thould be deemed prejudicial to our interests, or likely to
derange the finances of our country. As was remarked in
a former paper which slightly touched upon these points,
" manufactures might flourish and prosperity exist without

a single article of export ever being made." We do not take it as indicative of poverty in London, nay, rather as a proof of its wealth, that the articles it receives so greatly exceed those it parts with. We might even point out whole districts which, abounding in every token of wealth and luxury, are nothing but recipients, and why? Because there are congregated in these quarters those who draw thither the returns which labour, skill, and capital combine to produce at the different seats of our national industry. Let us look upon England as the metropolis of the world, the residence of those whose capital flows to every land, whose skill directs the employment of that capital in combination with the labour of emigrants from her own shores, still more of the workers she finds ready to her hands almost wherever she turns her thoughts; and she may go on receiving without payment those imports which thus serve to support her own population, and purchase all the products of their industry. Let the increase of our capital abroad, and the openings found for its profitable employment, only keep pace with, or exceed, the increase of numbers, wants, or desires at home, and there will ultimately be true reason to measure the prosperity of the nation by the amounts it can afford to receive without the necessity for sending their value away. But if, on the other hand, investments abroad lessen in productiveness, our manufactures cease to sell on profitable terms, and our consumption at home shall require increasing foreign supplies; we shall by degrees be eating up the wealth accumulated in the past, and the rapidity with which our imports increase will then be the measure of our national decay.

V.—*Preponderance of Imports in Recent Years.*

In 1872 the true excess would seem to have been on the side of exports rather than imports, to the extent of nearly £4,000,000; but in the following year the imports again predominated, and have continued to do so with increasing weight up to the present moment. The figures by which this is shown demanding particular investigation, another table has been prepared in which both imports and exports are separated into three classes. This division is necessarily rather a rough one, so many articles not belonging decisively to either class. Again, there are many substances not strictly food, which are yet entirely consumed in supplying our inner wants or inclinations, and leave nothing remaining but the bodily power they support, beyond that which, as unfortunately too often happens, they impair or destroy. The broad distinction between that which enters the mouth, and that which employs the hands, has decided whether each article should be classed as one of food, or a material for manufacture. Wine, spirits, tobacco, have all thus been deemed food, as well as wheat, meat, or sugar. Manufactured articles, and those which admit of no particular classification, form the third head under imports. With the exports it has been attempted to distinguish between those originating in foreign materials and such as are of home produce alone. However imperfectly this distinction may have been capable of maintenance, it is equally correct or incorrect for the different years, and may thus serve as a guide for comparison. There are some features in these figures which shed great light upon the main subject of this paper, namely, the growing increase of our imports and decrease of our exports.

Table IV.—*Classified Imports and Exports for the Years 1854 to 1876, Distinguishing Articles for Food from the Imports of Raw Materials for Manufacture and other Articles, and the Exports of British Manufactures Produced from Foreign Materials, and those of Home Growth.* [1877-9 *added.*]

[In Millions of £'s.]

	Imports.					Exports.			
Years.	Total Retained for Home Consumption.	Articles for Food.	Raw Materials for Manufacture.	Other Articles.	Real Excess of Imports.	Manufactured from British Materials.	Manufactured from Foreign Materials.	Articles of Food.	Total British Produce and Manufactures.
	£	£	£	£	£	£	£	£	£
1854	134	59·	61·	14·	—	27·	66·	4·	97·
'55	123	52·	57·	14·	—	25·	65·	6·	96·
'56	149	62·	72·	15·	—	31·	78·	7·	116·
'57	164	64·	82·	18·	—	35·	81·	6·	122·
'58	141	57·	68·	16·	15·	30·	81·	5·	116·
'59	154	56·	84·	14·	—3·	33·	91·	6·	130·
1860	182	80·	85·	17·	26·	34·	97·	5·	136·
'61	183	82·	79·	22·	32·	31·	88·	6·	125·
'62	183	89·	71·	23·	37·	33·	86·	5·	124·
'63	199	79·	94·	26·	29·	37·	104·	6·	147·
'64	223	79·	119·	25·	37·	37·	118·	5·	160·
'65	218	78·	112·	28·	29·	38·	123·	5·	166·
'66	245	91·	126·	28·	36·	42·	141·	6·	189·
'67	230	101·	100·	29·	27·	42·	134·	5·	181·
'68	247	105·	110·	32·	38·	42·	133·	5·	180·
'69	248	106·	108·	34·	29·	50·	135·	5·	190·
1870	259	100·	119·	40·	34·	53·	139·	7·	199·
'71	271	118·	117·	36·	15·	58·	155·	10·	223·
'72	296	136·	125·	35·	—4·	76·	173·	7·	256·
'73	315	147·	133·	35·	19·	85·	161·	9·	255·
'74	312	143·	130·	39·	29·	78·	154·	8·	240·
'75	316	157·	118·	41·	54·	67·	149·	7·	223·
'76	319	159·	119·	41·	83·	57·	138·	7·	201·
1877	341	177·	121·	43·	94·	55·	136·	8·	199·
'78	316	167·	105·	44·	84·	53·	133·	7·	193·
'79	306	167·	100·	39·	67·	52·	133·	7·	192·

It may be observed in the first place, that articles for food which in 1854 were imported to a rather less value than those for manufacture, are now vastly in excess. In 1871 they were nearly equal to each other; by 1875 the one had increased from 118 to 157, the other scarcely at all. In the present year it is believed the disproportion will be greater. The total amounts of both are less than they would be but for the low prices which have prevailed—a cause, however, which has certainly not affected materials more than food. The conclusion that we are buying more food and selling fewer manufactured goods tallies with the diminution of our exports.

Again, it may be noticed that the exports of manufactures from foreign materials, which in 1854 only exceeded the value of the materials imported by 8 per cent. (66 to 61), were last year 18 per cent. in excess (149 to 118), seeming to comport with what we know of the increasing cost of labour.

These two circumstances—the growing expenditure for food, and the increasing cost of manufactures—cannot both arise from the prevalence of low prices, nor are they likely to be remedied by any revival of trade to which present indications point. If food become dearer it will not cheapen the manufactures we sell, and if at present prices we are being undersold by foreign producers, it is scarcely probable that a general rise in values will at all check the rapid growth of excess in our imports. To recur to the net balances which have to be adjusted; we find that they are larger than they have ever been before, that they are increasing in an accelerated ratio, and that our export trade furnishes no indication of being able to alter their amount, any more than our import does of their being reduced. Further, that all this occurs conjointly with default in remittances for dividends on foreign loans, and that on all sides we hear that this extended import and diminished export trade is unaccompanied by the usual rate of profits.

Unless, therefore, some radical change take place in the conditions of our trade and manufacture, or the system upon which they are conducted, these unfavourable symptoms will every year become more painfully apparent.

VI.—*Concluding Remarks.*

What, then, are the requisite changes? How may the growing evils indicated by the figures we have before us be checked or averted? These are questions for the political economist rather than the statistical inquirer. If, however, the investigation we have been pursuing has at all served to make clear facts of importance as regards our natural position as a manufacturing and trading community, I crave your indulgence for the utterance of a few thoughts which have arisen during its progress.

The gravity of the situation lies in the fact that whilst we are every year becoming more dependent upon foreign supplies for the support of our population, the products of its industry are becoming less necessary to the countries from which those supplies are drawn. Whilst fancied security in our ability to defy competition, and a knowledge of the large profits hitherto accruing to our manufacturers, have induced our artisans and labourers to grow more exacting in their demands, and their masters to be more lavish in their expenditure, other nations have been profiting by our experience, and rival manufactories have been springing up on all sides. Whilst we have been appropriating a large portion of our earnings to the increase of our productive powers, other nations have been calling forth and utilizing their natural advantages; so that, for a time at least, supply has overtaken demand, and competition has lowered prices to such an extent as to render a large recovery very doubtful. Whilst we have been freely lending our money to other nations, thereby enabling them to pay for their purchases from us, more than one of those deeply in our debt have been repudiating or neglecting their pecuniary obligations to us, and so acting that it seems uncertain whether national expenditure may not be forced upon us for their maintenance, or repression, as the case may be. Is it, then, for us to sit down in inactivity or despair? Such has not been the Anglo-Saxon character hitherto; such will not be the conduct of Anglo-Saxons now.   If we have been running riot in the "seven ears full and good," and are about to suffer from the "seven thin ears blasted with the east wind," we may learn such lessons from adversity as to lay the foundation of a higher state of prosperity than any we have yet attained to.

Our labourers must learn that if trade is to be maintained the cost of production must be limited. To this end wages will have to fall, but if so, the cost of living will fall also; and if not, there is no need for them to earn less, for temperance and economy of time will enable them to produce more. It is said that we spend annually 150 millions in intoxicating drinks, as much as all our food imports cost us.   At least one-half of this might be easily saved by the lower classes for better employment, and the country would be spared the expenditure of an enormous sum in the maintenance of poor-houses, hospitals, police, and gaols.

Our capitalists, and those who live upon them, need to restrain the heavy expenditure accompanying the cravings of ambition, the undue pursuit of pleasure and frivolous idleness.   They will seek to invest their money in places where new industries are to be established, and new markets to be found, whilst a large number of those whose brains are their only capital, must cease from the wild speculation by which so many strive to live; seeking to make their fortunes not by honest industry, but by being sharper than their neighbours, thus, in truth, enhancing the cost to the consumer of all that passes through their hands.

Our rulers, now that the days of heavier taxation are looming before us, may well endeavour to reduce the costly expenditure of preparation for war, and devote more attention to extending our peaceful influence upon, and intercourse with, the countries which want but this to become valuable customers and faithful friends.

But are we not all labourers, capitalists, rulers? and as such are not these lessons for ourselves?   The food we eat, the water we drink, the air we inspire, are but so many constituents in creating and maintaining the physical power and the nervous energy which must be expended in labour of some sort, or they become inert; are there not abundant fields for their employment, as so many have already found, in new countries, or in old ones capable of being renewed?

Are we not all capitalists? The knowledge we have imbibed, the experience we have inherited or acquired, the brain power we possess, are but so much capital capable of profitable investment; especially when accompanied with, or supported by, the money capital of which there is no lack for promising uses.

Again, are we not all rulers? The liberty for self-govern-ment, the parental, conjugal, and social relationships in which we stand, are so many powers to be wisely employed in ruling ourselves and others, for our own and their advan-tage, which need but to be so devoted for the economizing of our present means, and the production of material addi-tions to our varied resources.

I firmly believe that Britain now stands tottering on the eminence to which she has attained, and that it rests entirely with her sons whether a further rise or a rapid fall is to mark her future history. It may be said that no nation has hitherto stayed in its upward progress without suffering a speedy descent. Other nations have possessed wealth, science, art, but none have ever combined with these the higher gifts which we enjoy. Let these but be consecrated to the advancement of civilization and Christianity through-out the world, and I, for one, have no fear for our lasting prosperity or enduring glory. Say not these are but the visions of an enthusiast: such enthusiasm has had its share in making us what we are, it may yet play an important part in the salvation of our country, and the regeneration of the world.

IV.

On the Increasing Dependence of this Country upon Foreign Supplies for Food.[1]

HAVING occasion, in preparing a recent paper for the Statistical Society of London, to divide the value of the Imports, under the several headings of Food, Raw Materials, Manufactures, &c., I was surprised to find how large a proportion of the whole fell to the first of these, viz., Articles for Food :—and having been honoured by a request from your President that I would contribute a paper to the Transactions of this Society, I felt that I could not well choose a more appropriate subject than the one which stands for to-night's discussion. To citizens of this northern metropolis, which has so large a share in providing clothing, not for our own country alone, but for the inhabitants of the whole world, the question of how its workers are supplied with food can scarcely fail to be one of the greatest interest ; whilst the present position of our trade and manufactures renders its due consideration of the highest importance to the national progress and well-being.

In treating this matter, I propose first to inquire what are the actual facts as to our present consumption of food from abroad, and to trace the growth of the provision imports in their several subdivisions. Next, to compare the foreign supplies with those of home growth, touching upon the sources from which our necessities are supplied.

[1] Read before the Manchester Statistical Society, April 11th. 1877.

Then to consider briefly some points of special importance as regards the interests of both consumers and producers ; and, lastly, to view the question in connection with the financial and other relations in which this country stands to the rest of the world.

I. That we may get a connected and comparative view of the food imports for a series of years it will be well, in the first place, to look at them in their total money value, that being the only denomination under which the various weights, measures, &c., can be collected together. Yet this is in some measure faulty, for the fluctuations from year to year in the prices of the different articles prevent the value from being a strictly true representative of quantity. This we shall be able to see for the several articles, but not quite accurately for all together. In the paper referred to, I started with 1854, that being the earliest year in which the values were collected on a system at all analogous to that now adopted, so that one period could be compared with another. For the present purpose I commence with 1857, as being just twenty years back, and the first also of the peaceful era which followed on the termination of the Crimean War. In that year the total value of the foreign and colonial goods retained for consumption in this country amounted to £164,000,000, of which 64 was for articles of food, 82 for raw materials for manufacture, and 18 for manufactured articles.[1] Last year, (1876) these amounts were a total of £319,000,000, of which 159 was for food, 119 raw materials, and 41 other ; from which it will appear that 39 per cent. of the whole in the former year, and 50 per cent. in the latter, went for food. In making this separation of food from other articles it is not possible to be absolutely correct, for so many substances admit of a two-fold use. Take, for instance, olive oil, which is actually used both as food and in manufactures ; or the fat of animals, which may appear on our table at meal-times for food or in the shape of candles to lighten its darkness.

[1] Vide p. 72.

Again, it may be asked what is food ?   Meat and tobacco are totally different in their use or abuse, but both enter the mouth and are there consumed ; both therefore are classed under this head, together with wines, spirits, &c.

In the following table the figures for each successive year since 1856 are set forth in millions (to two decimals,) and placed alongside the ascertained population of the United Kingdom ; and as it would be unsafe to take for comparison the amount of either in a single year, an average for the first and last three years has been worked out, showing that whilst the number of consumers had increased from 28$\frac{7}{8}$ to 32$\frac{1}{4}$ millions, the food furnished from abroad had advanced from 59 to 153, a growth of the one by 16, of the other by 160 per cent.   This means that on an average each member of the community now consumes to the value of two and a half times as much foreign food as he did twenty years back, somewhere about £5 for £2.

TABLE I.—*Showing the Total Value of Food imported between 1857 and 1876, under the several heads of Animal and Cereal Food, Sugar, &c., and Beverages, Alcoholic, and other.*

[In million £'s to two decimals.]

Years.	Population.	Total Value.	Animal.	Cereal.	Sugar, Fruit, &c.	Beverages.		Miscellaneous.
						Alcoholic.	Other.	
1857	28·19	64·00	7·60	20·51	19·52	5·68	5·63	6·06
'58	28·39	57·00	6·00	21·50	15·81	1·13	5·90	6·66
'59	28·59	56·00	6·77	18·24	14·83	3·69	6·59	5·88
'60	28·78	80·00	11·15	32·13	13·90	5·43	7·59	9·80
'61	28·97	82·00	12·46	35·94	15·62	5·07	7·25	5·66
'62	29·26	89·00	13·28	39·54	15·20	4·88	8·60	7·51
'63	29·43	79·00	14·01	26·99	15·15	5·51	10·39	6·95
'64	29·63	79·00	16·96	20·92	18·94	6·63	8·56	6·99
'65	29·86	78·00	20·05	21·28	15·30	4·96	8·83	7·58
'66	30·08	91·00	20·40	31·00	14·86	6·45	10·04	8·25
'67	30·33	101·00	17·28	42·67	16·31	7·78	9·20	7·76
'68	30·62	105·00	16·65	41·29	18·54	7·32	10·83	10·37
'69	30·91	106·00	21·37	39·61	19·45	7·34	9·22	9·01
'70	31·21	100·00	20·08	34·39	20·37	7·63	9·17	8·06
'71	31·51	118·00	23·53	42·60	22·05	9·39	9·40	11·03
'72	31·84	136·00	22·27	52·89	28·04	9·15	10·71	12·94
'73	32·12	147·00	28·41	52·69	27·06	10·75	10·64	17·45
'74	32·43	143·00	30·44	51·47	26·21	9·09	11·20	14·59
'75	32·75	157·00	34·14	54·74	27·34	9·48	13·26	18·04
'76	33·09	159·00	37·20	53·04	27·69	10·54	11·43	19·10
In 20 years	—	2027·00	380·35	733·43	391·19	137·90	184·44	199·69
Averages	30·40	101·35	19·02	36·67	19·56	6·90	9·22	9·98
1st 3 years	28·39	59·00	6·79	20·08	16·39	3·50	6·04	6·20
Last 3 years	32·75	153·00	33·93	53·09	27·08	9·70	11·96	17·24
Increase per cent.	16	160	403	165	62	184	101	174
1877	33·45	177·00	35·62	65·29	35·98	9·50	13·00	17·61
'78	33·88	167·00	39·98	60·11	29·15	7·84	12·08	17·84
'79	34·16	167·00	39·14	63·23	30·30	7·99	11·79	14·55

The further columns of this table subdivide the total values under the different heads of animal, cereal, and other vegetable food used in a solid state; such as are employed for beverage are divided into alcoholic, and non-alcoholic : with another column (partly estimated) of such as scarcely fall under either definition, or are not sufficiently distinguished in the official accounts to be assigned to their proper heads.   Amongst these latter we have tobacco, spices, oil, &c., and also a class of articles which at first sight may appear most improperly placed—namely, guano, manure, &c.   These, however, are mainly employed to stimulate the soil in its production of food, and therefore add to the supply just as much as they would if by their means the larger crops were raised for our use abroad instead of at home.   Thus much of explanation is necessary to guard against undue conclusions being drawn from these figures, and it must also be remembered that as in the selection of food from other substances, so in this further separation complete certainty is not attainable ; but as in each year the same rule has been followed, the progress in each class may be truly traced.   A few words on each heading may be desirable, reserving closer remarks till we come to deal with quantities.

In none of the classes has the value risen to anything like the extent that it has in animal food, the average for the first three years being under 7, for the last three nearly 34 millions, fully five times as great as in the former.   In this class there are included living animals, fresh and salted meat, fish and poultry, and their products, butter, cheese, eggs, lard, &c.   The increase in price on live and fresh meat being neutralized by reductions in other descriptions renders the comparison between the two periods fair.

Under the head of cereal produce is included every description of grain, flour, rice, and farinaceous substances generally, no distinction being made between that which is adapted for human as distinct from animal food.   That which is consumed by oxen, sheep, and poultry is in fact but human food under another form ; but it would have been desirable, had it been possible, to have excluded at least so much as serves for the support of horses.   Another deduction also is requisite on account of the grain used for malting and distilling. The quantities thus employed cannot be ascertained, but an estimate is possible of the whole consumption for these purposes of home and foreign produce taken together, and since whatever of home growth is converted into beer or spirits has to be replaced by importations from abroad, it will not be unfair to deduct it all from the heading of cereal food, and add it to that of alcoholic beverage. The following table shows both quantity and value of the grain thus converted, and in addition those of sugar and molasses which are devoted to the same use.

TABLE II.—*Quantities and Value of Grain converted into Beer and Spirits, also of Sugar and Molasses.*

[Millions to two decimals.]

Years.	Grain.	Value.	Sugar and Molasses.	Value.
	Cwts.	£	Cwts.	£
1857	25·60	10·88	·03	·05
'58	24·40	9·13	·06	·06
'59	25·90	9·20	·08	·07
'60	23·60	10·02	·11	·12
'61	24·35	9·91	·34	·24
'62	23·62	7·36	·51	·30
'63	25·76	9·05	·31	·19
'64	28·61	9·55	·05	·05
'65	28·46	9·50	·08	·07
66	29·34	11·25	·22	·18
'67	26·77	12·19	·47	·45
'68	27·88	13·43	·47	·44
'69	30·07	11·55	·46	·47
'70	32·11	12·32	·34	·31
'71	30·11	11·74	·41	·42
'72	33·81	12·84	·56	·53
'73	35·31	13·77	·84	·84
'74	35·03	15·41	1·04	1·06
'75	35·41	14·87	1·01	1·04
'76	37·43	13·10	1·08	1·01
	583·57	227·07	8·47	7·90
Average......	29·18	11·35	·42	·40

The correction thus made under this head materially reduces the value of the cereal supplies, making the

average of the first three years to be 10·34 millions instead
of 20·08 as shown in Table I., and that of the last three
38·61 instead of 53·07. The increase of one period over
the other being 273 per cent. instead of 165 per cent.

Next in order is the class of sugar, fruit, and vegetables,
which are thrown together as being all of them vegetable
products occupying a subsidiary place to that of the staple
articles of bread and meat. A transfer from this head to
that of alcoholic beverage, similar to that from the previous
head, must also be made here, though not to anything like
the same amount, for as yet the quantity of saccharine
produce used in brewing and distilling is but small in
comparison with that of grain. The two averages will be
16·33 millions instead of 16·39, and 25·59 instead of 26·63.
The rate of increase 57 instead of 62. Sugar forms by far
the larger amount of value under this head, and though the
increase is less than with meat, it would have been somewhat more than it is but for the extensive reduction in the
price consequent upon the diminution first, and total abolition of the duty afterwards. This is one of the articles,
the consumption of which is likely to grow rapidly, and to
continue at a low price.

The various substances in use as beverage, whether
imported in the liquid form fit for drinking, or as the
materials to be subsequently prepared for consumption,
admit of division into the two sub-classes of alcoholic and
other liquors. Making the necessary transfers from cereals
and sugar, we find that the first three years averaged 13·30
millions for the one and 6·04 for the other, whilst the last
three show totals of 25·43 and 12·15 respectively, the increase upon the one having been 91 and the other 101 per
cent. This, it must be remarked, does not represent either
. the total or the comparative expenditure by the consumers
of alcoholic as compared with non-intoxicating fluids, for
the major part of the value assigned to the former is simply
that of the raw material from which the liquor is prepared.
This, in the case of spirits and beer, is a very small propor-

tion of the outlay, the chief cost being in the manufacture of the finished liquor, whilst tea, coffee, &c., require little or no expense to fit them for immediate use.

Thus far we have been dealing with values only, and find that during the period of twenty years the total cost of our foreign food has been rather more than two thousand millions of pounds sterling, thus made up :—

	£			
Cereals..	506 millions.	Average		25·3
Sugar and Vegetable Products.........	382	,,	,,	19·1
Animal Products...........................	381	,,	,,	19·05
Beverages—Alcoholic....................	374	,,	,,	18·7
,, Non-alcoholic..............	185	,,	,,	9·25
Miscellaneous	199	,,	,,	9·95
	2,027	,,	,,	101·35

Or, if we take the averages of the two triennial periods as the present and former consumption, we should say the expenditure is in round numbers, for—

	£			£	
Cereals	39 millions, as against			10 formerly.	
Animal Products.................	34	,,	,,	7	,,
Sugar, &c.......................	26	,,	,,	17	,,
Beverages—Alcoholic...........	25	,,	,,	13	,,
,, Non-alcoholic	12	,,	,,	6	,,
Miscellaneous...................	17	,,	,,	6	,,
	153			59	

The true measure, however, of our dependence upon foreign supplies is furnished by quantities rather than values. The principal ones are set forth in the following table, in which wheat is divided from other grain and from rice ; the living animals are reduced to their weight in meat, and added to the importations of that coming here either salted or fresh ; including also fish, but excluding poultry, the weight of which is not ascertained. Butter, cheese, and lard are separately shown, as also sugar and dried_fruit (currants and raisins). These several articles make up the bulk of the food, properly so called, received from abroad. Those used exclusively as beverages, find a place in a separate table, both being constructed upon the same plan as that relating to values; and showing the results, as before, in millions to two places of decimals :—

TABLE III.—*Showing the Quantities of the principal Articles of Food.—Imports retained for Home Consumption*, 1857-76.

Years.	Animal.		Cereals, &c., &c.			Other Vegetables.	
	Meat.	Butter, Cheese, and Lard.	Wheat.	Other Grain.	Rice.	Sugar and Molasses.	Currants and Raisins.
	Cwts.	Cwts.	Cwts.	Cwts.	Cwts.	Cwts.	Cwts.
1857	1·35	1·00	17·23	18·09	2·24	8·01	·44
'58	1·17	·86	23·16	21·50	2·56	9·56	·64
'59	1·21	·92	21·43	18·99	·33	9·56	·78
'60	1·85	1·61	31·81	33·43	·35	9·33	·92
'61	1·81	2·01	36·26	27·90	1·61	10·26	·91
'62	2·46	2·21	49·95	25·86	2·65	10·49	·98
'63	2·99	2·20	30·74	30·25	1·46	10·19	1·08
'64	3·31	2·04	28·74	19·31	1·53	10·24	1·03
'65	3·48	2·04	25·79	24·63	·57	11·17	1·09
'66	3·16	2·23	29·30	34·82	1·13	11·70	1·06
'67	2·55	2·27	38·88	27·79	1·76	12·09	1·07
'68	2 29	2·17	36·19	31·27	2·85	12·22	1·15
'69	3·22	2·45	44·36	36·83	3·74	12·47	1·15
'70	3·08	2·36	35·34	38·40	2·25	13·86	1·11
'71	3·96	2·93	43·31	40·59	2·37	13·86	1·23
'72	4·07	2·60	47·39	55·68	4·03	14·08	1·35
'73	5·48	3·15	50·53	44·32	3·33	15·35	1·23
'74	5·11	3·39	48·47	45·23	3·00	15·47	1·30
'75	5·69	3·55	59·45	49·51	3·48	17·91	1·25
'76	6·31	3·65	50·97	67·14	3·05	16·62	1·46
In 20 years.	64·55	45·64	749·30	691·34	44·26	244·44	21·23
Average	3·23	2·28	37·47	34·58	2·21	12·22	1·06
First 3 years.	1·24	·93	20·61	19·53	1·71	9·04	·62
Last 3 years.	5·70	3·53	52·96	53·96	3·18	16·66	1·34
Increase per cent.	360	280	157	176	86	84	116
	325		163			86	

Looking first at the animal food, and especially at the meat, we shall see that the quantity now imported is very nearly five times as great as it was twenty years since, the exact increase being 360 per cent., and that this has been reached by tolerably steady progress. Each year, with a few exceptions, has advanced upon its predecessor in an accelerated ratio, until now we have a total supply of more than 6 million cwts. which, if equally divided amongst all the inhabitants of the United Kingdom would give rather more than 21½lbs. per head per annum. Although not shown in the table, the proportion of live to dead meat was last year as 6 to 15, one which will be speedily altered if the importations now taking place from America are continued. During the three months of this year already elapsed, the beef fresh or slightly salted has been 132,000 cwts., and meat preserved otherwise than by salting, 125,000 cwts., as against 24,000 cwts. and 38,000 cwts. in the same period of last year, more than quadrupling the amount.

With butter, cheese, and lard, the growth has been equally continuous, though not so large. The increase is 280 per cent., or nearly four times, the total quantity at present being rather more than half the weight of meat—if equally divided 12¼ lbs. per head. Taking the two together the increase is 325 per cent., and the weight falling to the share of each individual about 1½ oz. per diem throughout the year. The bearing of these calculations will be seen further on when comparing the foreign supply with home produce. But even this scarcely represents the full accession to the stock of animal food for which we are indebted to foreign supplies, since a considerable portion of grain, notably barley, peas, and maize, as well as oil-cake, is employed in feeding home-raised cattle and pigs. We have seen that of the farinaceous articles imported last year some 37 out of 67 million cwts. are probably appropriated to alcoholic production, either directly or to compensate for home produce so employed. The balance may

perhaps bo equally divided between feeding for horses and
meat-producing animals. To what extent, however, this
may increase the home-grown animal food there are not
sufficient data for determining. We may here notice the
different rate of increase in the quantity and the value, 325
per cent. against 403, showing an advance in price on the
whole equal to 19 per cent.

Of the corn and grain, other than wheat, very little can
be deemed directly available for human food, although most
of it, as we have stated, virtually serves this purpose, and
what does not, leaves the land at home free to grow that
which does; but rice, of which only a small quantity is used
for distilling, may fairly be classed with wheat. Taking
these two together, we find that the average of the first
three years, 23 million cwts., has grown to 56 in the last,
more than doubling the supply. This quantity, divided
amongst the whole population, would · provide a daily allowance of rather more than half a pound weight of bread
for each person. In this class of food the advance in price
has been almost identical with that in quantity.

The quantity of wheat shown in the table includes flour,
of which 1 cwt. is reckoned equivalent to 1¼ cwt. of wheat.
The quantities of this and other descriptions of grain vary
from time to time more than most articles—a necessary
consequence of fluctuating yield in home produce and varying harvests in the countries with which we deal. Dividing
the twenty years into periods of five, we find the supply
from abroad to have averaged per head :—

1857-61 .	. 97·73 lbs.	Price per cwt. . .	11/3
1862-66 .	. 119·71 ,,	,, . .	9/9
1867-71 .	. 139·84 ,,	,, . .	11/10
1872-76 .	. 173·01 ,,	,, . .	10/10
1857-1876	132·52		10/11

How far this rate of increase results from greater population, combined with stationary or diminished home growth, will be seen when the two are considered together.

Of the rice imported, some portion, perhaps a considerable one, is employed for other purposes, such as the manufacture of starch, &c., but the whole quantity 3·18 million cwts. is so small compared with that of wheat, that any allowance for these purposes, or for distillation, would but little affect the average.

Coming then to the last class, sub-divided into sugar and dried fruit, we find that the first average of 9·66 millions has grown into 18·00 in the latter, the increase of 86 per cent. being far lower than in the classes of animal food and of wheat. Of sugar, itself, after allowing for that converted into alcohol, the difference between the first and the last years of the series is that between 7·98 and 15·54, equal to 96 per cent. In value, the variation has been in a contrary direction, 14·41 having only grown to 17·09, or but 12 per cent., the difference of the two rates thus showing a fall in price equivalent to 40 per cent.

The several articles thus enumerated constitute the bulk of the solid food imported, but there are two others, of some importance, included in the value table (though to save space not particularized in the quantity one), eggs under animal, and potatoes under vegetable.

Of these we imported :—

		£
In 1857—Eggs 126·82 millions.	Value	·32
„ 1876— „ 753·36 „	„	2·61
„ 1857—Potatoes ·96 „	„	·18
„ 1876— „ 6·03 „	„	1·74

In the next table there are shown those articles which are imported in the liquid form, or are designed for use as beverage ; and one other, not belonging either to food or drink, but yet properly classed amongst those pertaining to the ordinary consumption of a large portion of the population.

TABLE IV.—*Showing the quantities of the principal Imported articles retained for home use as Beverages; also of Tobacco.*—1857-76.

Years.	Alcoholic.		Non-Alcoholic.			Tobacco.
	Spirits.	Wines.	Tea.	Coffee.	Cocoa.	
	Gals.	Gals.	lbs.	lbs.	lbs.	lbs.
1857	4·73	6·60	69·13	34·35	2·65	32·68
'58	4·58	6·27	73·20	35·21	2·86	33·92
'59	4·93	6·78	76·30	34·33	3·01	34·63
'60	5·52	6·72	76·82	35·50	3·23	35·23
'61	5·19	10·69	77·93	35·20	3·41	34·83
'62	5·19	9·76	78·79	34·45	3·62	35·42
'63	5·57	10·42	85·18	32·76	3·71	37·37
'64	6·30	11·40	88·60	31·36	3·86	38·01
'65	6·74	11·99	97·83	30·51	3·83	38·90
'66	7·80	13·24	102·27	30·63	4·05	40·50
'67	8·34	13·67	110·99	31·28	4·23	40·72
'68	8·40	15·06	106·82	30·36	5·11	40·98
'69	8·17	14·73	111·80	28·84	5·70	41·37
'70	8·44	15·08	117·55	30·23	6·15	41·37
'71	8·93	16·14	123·40	30·60	7·25	42·50
'72	9·07	16·77	127·66	31·17	7·79	43·68
'73	10·26	17·91	131·88	31·79	8·28	45·48
'74	10·68	17·17	137·28	31·26	8·85	46·58
'75	11·85	17·24	145·33	32·05	9·96	47·82
'76	11·55	18·66	149·13	33·34	10·43	48·57
In 20 years...	152·24	256·30	2087·89	645·22	107·98	800·56
Average	7·61	12·81	104·40	32·26	5·40	40·03
,, first 3 yrs.	4·75	6·55	72·88	34·63	2·84	33·74
,, last 3 ,,	11·36	17·69	147·25	32·22	9·75	47·66
Increase per cent.	140	170	102	—7	243	41
		157		71		

We have already (Table II.) seen both quantity and value of the grain, &c., converted into alcoholic beverage, and in this table only deal with the spirits and wine imported in a completed state; the amount of beer brought hither being quite inconsiderable, not more than two to three thousand barrels a year. Taking wine and spirits together, the growth since 1857 has been from 11·30 to 29·05 million gallons, or 157 per cent. That of spirits alone from 4·75 to 11·36, or 140 per cent.; and of wine from 6·55 to 17·69, or 170 per cent. The total value has risen from 3·50 to 9·93, or 184 per cent., not so great a difference as to render particular observation necessary. Both have fallen in price, spirits more than wine, but wine being the dearer article and the one which has increased the most, has tended to raise the whole value.

The class of non-intoxicating drinks, or rather the materials from which they are derived, manifests on the whole an increase of 71 per cent. only. This arises mainly from the declining use of coffee, which is now actually 7 per cent. less than it was in 1857. Tea has increased 102 per cent., and cocoa 243, or together 107 per cent., considerably less than the alcoholic liquors have done. The average quantities in the first and last years having been :—

| Tea............ | 72·88 | Coffee............ | 34·63 | Cocoa............ | 2·84 |
| and .... | 147·25 | and............ | 32·22 | and .... | 9·75 |

Comparing this increase of quantity with that of value, it appears that tea, by far the larger of three articles, has increased in weight almost in the same ratio as the whole has in cost, that is, in both instances almost exactly double.

Of tobacco, the growth has been from 33·74 millions to 47·66, or 41 per cent., happily a less rate of progress than (excluding coffee) in any other article. Its price has not very materially altered, nor, being in its imported state a cheap article (8d. to 1s. per lb. for the principal portion), is its value sufficient to affect greatly any calculations of our total imports. Yet as an indication of the tendency of the popular taste, it becomes no less important than it is to the revenue as one of our highly remunerative tax-paying articles.

II. In endeavouring to compare the extent of foreign supply with that furnished by home produce, it will be necessary to take a lesser range of years, since the infor-

mation of the earlier period embraced in the tables was not
collected with the same detail as it now is, but a fair comparison can be drawn for the last ten years.   In 1868 Mr.
Caird thus calculated the average value of the agricultural
produce of the United Kingdom, consumed annually:—

Corn of all kinds	£84,700,000
Beef and mutton	47,200,000
Butter and cheese	30,100,000
Potatoes	18,000,000
	£180,000,000

The foreign supplies for the same articles he placed at
£40,000,000, giving a proportion of one-fifth of the total
supply.   Since that period it is not probable that there has
been much variation in the home produce, but the foreign
supplies have increased 80 per cent.   The average of the
two columns, Animal and Cereal, in Table I., during the first
ten years, gives £39·67, singularly near to Mr. Caird's estimate, and for the last ten years £71·78.   This proportion
agrees well for the total value of the food imports, which,
as we have seen before, has, during twenty years, risen 160
per cent., or, assuming an even progress, 8 per cent. per
annum.   For the past year, however, these two classes give
a total of £91,000,000, and if we add to this £2,000,000 for
potatoes, we shall have £93,000,000; rather more than half
the estimate for home produce.   On this showing we at
present depend for corn, meat, and potatoes together, on
foreign supplies for somewhat more than one-third the value
of that we consume.

Turning, however, to quantities, we descend into closer
comparison as regards the two staple articles of bread and
meat.   In the following table a careful estimate has been
made of the relative weights drawn from the two sources.
Mr. Caird has kindly furnished me with estimates of the
average produce of wheat per acre in this country for each
year since 1867, and applying these to the number of acres

shown by the Agricultural Returns to be in cultivation, I arrive at the quantities given, averaging a growth of 54,000,000 cwts. Against this there is a foreign supply at the average of 45,000,000 ; but if we take the foreign importations for the last three years we get an average of 53,000,000, from which it may be safely inferred that our bread is equally of home and foreign origin.

TABLE V.—*Quantities of Home-raised Wheat and Meat, compared with Foreign Importations, during the last ten years.* [1877-9 *added.*]

Years.	Wheat.		Meat.	
	Home.	Foreign.	Home.	Foreign.
	Cwts.	Cwts.	Cwts.	Cwts.
1867	40·65	38·88	25·22	2·55
'68	74·26	36·19	24·61	2·29
'69	62·27	44·36	24·11	3·22
'70	65·22	35·34	24·96	3·08
'71	53·62	43·31	25·37	3·96
'72	54·53	47·39	26·13	4·07
'73	44·77	50·53	26·23	5·48
'74	62·43	48·47	26·46	5·11
'75	42·12	59·45	26·04	5·69
'76	43·99	51·06	25·87	6·31
	543·86	454·98	255·00	41·76
1877	37·27	62·54	25·63	6·24
'78	53·35	58·76	25·00	6·99
'79	28·00 ?	70·32	24·00 ?	7·94

As regards meat, an eminent agriculturist, Mr. H. Thompson, in "The Journal of the Royal Agricultural Society," 1872, entered into an elaborate calculation of the annual produce of our flocks and herds. Applying his data, as to numbers and weight of those killed for this purpose, to the existing number in each year—as stated in the Board of Trade Returns, I obtain the weight given in the table,—averaging 25½ million cwts. per annum. The weight thus derived is less than it would be were the data employed those on which Dr. Playfair founded his calculations in a

paper published in 1870; but as the object here is to compare
the British and foreign supplies, rather than to ascertain the
actual amount, and Mr. Thompson gives data for estimating
both, it is safer to adopt his figures.   For two reasons,
however, it is probable that an addition should be made to
the home weight,—the cattle are brought to market at an
earlier age, and therefore the proportion slaughtered is
greater,—and they are fed to an heavier weight.   It will be
right, too, to take into consideration the supply of fish which
takes the place of meat.   It may not, therefore, be incorrect to set down the whole supply at 36 million cwt., of
which one-sixth comes from abroad.

In calculating their relative worth as " flesh formers " it
is estimated by Dr. Playfair that the requisite daily allowance of albuminous material is three ounces per head, which
for the year will be found in 480 lbs. of corn, or 550 lbs. of
meat, that is 8 lbs. of meat will only go as far in support of
the animal frame as 7 lbs. of corn.   On this supposition our
30 million cwt. of fish and flesh is equivalent to about 26 of
corn, and our 6½ millions of foreign to 5¼.

Of potatoes, Mr. Caird estimated the weight consumed in
1867 to be equal to that of bread, about 1 lb. daily for each
person; but there were then 1,500,624 acres under crop, and
now only 1,394,254.   In converting wheat into flour there
is a loss of one-fifth, and flour into bread a gain of one-
third.   This would give a consumption of 90 million cwts.,
but as compared with grain, Dr. Playfair estimates the feeding power to be but one-tenth, equal, therefore, to 9 millions
cwts. of wheat for home, and half-a-million for foreign.

Of other grain, some portion enters into the supply of
human food, and so does rice; but in the absence of any
data on which to make calculation, I assume that these on
either side follow the proportion of wheat, &c.   Butter and
cheese also enter largely into consumption, the home produce
of the latter has been estimated to me by a good authority
at 100,000 tons, and butter at half the cheese.   The importations of last year amounted to 75,000 tons of cheese and

81,000 of butter, together rather more than that of native manufacture.

To sum up these several estimates for reducing the various descriptions of food to their equivalent in wheat, our consumption may be thus stated :—

	Home produce.		Foreign supply.
Wheat	54 million cwts.		53
Meat, equal to . .	26 ,,	,,	5¼
Cheese and Butter =	3 ,,	,,	3
Potatoes . . . =	9 ,,	,,	¼
	92		62

The conclusion thus arrived at would appear to be that for absolute sustenance we rely upon home and foreign produce in somewhere about the proportion of three to two-fifths. The articles which hold a secondary place as means of support are more foreign than British, and adding these to those of higher importance, it is probable that both in value and quantity, about one-half of our food is of foreign origin.

One more calculation may be made. If the nutrition to be found in wheat is such that 480 lbs. suffices for a year's food, and in meat that 550 lbs. is necessary, then

53 million cwts. wheat will support 12¼ millions people.

6¼ ,,	,,	meat	do.	1¼ ,,	,,
6 ,,	,,	potatoes do.		⅓ ,,	,,
3 ,,	,,	butter and cheese		2/7 ,,	,,

14⅚

Hence on this computation of the 33 millions of inhabitants in the United Kingdom, 18 millions may be sustained on food grown at home, and 15 on that received from abroad.

The results obtained by these different processes, though

not identical, are sufficiently near to each other to justify the opinion that neither can be very far from the truth.

If such be the case as it at present stands, the question arises what alterations are likely to take place in the future? Our capacity for home production is by no means exhausted. If we were wise enough to retain the refuse which now pollutes our rivers and is lost in the ocean, the soil would yield larger returns. Higher cultivation and the reclamation of waste or imperfectly drained lands might add to the average under crops, and increase the fertility of that already so employed; but we can scarcely expect any of these measures to be extensively adopted. They are all dependent upon the cost, and every day's experience seems to show that it is cheaper to bring from abroad than to force production at home. Were it even otherwise, should our country continue a prosperous one, the growing demands for space to build on, to plant for pleasure grounds, and to cover with roads, are likely to outstrip any additions which can be made. Neither can it be desired that we should be content with diminished or stationary supplies. The population ought, under the influence of sanitary regulations, and the spread of hygienic knowledge, to increase more rapidly than it has hitherto done, and to substitute meat food for alcoholic drink.

From the combined influences of these several causes we must calculate upon an extended rather than a diminished demand upon the productions of other countries, and every year look to depend less upon our own resources.

III. To be thus dependent upon extraneous sources for so large a portion of the national food may probably to some minds be the occasion of much anxiety, as rendering our very existence precarious, and as being derogatory to our national pride; but provided our circumstances be such as to preclude it resulting in financial embarrassment, we shall find it to be in every respect advantageous, or at least to have so many benefits connected with it as to far outweigh any considerations of an opposite character. Leaving for the present the question of finance, it may not be out of place to briefly state some of the reasons why we should welcome rather than deprecate such a condition.

In the first place, as a manufacturing nation, having something to offer in exchange for the products we require, it is a powerful inducement for other nations to become our customers. Large portions of the world as yet less civilized than our own, where labour is consequently cheaper than with us—having climates more suitable than that of England for producing the food we need—are enabled to raise wheat, to feed cattle, and to grow sugar on easier terms than we, and thus the whole world may, in one shape or another, become tributary to our necessities. With our command of shipping, there need never be any real difficulty in transporting their produce to our shores, and the cost of conveyance, instead of being so much paid out of the country, repays our own sailors and shipowners for the labour they bestow and the capital they employ. By this means we are brought into close and constant communication with various nations, to whom, but for the necessity for intercourse, we should remain strangers. From many of them we may learn much, and to many more we may be the instruments, as we have been and now are, of conveying the knowledge of the arts and sciences, the blessings of civilization, and the truths of religion. There is nothing like extended intercommunication for enlarging the mind, sharpening the intellect, and warming the heart.

For ourselves, confined as we are within a few degrees of climate and limited, so long as we maintained our insular isolation, to the vegetable and animal products of our own narrow sphere, it is something to have almost all the varieties of meat, fruit, and vegetables which the world brings forth, placed within our reach. Variety of food is no less beneficial to the health than pleasant to the taste and gratifying to the sight. It is generally admitted that we owe most of our national vigour to the admixture of class and race, and when properly adjusted there can be little doubt

that a variety of food is conducive to bodily health and enjoyment. With the present search after appliances for the
removal of perishable substances from one side of the ocean
to the other, there is no saying to what extent this may be
pursued, or that the most delicate products will not ere long
be capable of being transported hither from the very ends
of the world. If meat can be brought from America, in such
perfect preservation as that which is now arriving daily, the
game, the fish, the fruit, the vegetables of every clime may
be furnished to our tables. New markets being thus found
for the superabundance of other people, we shall also find
new openings for the sale of our manufactures. The natural
advantages of more favoured countries will thus be shared
with us, and the acquired comforts which we possess may
be participated in far more largely than they otherwise
would be by those who are separated from us by the longest
distances.

Again, nothing is more likely to prevent war than the
mutual dependence of one nation not on another only, but
upon all others. Where commercial relations exist, and
friendships arise, there will ever be a desire for the peaceful
settlement of all differences; and in this respect, the nation
which is the strongest, whether it be in money, in manufacturing skill, or in productive power, will always have more
depending upon it than it has upon others. The larger
the sphere over which its operations extend, the less the probability of any one country being able to interfere with its
dealings with others.

It would be very easy and pleasant to enlarge greatly on
this head, but to pursue it further would unduly extend the
limits of this paper. We proceed therefore to the last topic
with which I propose to tax your attention.

IV. There remain for consideration, then, the financial
relations of this country with the rest of the world, resulting
from this importation of food. During the past year (1876)
the value of goods of foreign origin retained for use in this
country was, as shown in the official returns, £319,000,000;

and that of the produce of this country's growth and manufacture exported from hence £200,000,000, showing an apparent excess of imports to the extent of £119,000,000.
Certain revisions of these figures have, however, to be made,
such as allowances for freight, &c., &c., which justify the
assumption that the real excess of imports for which we have
in some way or other to make provision is somewhere about
£75,000,000. The connection between this balance and the
food question will be best seen by an examination of the
figures for the last ten years. The original values are derived from the publications issued from the Custom House
and Board of Trade, representing the worth of the foreign
goods retained for home use at the time of their arrival in
this country; and in like manner of the British exports at
the time of their departure. The revised figures do not in
any way conflict with the official. They are an estimate of
my own, based upon reasons on which it is not necessary
here to enter, but which will be found fully detailed in a
preceding paper. They are presumed to represent the cost to
this country of the goods it receives, and of those with which
it parts; the difference between the two being the amounts
which have to be met by actual payments in money, or by a
set off in the adjustment of accounts between this nation and
those with which it trades. The sums are shown in millions
of pounds only.

	1867.	1868.	1869.	1870.	1871.	1872.	1873.	1874.	1875.	1876.
	£	£	£	£	£	£	£	£	£	£
Original Values.										
Imports	230	247	248	259	271	296	315	312	316	319
Exports	181	180	190	200	223	256	255	240	224	201
Excess of former.....	49	67	58	59	48	40	60	72	92	118
Revised Estimate.										
Imports...............	205	220	221	231	240	263	281	278	281	284
Exports	188	187	196	207	230	266	267	251	233	209
Balance...............	17	33	25	24	10	—3	14	27	48	75

The total of these balances gives an average of 27 millions a year, but the steadiness and rapidity with which they have latterly grown forbids the expectation that so small an amount is all that will have henceforth to be provided for. Judging by the indications the trade of the past quarter affords, a further increase of 25 millions on that of last year is by no means unlikely. Be it, however, 75 or 100 millions, the sum is so large that it may well excite uneasiness as to how it is to be met. The connection of this with the outlay for food is obvious. It is evident that this country, not being one in which the precious metals are found, cannot pay for its purchases in gold or silver; it may do so for a limited period by suffering a drain upon the bullion previously accumulated, but this has not been the case hitherto. Out of the past twenty years there have been only three in which the import of bullion has not exceeded the export, the average rate of addition to our stock having been five millions per annum, a quantity not more than requisite to meet the extensions of our circulation and the absorption in the arts and manufactures. This year, from the fulness of our coffers, and the diminution of our exports of goods, is likely to be one in which some considerable amount of treasure may be sent away.

The other sources from which the country may derive the means of meeting its obligations are two-fold—the dividends or interest of capital lent or accumulated abroad, and the profits or earnings remitted to this country for use or investment. Of neither is it easy to estimate the amount, nor, however valuable or interesting such information would be, is it necessary for the present argument, which is, that it cannot be increasing in the ratio of our liabilities. We have but to note the defaults of the nations to whom we have lent largely, to see that the stream from the first source is not enlarging; and to listen to the universal chorus of complaints as to the diminished profits of trade abroad to understand that the flow from the second source must be lessening. I am quite aware that it is now a received axiom in the science of political economy that a prosperous country should import more than it exports, otherwise its trade cannot be profitable; but we are not simply traders sending out so much to sell at a profit, and with the proceeds to purchase that which will be of greater value when it reaches our shores than when it left the place from whence it came. We are capitalists also, investing our means in foreign countries to which we can only remit them in the shape of goods exported, or by suffering the profits accruing abroad to remain for employment there instead of at home. Were all our capital absorbed in investments here, the excess of imports of goods and bullion would represent the gains of trade, but scattered as our capital is all over the world, the excess may arise either from increased income accruing abroad or from capital withdrawn from foreign uses. Another explanation may be offered, and probably this is the right one, that in the five years in which our exports were the largest, 1871-75, we were lending or had lent largely to foreign nations, and that those loans were remitted partly in goods —money we did not send—whilst a large portion never went out at all, being absorbed in commissions, &c., by operators at home. But if so, what does this prove? That the trading and manufacturing prosperity of those years were at the expense, not so much of the foreigners who bought our goods, as of our capitalists at home who lent the money with which they were paid for, and that to revive our trade we must resort again to reckless lending.

In whatever light, therefore, we may view these growing balances, it would seem to be sound policy—it may shortly become absolutely unavoidable—that we should seek to reduce them in one or both of two ways, by buying less or by selling more. It is with the former of these expedients we have to deal in relation to our present inquiry, yet a few words on the latter way may not afterwards be out of place.

The following figures for the same period will show the proportion of the above total imports, which are due to articles for food, raw materials for manufacture, and other articles respectively :—

	1867.	1868.	1869.	1870.	1871.	1872.	1873.	1874.	1875.	1876.
	£	£	£	£	£	£	£	£	£	£
Food	101	105	106	100	118	136	147	143	157	159
Raw Materials	100	110	108	119	117	125	133	130	118	119
Manufactures	29	52	34	40	36	35	35	39	41	41
Total Values	230	247	248	259	271	296	315	312	316	319
Percentage of Food	44°	43°	43°	39°	44°	46°	47°	46°	50°	50°
Percentage of Food to Raw Materials.	101	95	98	84	101	109	111	110	133	134

An examination of this table will show that of 319 millions worth of imports for last year 159 were for food, 119 for raw materials, and 41 for manufactured and miscellaneous articles, and that of these the past ten years' growth has been the most rapid in articles for food. We must not wish for any reduction in the supply of raw materials, lest thereby we reduce also the manufactures we have to sell. Of manufactured articles we may somewhat curtail the supply from abroad by reverting to a less extravagant style of living, but even then we shall lose in the customers from whom we take them. In food, as we have already seen, there is no probability that we can do without the staple articles of which our imports are largely composed, but in one branch we may, and I believe we must retrench, that is in our consumption of alcoholic liquors, both those which are imported as such, and those which are manufactured from grain, whether imported or of home growth.

Referring back to Table I. we shall see that the value of alcoholic beverages imported last year amounted to £11,230,000, and in Table II. that grain to the value of £13,100,000, with sugar and molasses to the value of £1,010,000 were converted into beer and spirits, giving a total of more than twenty-five millions of money. This it must be remembered is not the expense to the consumer, that is something far beyond; but the simple cost to the nation of the materials of which its " drink " is composed, and just in proportion as the use of alcohol is lessened may this charge upon its resources be diminished, or, what would be far better, devoted to productive uses. Of food proper, that which nourishes life and creates the force, which, rightly employed, produces the manufactures with which to purchase food, we cannot have too much; but whatever opinions may be held as to the use of alcoholic liquors at all, it is undeniable that the greater portion of our consumption goes to impair life, health, strength, and thus to curtail the productions we need to exchange for our food. Nor is this all, it exhausts our resources in providing for repression of crime and the relief of destitution,— it diverts from profitable employment the time, thought, talent, on the right use of which our national prosperity depends; and by debasing the character, and destroying the skill of our workers in all ranks, it unfairly weights us in the race of competition with countries where temperance is the rule and intemperance the exception. If it be thought that I dwell unduly upon this point, I do so from the thorough conviction that it is to a radical reform in our national ideas and habits in this respect that we must look for a revival or maintenance of our manufacturing and trading prosperity.

Something further than this is, however, necessary. We must not only utilize our food supplies by converting them, through the bodily and mental power they maintain, into products wherewith we may trade with other nations; but must seek, as well, to enlarge the sphere of our mercantile operations. At present it would seem as if our produce and manufactures had exceeded the wants of the world, or at least its power to pay for them, and it is of little use to manufacture more if customers are not forthcoming. This evil can only be met by opening up new markets, by sending forth our brains and our bullion to find employment in places, such as those in Africa, where there are lands of surpassing fertility, rich in vegetable and mineral wealth. These countries are teeming with peoples, wanting but our help to raise them from the degradation in which they are sunk to the level at least of such civilization as may create the wants which we have the power to supply, and enable them in return to bring forth the food and other commodities which our growing population and increasing desires may enable us to consume. Let us as a nation become thrifty and temperate; cherish the character for honesty and justice which the greed of gain has gone far to destroy, and there are untold stores of wealth ready to be brought to our shores. There are unnumbered blessings ready to be poured out upon us, if we will be but true to our creed; and whilst not unmindful of the advantage to ourselves, strive to cultivate higher aims in colonizing, civilizing, and Christianizing the lands and people which geographical discovery and scientific research are daily bringing within our reach.

V

The Nature and Extent of our Foreign Food Supplies, and the Sources from whence they are Derived.[1]

THE latest published official returns of the trade of the United Kingdom show the total value of the imports during last year to have been very little short of £394 millions, that of the preceding year having been a trifle over 375. Looking back for a period of twenty years, it will be seen that in 1857 the value was £188 millions. Of this amount £24 millions was exported, thus leaving 164 for consumption or manufacture at home. The proportion thus taken away in 1877 is not yet ascertained, but that of 1876 having been rather more than £56 millions, that of last year may, allowing for the slackness of trade, be safely estimated at 53, which would leave the value retained in the country at £341 millions, being £22 millions beyond that of 1876, and more than double that of 1857. The goods thus allowed for as re-exported are only those which leave the country in an unaltered state, having simply come to it as a market from whence other nations draw their supplies. Dr. Forbes Watson, in a very interesting paper recently read before the Colonial Institute, has carried this deduction a step farther, and reasoning from reliable data, estimates that in 1876 foreign raw material to the value of £58 millions was worked up into goods which, having undergone manufacture here, were exported as British. Applying

---

[1] Supplement to the "Statist," March 23rd, 1878, and "Journal of Statistical Society," June, 1878.

the same method of calculation to the exports of 1857, we may assume that the value of foreign goods thus dealt with would then have been £36 millions. Again, dealing with the figures for 1877 in the same manner, we may assume that in addition to the foreign goods exported in their original condition there were those converted into British manufactures of the value of £56 millions. The comparison between the two periods will stand thus :—

[000,000's omitted.]

			1857.	1877.
Foreign and Colonial Goods Imported			£188	£394
,,	,,	Exported unchanged	24	53
,,	,,	Exported worked up	36	56
			60	109
		Retained and consumed at home	£128	£285

Such being the full value of the goods for which we are indebted to foreign producers, the portion in each of these years which consisted of food has been shown in the previous paper, in which the growth of consumption and population were compared.

Without pretending to very strict accuracy of detail, the total values of the first and last year in the series may be thus subdivided :—

[000,000's omitted.]

	1857.	1877.
Animal	£8	£36
Cereal	10	52
Sugar and other Vegetables	18	36
Beverages—Alcoholic	16	23
,, —Other	6	13
Miscellaneous	6	17
	£64	£177

The extreme importance of these figures, and the great disparity between those of the two periods, become more

apparent when brought into juxtaposition with the value of
goods exported at the same dates ; thus :—

[000,000's omitted.]

	1857.		1877.
British Produce and Manufacture	£122	...	£199
Deduct Foreign Material in them	36	...	56
	£86	...	£143
Foreign Food Consumed	64	...	177
Other Foreign Goods retained	64	...	108
	£128		£285

In the former year we exported, as the produce of British
labour and capital, £86 millions, to meet an import of food to
the extent of £64, an excess of £22. In the latter, £143,
to meet £177, a deficiency of £34 millions.

Although for the purpose of comparing one description of
food with another and the several years one with the other,
as well as for viewing the whole subject in its financial
bearings, it is necessary to express the whole in money value,
the true measure of our dependence upon foreign supplies is,
since the prices vary so much from time to time, best furnished by quantities rather than cost. The staple articles
obtained from abroad were fully shown in the tables of the
preceding paper (pp. 84, 88).

The Sources of Supply.

Coming now to consider the sources from whence these
supplies are derived, and following the same subdivision of
articles under the principal heads into which the various
descriptions of food may be conveniently divided, the table
here given will show the value of each kind which we
received from the different countries to whom we are
customers for the year 1876. The several totals will not
altogether agree with those of the former totals, because
in both many small items fail to be included and get sunk

among the miscellaneous.   Neither is it possible to deduct
from each country the amount of its produce which is
re-exported.   This, however, is of little importance, the
object being not altogether to see how much from each producing country we keep to supply our wants, but how much
there is available if we should wish to keep it.   The miscellaneous items not being shown here, the comparison must be
with the total of the first of the tables already referred to, less
those there included; and deducting 18·42 from 159·00, we
have 141·58, an almost identical total with that of 141·29
arrived at in the latter table after deducting from the full
value of the goods re-exported the whole amount stated as
imported.   The totals of the different kinds come sufficiently near to the former ones to establish the substantial
accuracy of each compilation.

Table showing the Countries from which the specified Articles of Food Imported in 1876 were obtained, with the respective values of each class.

[In million £'s to two decimals.]

Countries.	Total Value.	Animal Produce.	Cereal and Farinaceous.	Sugar, Fruit, and Vegetables.	Beverages.	
					Alcoholic.	Other.
Russia	7·16	—	7·15	—	·01	—
Sweden	2·38	·30	2·08	—	—	—
Norway	·20	·16	·04	—	—	—
Denmark	3·74	2·64	1·10	—	—	—
Germany	10·33	4·87	2·67	2·24	·53	·02
Holland	8·56	5·56	·27	1·87	·76	·10
Belgium	3·35	1·72	·02	1·34	·21	·06
France	18·12	6·23	1·90	4·48	5·51	—
Portugal	1·93	·34	—	·31	1·28	—
Spain	4·39	·42	·17	1·72	2·08	—
Italy	·95	·02	·42	·38	·13	—
Austria	·56	—	·56	—	—	—
Greece	1·59	—	—	1·59	—	—
Turkey	5·74	—	4·99	·75	—	—
Other Places	1·08	·13	·51	·41	·03	—
Europe	70·08	22·39	21·38	15·09	10·54	·18
British India	13·34	—	4·84	1·54	·02	6·94
Australia	1·98	·36	1·60	—	·02	—
China	10·54	—	—	·40	—	10·14
Japan	·07	—	·06	—	—	·01
Other Places	2·49	—	·13	2·30	·02	·04
Asia & Australia	28·42	·36	6·63	4·24	·06	17·13
Egypt	2·41	—	2·15	·25	·01	—
Cape Mauritius, &c	·98	—	·02	·86	·04	·06
Other Places	1·03	—	·50	·44	·07	·02
Africa	4·42	—	2·67	1·55	·12	·08
United States	36·48	13·90	21·41	·75	·31	·11
Canada & Newfoundland	4·66	1·80	2·81	·05	—	—
South America	4·59	·09	·54	2·23	—	1·73
West Indies	8·71	—	·06	6·65	1·01	·99
America	54·44	15·79	24·82	9·68	1·32	2·83
Imported	157·36	38·54	56·00	30·56	12·04	20·22
Re-exported	16·07	1·54	2·42	2·55	1·29	8·27
Total	141·29	37·00	53·58	28·01	10·75	11·95

Looking first to the magnitude of our demands upon the several producing countries, we find that the United States stands far before any other ; next in rank comes France, British India, China, and Germany ; then the West Indies, Holland, Russia, Turkey, and British North America—the values from these ten standing relatively in the following order :—

[000,000's omitted.]

United States	£36	West Indies	£9
France	18	Holland	9
British India	13	Russia	7
China	11	Turkey	6
Germany	10	British North America	5

These together amount to £124 millions, very nearly four-fifths of the contributions to our necessities from the whole world.   Of these, Germany and Holland, more particularly the former, are to a great extent not the real sources of supply, but only the countries through which the rivers and railways of the Continent pass their supplies to our shores. It is probable that some portion of the receipts from the United States are really the produce of Canada, shipped from Portland during the month when the navigation of the St. Lawrence is closed.   Turkey too gets the credit of much Austrian produce which finds its way down the Danube. China, on the other hand, sends, to the extent of perhaps a million, by way of Hong Kong.

Pursuing another mode of division, and collecting together those which come from our own Indian and Colonial possessions, we shall find about £31 millions, or one-fifth of the whole, to come from places which own our sway ; this proportion being nearly equally divided between India and the Colonies, both together, however, falling short of that which the United States alone sends us.

·   The geographical division between the four quarters of the globe will be apparent from an inspection of the table itself ; Europe, as would be expected from its contiguity and its more ancient settlement and populous condition, being the largest supplier. America, however, is rapidly advancing upon her, and will doubtless before long do more towards provisioning us than the older continent. Asia and Australia are yearly becoming of more value to us in this respect, but the development of Africa as a granary and grazing territory yet remains to be accomplished.

The Different Kinds supplied by Different Countries.

Passing from the extent of our whole supplies to the nature of those which each country furnishes, it appears that of animal food the United States again sends us the most—14 millions out of 39; and judging from the speed with which she is taking up the trade of butcher as well as of provision merchant, her superiority in this branch of supply will yearly advance. Next to her comes France, with 6 millions, largely derived from the poultry yard, 2 millions being in eggs and chickens, with nearly 4 in butter. Holland figures for between 5 and 6 millions, of which 3 millions are in dairy produce and 2 in meat, mostly alive; Germany for nearly 5 millions divided much in the same proportion as Holland; Denmark for nearly 3 millions, and Belgium less than 2. Our own Canadian Dominion sends nearly 2 millions.

As supplying grain and flour, the United States again heads the list with 21 millions, her vast and luxuriant corn-fields enabling her to send from both sides of the continent; nearness of access from the Atlantic being as much to her advantage there as the superior quality and ability to bear the transit in a marketable condition is to the Pacific. Russia does not send us in an appreciable quantity any food other than grain, of which we took from her in 1876 to the value of £7 millions. This quantity was largely increased in 1877, probably by 50 per cent., her desire to anticipate a blockade of her ports pushing forward the supplies which pecuniary necessities rendered it very desirable to convert into cash, and inducing the forwarding of considerable quantities by way of internal communication through other

Continental ports. Turkey, including of course the Roumanian provinces, has sent us £5 millions, of which some considerable portion will be of Austrian or at least Hungarian growth. British India stands next, with not far from £5 millions, having always largely supplied us with rice, and thanks to railways and irrigation she is now becoming a considerable exporter of wheat. Our own North American province stands for nearly £3 millions; Germany for almost as much; whilst Sweden contributes rather more, and Australia rather less, than £2 millions each.

Our next class is that of sugar, fruit, and other vegetable productions not being either cereal or for use as beverages. To this the West Indies, our own colonies, in the proportion of about two-thirds, contribute nearly £7 millions, the produce of their cane-fields. France more than £4 millions, the outcome of her State-subsidized manufacture, to which also Germany, Holland, and Belgium largely owe their ability to find purchasers with us to the extent together of £5½ millions. The contributions of Spain, Greece, and Turkey to that class consist mainly of dried fruits. And it must not be forgotten that considerable supplies of sugar come from our own Eastern possessions, as well as those of Java and the Philippines and even China, as well as from the ancient settlements on the continent of South America.

Of beverages containing alcohol there are but three chief producing countries, and France yields one-half the whole supply, namely, £5¼ out of £12 millions, rather more than half being wine, the remainder, with the exception of a few liqueurs, brandy. Spain contributes £2 in wine, and Portugal rather more than half as much in the same; Germany and Holland together £1 million in Geneva and potato spirit; the West Indies, principally our own, £1 million in rum.

Of other substances for producing beverages, China sent £10 millions in tea, of which one-fifth is again exported; India £2½ millions in the same, and more than as much in coffee from Ceylon, in all nearly £7 millions. Central and South America £1¼ millions; and the West Indies £1 million in coffee and cocoa, the larger proportion of these articles being again exported, principally to the Continent.

Comparison of Foreign with Home Supplies.

The most obvious impression on perusing these details is one of surprise at the extent to which the wants of the country are supplied from abroad, and the ease with which the provision is made; not unmixed with a measure of anxiety at the dependence in which it places us upon other countries, and the inconveniences which might ensue upon interference with peaceful relations or other national disturbances. Nor is the force of this impression lessened by a comparison of the quantities produced at home with those received from abroad, as seen in the table of the quantities of home-raised wheat and meat, compared with foreign importations, also contained in the former paper (p. 91).

[The conclusions thus forced upon us would seem to be that of substantial food the proportion drawn from abroad is at least two-fifths of the whole; that the actual consumption is in value about equal; or by a computation based upon the flesh-forming constituents of the quantities imported, some fifteen millions out of the thirty-three inhabiting the United Kingdom are sustained upon foreign supplies.] Since, therefore, we are making no material progress in extracting more food from our own soil, and the population goes on to increase; could anything happen to deprive us of access to our neighbours' stores, more than half of our population would be destitute of food. The bare possibility of such a catastrophe need not, in the face of its extreme improbability, excite more alarm than the apprehension that our coal-fields are on the verge of exhaustion; for if, on the one hand, our demands are enormous, on the other, the sources from whence they can be met are practically boundless. Although at present the Eastern Hemisphere yields the larger proportion of both animal and cereal produce, two-thirds of our vegetables, nearly all our alcoholic and other beverages, the Western is pressing forward in the race for custom. Were the Northern Latitudes to fail in their accustomed tribute to our necessities, the Southern would soon step forward to meet our wants. Whilst, should the old countries lose their power or their will to fill our storehouses, the new ones would not be long in laying their treasures at our feet. Our insular position has facilitated approach to our shores from every quarter of the globe, and hitherto our wealth and our enterprise have drawn to us sufficient for every need.

With all this, however, there are not wanting signs that times of distress may be at hand, and it is too evident that we are already in the vortex of a severe crisis. It is on our trade in times past that we have had to rely for progress, and whatever grounds there may be for confidence in the future, it is clear that at present this is far from being as productive as it has been. A reference again to the official returns from which the figures already used have been compiled, will enable us to see to what extent the countries from whom we buy so largely are taking from us in exchange. The ten previously stated as standing highest on the list thus show the values of British produce and manufacture which we exported to them during the last year :—

[000,000's omitted.]

United States	£16	West Indies	£6
France	14	Holland	10
British India	29	Russia	4
China and Hong Kong	8	Turkey	6
Germany	20	British North America	7

These together amount to 120 millions, or 4 millions less than the food we take from them, to say nothing of all the raw material and manufactured articles we also purchase.

Coupling this with the great difference in the total values of the food imports for the two years compared on a former page, viz., 1857, £64, and 1877, £177 millions (which periods most fairly compare with each other from the similarity in the price of wheat ruling in those years), the whole situation is one of extreme gravity, and well worthy of the closest consideration. It is quite evident that there is no lack either in the will or the power of other nations to produce all the food we may need for the support of our population, and equally so that we have both the means and the desire to manufacture more than sufficient goods wherewith to make payment for the supplies they send; but this ever-increasing divergence between the amount of our purchases and our sales cannot continue growing to an indefinite extent. Whatever may be our accumulations of wealth at home, they will not suffice to ward off a scarcity of food, if those who have it to give us will not take the produce of our labour and capital in exchange; and viewed in this aspect the problem seems difficult of solution. True wisdom points, therefore, to economy in the use of food, especially in cutting off such articles of consumption as are not really of any use in sustaining life; in endeavouring still further to cheapen the goods we manufacture for sale, so as to induce customers to come to us; and beyond this in seeking to open up new markets in which we may find purchasers on more profitable terms than the old ones are disposed to accord. Whatever wealth we may derive from our investments or our earnings abroad, it cannot be a satisfactory state of things that all the exertions of our labourers, all the skill and capital of our manufacturers, all the enterprise of our traders, fail to provide the food they consume; not because we are slackening in our efforts, but because our customers cease to require what we are willing to sell them, or to give us such prices as will prevent the necessity for our drawing upon other resources.

VI.

ON THE GROWTH OF POPULATION WITH RELATION TO THE MEANS OF SUBSISTENCE.[1]

FROM the time when Malthus propounded his theories on population, the minds of many have been concerned with the question whether such a growth as he deprecated is not indeed an evil to be warred against.

These theories appear to have been—

1. That growth of population must follow or be regulated by the means of sustenance.

2. That the tendency of population was to increase in geometrical, that of subsistence in arithmetical, progression, and therefore that without some corrective the one must of necessity outstrip the other, and the world become unable to support the lives thus produced.

3. That this correction was found in the natural or unnatural occurrence of famine, pestilence, and war, at the cost of much misery, which it would be wise to prevent by restraining the natural increase of population through the avoidance of early marriages.

In later times our sense of decency has been shocked by the outspoken denunciation, not of marriage, but of its consequences; and the bold inculcation of means whereby the gratification of natural inclinations may be conjoined with the violation of nature's laws and the frustration of nature's ends. Upon the consideration of such a question

[1] Read in Section F, British Association, at Plymouth, 1877.

it would be manifestly improper to enter here. If, indeed, any place or time be fitted for such discussion, it must be some other than this one. But whatever opinion may exist as to the means thus proposed for our adoption, it is a thoroughly legitimate subject for inquiry, whether the growth of population is, as these *philosophers* (?) assume, an evil to be averted ; or, as others assert, a burden to be borne ; or, as many believe, a source of wealth to be prized.

Again, looking at the trepidation which Malthus felt at the misery certain to follow upon any large accession to the seven millions of inhabitants which England then supported, and comparing the condition in which it now holds and maintains more than three times that number, we may smile at the folly of his forebodings. Yet the question is still an open one, whether the limits of sustenance may not have been reached, and the time have arrived when to follow his counsels would be true wisdom. It is a desire to see what light can be thrown upon these two subjects for investigation, that has suggested the attempt made in this paper to ascertain how the various sections of our population are distributed as to occupations, and the proportions engaged respectively in providing food, other necessaries, and luxuries.

Taking as a basis in our inquiry the Census Reports for the year 1871, we shall find the population for the three divisions of the United Kingdom thus stated :

England and Wales . . .	22,712,266
Scotland	3,360,018
Ireland	5,412,377
	31,484,661

Since that date it is estimated to have increased by 1,604,576, so that at present it amounts to slightly more than 33 millions. But as there are no means of distributing these additional inhabitants amongst the several occupations, it will be necessary to confine our attention to the figures furnished for the census year. These are divided by the Registrars-General into six classes, in this order:

i.	Professional .	.	.	891,160
ii.	Domestic	.	.	6,804,769
iii.	Commercial .	.	.	1,035,737
iv.	Agricultural	.	.	2,989,154
v.	Industrial	.	.	6,425,137
vi.	Indefinite	.	.	13,338,704

31,484,661

The individuals composing these classes are alike in one respect—that they are all consumers, and need to be provided with the means of subsistence. They differ, however, greatly in another—in that only a portion are producers, and on the productive power of this portion must the whole rest for support. It is impossible minutely to separate the one from the other; but we cannot greatly err in adopting the above division into classes, and for the present purpose may include the third, fourth, and fifth as the productive, and the remaining three—the first, second, and sixth—as those whose labour does not actually contribute to the supply on which they, in common with the producers, depend for sustenance. This, in a sense, the commercial class does. Strictly speaking, the merchant may be no more essential to the welfare of the community than the schoolmaster; but the one assists in procuring the means whereby life is supported, whilst the other, in this respect, does but consume a portion of that on which existence depends. Thus, separating the population into two divisions, we shall have—

Producers .	.	.	.	10,450,028
Non-producers .	.	.	.	21,034,633

31,484,661

The latter being very nearly double the former.   Further dividing the class of producers, we find those engaged in agricultural operations to be 2,989,154, and the industrial and commercial together 7,460,874; in round numbers three, and seven and a half millions respectively.

I. The agricultural class embraces those engaged in the cultivation of the soil, whether " in fields and pastures, 1,447,481 ; " " in woods, 7,861 ; " or " in gardens, 103,695," including not alone the actual agricultural labourers, shepherds, farm servants, and gardeners, but all those returned simply as landed proprietors; all farmers, graziers, bailiffs, agents, and others whose sole or principal employment is upon or about the land.   It further comprises all persons engaged about animals, such as horse-keepers, game-keepers, drovers, cattle-salesmen, fishermen, and others, the business of all of whom is the capturing, rearing, and dealing in beasts, birds, and fishes; the whole class thus comprehending all whose manual or mental labour, whose time, thought, and capital, are devoted to calling into existence and utilizing the various products of animal and vegetable life.   It is obvious, however, that not all of these are engaged solely in the production of human food, which numbers, for our present purpose, it is important to ascertain.   The value of the wool and flax grown at home has been estimated at 6 per cent. of the whole produce, that of the oats at 13 per cent., of the barley at 11 per cent., of the peas, beans, and rye at 4 per cent.; in all, 33 per cent. The corn and hay for the support of horses not employed in farming operations is of considerable value, whilst a large number of woodmen and gardeners, grooms and game-keepers, are solely engaged in ministering, not to subsistence, but to enjoyment, or in other useful operations. To discover the exact proportion thus employed would be difficult; but it cannot be deemed an undue estimate if we say that one-fourth at least must devote their labours to other objects than the raising of food.   If we make a deduction to this extent, it follows that two and a quarter

millions of the population are sufficient to produce all the
home-grown food. This is estimated at about three-fifths
of the whole consumption of the kingdom, the remainder
being derived from foreign supplies, received in exchange
for the produce of our mines and manufactories. Assuming,
as may fairly be done, that each individual employed in
manufacturing operations will produce goods for export
equivalent at least to the food which he could raise directly
from the soil, we arrive at the conclusion that two-thirds
of two and a quarter millions, say one and a half million,
should be deducted from the industrial and added to the
food-producing class, and thus that three and three-quarter
millions are actually engaged in producing or procuring
food for all the inhabitants of the United Kingdom.

But we must go a step further. There are other things
which are absolutely essential for those who thus labour:
houses to live in, clothing to wear, and several minor articles
of food, over and above that which is raised at home. To
provide these, some of our mechanics and operatives must
devote their time either directly to their production, or indirectly to producing that which will procure them from
abroad. For reasons which will be better explained when
speaking of the industrial class, the number thus employed
may be computed at half a million of workers. The result
of these calculations may thus be stated in round numbers:

Census return of agricultural class . .	3,000,000
Less ¼, producing hay, wool, flax, hides, oils, &c.	750,000
	2,250,000
Add, manufacturers of goods to be ex- changed for food . . .	1,500,000
Ditto, of necessaries for food-producers .	500,000
Giving a grand total of .	4,250,000

whose labour in one shape or another sufficed to maintain

in food the 31,500,000 ascertained inhabitants of the kingdom in 1871.

II. The industrial class, numbering six and a quarter
millions, includes all persons engaged in art and mechanic
production, and those working and dealing in textile fabrics
and dress, in foods and drinks, and in animal, vegetable,
and mineral substances.   To these we may, as before stated,
add the commercial class, one million; not that they are actual
producers, but because their employment is necessary for
the distribution and exchange of that which others produce,
and which without such assistance could not be utilized.
To these seven and a quarter millions we must add the
three-quarters of a million of the agricultural class, whom
we considered as employed in producing other articles than
food, but deduct the one and a half million the product of
whose labour we reckoned as applied to the purchase of
food imported from other countries; leaving six and three-
quarter millions of workers engaged in producing, for the
benefit of the whole population, substances *not* to be consumed as food.   In like manner, however, as we added to
the food-producers half a million for those providing articles
necessary to their existence, so must we deduct this half a
million from the industrial producers, together with, say,
three-quarters of a million similarly employed upon necessaries for these workers themselves.

These two numbers, thus transferred as necessary for the
workers, are to a certain extent conjectural, yet not altogether arbitrary.   A close examination of the sub-orders
and divisions of the Census Return under the various occupations of the industrial class leads to the conclusion that,
after making the deduction for goods manufactured to be
exchanged for food imports, one-half of the workers may be
assigned to the production of articles of necessity, and as this
would give some three or three and a half millions, the proportion for the consumption of the workers themselves
would be about a quarter of a million for the agricultural
and three-quarters of a million for the industrial.   Thus we

get five and a half millions, the products of whose labour supply themselves with food and necessaries, and the rest of the community with everything it uses, beyond the absolute food on which it subsists.

Assuming that the necessary supplies for the wants of the non-productive population (including most of the women and all the children) will absorb the labour of two and a half millions more, we shall have left some three millions for the production of luxuries or superfluities, and the accumulation of wealth; nearly one-third of the total workers.

These calculations may be tabulated in round numbers thus:

Census return of industrial and commercial   .   7,500,000
Add ¼ of agricultural class who do not produce
    food   750,000

                                8,250,060

Deduct—
  Producers of foreign food   .   1,500,000⎫
      „   necessaries for pro-   ⎬   2,000,000
          ducers .   .   500,000⎭

                                · 6,250,000
      „   necessaries for industrial workers   750,000

                     Leaving   .   .   5,500,000
Assumed to be employed in manufacturing ne-
    cessaries   2,500,000

Leaving for the production of superfluities   .   3,000,000

The powers of the whole population will thus be expended:

In the production of food	.	.	4,250,000
„ „ other necessaries	.	.	3,250,000
„ „ superfluities	.	.	3,000,000
			10,500,000
Consumers only	.	.	21,000,000
			31,500,000

Although resting upon a sound basis, as regards the numbers employed and the class of occupation, these calculations can only claim a presumptive accuracy as to the purposes which such employment serves. There is not much reason to question the proportion of the nation's power assigned to the production of food; but opinions may differ as to how much is required for the supply of its necessities, and the degree in which the product of the remainder is to be considered essential to comfort and happiness, or to be looked upon as unnecessary or even hurtful. It is not, however, requisite that there should be precise agreement on these points. Let it be granted that, after providing the means of subsistence (whatever that may be deemed to include), there is any surplus at all, the national welfare cannot really be imperilled by its existence. That such is the case needs no proof. The rapid growth of its wealth, the luxurious living of so many of its members, and the ability of so many to exist and spend without any labour, all prove that the means of subsistence have hitherto kept ahead of the increase of the population.

III. Another line of argument, founded also upon the Census Returns, will lead up to the same conclusion. Dividing the whole population, as ascertained in 1871, according to sex and age, we find that there were 15,301,830 males and 16,182,831 females; viz.:

	Males.	Females.	Both Sexes.
Under 15 years .	5,706,589	5,383,683	11,090,272
Over 65 ,, . .	721,997	501,306	1,223,303
Wives and Women performing house-hold duties .	......	5,058,298	5,058,298
	6,428,586	10,943,287	17,371,873
Between 15 and 65, excluding house-hold women .	8,873,244	5,239,544	14,112,788
	15,301,830	16,182,831	31,484,661

In making this division, it is assumed that the working period of life is between 15 and 65, whilst all under and over those ages are unable to labour for their own support or that of others. It is true that many children below 15, and aged persons beyond 65, do in part earn the means of subsistence; but there is probably an equivalent number between 15 and 65 who do not actually work, and thus one may be set against the other. Married women, too, and those engaged in household duties, although in some instances assisting as bread-winners, must, generally speaking, be excluded from the class of productive workers. These together amount in round numbers to 17½ millions, leaving 14 millions of an age and position to be profitably employed. So far, however, as being actually productive members of the community, we must except the professional class and those engaged in domestic service, together numbering 3½ millions. Deducting these from the 14 millions at the working age, we have 10½ millions to perform the various agricultural and industrial operations on which the nation depends for its sustenance (necessary and superfluous) and its growth in wealth. By the former separation into productive occupations, we found that 10½ millions were so classed—a number so singularly near to the 10½ millions arrived at by the division into ages, as to confirm the accuracy of the reasoning by which we arrive at the following results; viz.:

1. That one-third of the population is capable of labouring, and actually does labour for its own support, and that of the remaining two-thirds which are dependent upon it.

2. That of the productive portion of the community about 40 per cent. are either directly or indirectly engaged in the production of food, from 25 to 30 per cent. in that of other necessaries, leaving 30 to 35 per cent. free for those occupations which furnish us with luxuries for consumption, or wealth for accumulation.

3. That therefore the growth of population in this country has not hitherto unduly pressed upon or overtaken the means of subsistence.

IV. If then, as these two sets of figures seem conclusively to show, one worker, besides procuring food and necessaries for his own support, can and does produce the food which nourishes six or seven others ($4\frac{1}{2}$ to $31\frac{1}{4}$ millions), whilst there are on the average no more than one adult and one child dependent upon each producing member of the community ($10\frac{1}{4}$ to $10\frac{1}{2}$ over, and 11 under 15 years), there can be no doubt whatever that the power employed in raising the means of subsistence is far below what might be made available should more be required. If again the strength of the nation can, after allowing for the employment of nearly one-half of its producing power (5 out of $10\frac{1}{4}$ millions) in labour for their own necessities and the food of others, have more than the other half ($5\frac{1}{2}$ millions) left to supply the remaining wants of the other 21 millions, and the further desires of the whole $31\frac{1}{4}$ millions, there can be no true reason why the growth of the population needs to be restrained. Neither is there any room to fear that such a ratio of increase as the present progress furnishes can do other than add to the productive power of the nation. If such restriction be advocated, let it be honestly done with the object of confining the use of the nation's wealth

in undue proportion to a part of the community, or of substituting luxurious self-indulgence for the natural use of our
powers and privileges.

The numbers and the conditions of existence with which
we are now dealing are those of the present time, when it
is admitted that much room exists for sanitary, hygienic,
and moral improvement, the beginnings, or rather some
advance in which we already witness. From such improvement there would certainly result a strengthening of our
position. Disease lessens the power of those who live, and
premature death destroys the power which has cost much
to rear. The children under fifteen years of age are rather
more in number than the productive workers, and reckoning the average consumption of each as equal to half that
of an adult, they must absorb one-sixth of the food and
necessaries produced by the workers. This they more than
repay during mature years. If, however, life is cut short
before maturity, every year that it has lasted has been a tax
upon the means of subsistence, for which there is no recompense. Infant mortality is confessedly higher than it ought
to be. Every life which knowledge or care can rescue is
an addition to future producing power, and so to the surplus
which makes the nation's wealth. Still more is this the
case with improved health amongst producers, because to
the extent which disease exists it not only destroys power
in the sufferer himself, but draws upon the resources of
those whose own power is thus directed to unproductive
uses. It is not too much to hope that an improvement
in this respect is taking place, by which a considerable gain
may ensue, the whole of which will be that of surplus power.

Beyond this, the constant increase of mechanical power,
and of economy in its uses, largely adds to the producing
capacity of those who call it to their aid. Whatever is
thus applied to the actual forcing of a greater yield from
the soil, or to the manufacture of the necessaries for home
use, must be a clear gain; but so much as increases the
product of manufactures for exchange with other nations

may not really be any gain, if thereby, through competition or other causes, the value of the articles produced sustains an equivalent diminution.   To make this plain, the reaping-machine will set free so many reapers to reclaim and plant other land, but an improved steam-engine may only increase the produce of the loom without ensuring its value in exchange for food being any greater.   The whole tendency, however, of growing intelligence, knowledge, and wealth, is to render the employment of power more productive, and thus to increase the available surplus.   If therefore there be any surplus at all at present, and we have seen that there is a considerable one, increase of population should cause it to become still greater.

V.   Two objections, however, may arise, which it is important to meet.   It may be asserted that there must be a limit to the numbers which our country can hold and maintain, and that the time when this limitation makes itself felt has arrived, or is soon to come.   Again, many will maintain that we have even now no true surplus of productive power, because the producers and their dependents are both straitened in their consumption, and overstrained by the amount of labour which is necessary to procure even that they have, whilst a proper supply of necessaries and a just limitation of labour would consume or lessen the surplus now produced.

To deal first with this latter argument in both its branches.   If we look at the so-called working classes, it is impossible not to see that in both the quality and quantity of food they consume, in the sufficiency and finery of the clothes they wear, and in the comfort and size of the houses they inhabit, they are better off at this time than at any previous period.   There may be much of squalid poverty, many ill-filled stomachs and ill-clad backs, uncomfortable houses and miserable homes; but there is still more of lavish expenditure in drink and tobacco, of wasted food and unsuitable clothing, of ill-kept habitations and mismanaged homes.   The relief from want is to be obtained by the

repression of extravagances, and comfort is to be procured
by the economic use of time and money ; for there can be
little doubt that the wages earned, if properly employed
and fairly distributed, are amply sufficient to purchase food
and necessaries for a larger population than they now support.   With the middle class the strain and privation, not
perhaps of the absolute necessaries, but in those which habit
and education have made such, is probably much greater than
in the lower strata.   There is more difficulty in finding profitable employment for sons, and fitting homes for daughters ;
but here, too, the cause is to be found in the improvident
expenditure of money and time, ill-regulated desires and
undue aspirations; not indeed here or in the lower classes
always on the part of those who suffer, for the misery-
maker is too often not the one who endures the suffering.
With the higher classes there can be no question as to the
actual means of subsistence or of comfortable existence ; it
is one of maintaining their present position, or of failure in
attaining a higher one, should the numbers amongst whom
existing or prospective means are to be divided greatly
increase.   Looking to the rapid growth and concentration
of wealth on the one hand, and the equally rapid increase
of luxurious expenditure on the other, it cannot be for a
moment maintained that, even supposing this accession of
means not to keep pace as it has hitherto done with the
growth of population, there is not ample for division
amongst greater numbers.   Besides this there seems to be
some natural cause or effect whereby the accretion, possession, or expenditure of wealth is generally attended with a
stationary or decreasing family.

As regards the supposed undue amount of labour exacted
from those who produce for themselves or work for others,
almost the same course of reasoning may be pursued.   It
is not that the aggregate amount of exertion is more than
the whole body can well put forth, it is the unequal distribution among its various members.   There is scarcely a
family or neighbourhood—certainly not a town or county—

in which we do not see quite sufficient available power for the relief of those who are unduly pressed. The time which is devoted to pleasure, or spent in frivolity and idleness, and the strength which is wasted unnecessarily or exhausted by dissipation, is amply sufficient for lessening the strain put upon the overworked members of the community; nay more, it needs no argument, for it is self-evident to the most ordinary observer, that a just appropriation of time and a wise administration of power would produce far more than at present without at all limiting the hours which may rightly be devoted to rest, improvement, and enjoyment. Excepting for our follies and our pleasures, it cannot be said that as a nation we are on the whole overworked, or that we need to restrict the total time devoted to labour.

But granting, for argument's sake, that these evils do exist, are they to be removed or lessened by restraint upon marriage or increase? Is the disease one which may be cured by the prescriptions of either Malthus or Bradlaugh? Do we find that deferred matrimony or life-long celibacy really add to the productive power which the abstainers put forth? Is it not a fact, that as a rule the larger families thrive the best, and that a large number of those who have none dependent upon them, themselves become dependent upon others? Let a young man feel that he has no home to make or to keep, and he too often loses the stimulus to putting forth his productive power, and fails to preserve it by healthy exercise. He is tempted to expend his earnings in unprofitable or hurtful enjoyments, if even he does not exhaust his energies by dissipation and self-indulgence. Let a young woman feel that she is debarred from having a home of her own with those for whom she may expend her powers and cultivate the best feelings of her nature, and let her know that, instead of being provided for by the husband or sons on whom she may lavish her affections and her care, she must earn her own livelihood; and she is too often forced into uncongenial pursuits and exhausting labours, which go far to depress her vital powers, and ultimately extinguish her capacity, not so much for being herself a producer as a real helper to those who are such. When, on the contrary, the young of both sexes feel that they may possess a united home, in which the obligations of parental love may be an incentive to the preservation and development of their powers; they are supplied with the strongest inducement to the right use of the health and strength which makes them an addition to the nation's productiveness. There is nothing in this to enforce matrimony and its consequent multiplication of life upon those who are unfitted or unwilling to enter upon it, nor yet to encourage premature, imprudent, or ill-assorted unions ; on the contrary, the steady contemplation of the married state as a legitimate object to be attained, will be the best encouragement to prudent preparation. A knowledge of the duties it entails, and the noble self-sacrifice it requires, will be the most effectual restraint upon those to whom it has no attractions ; whilst those who realize the fulfilment of their desires will be far more likely to have healthy offspring, and in adding to the numbers of the population to give those who will be an increase of its productive powers.

VI. Thus far it has been assumed that an increase of productive power is a source of strength and prosperity ; but here the former of the two objections which were suggested requires to be met, and we need to be satisfied that with possession of increased power we have a sufficient field for its employment.

Malthus thought.that the prudential limit of population for our island was nearly reached, and trembled for the time when the world might have more inhabitants than it could possibly feed. The only possible justification for Bradlaugh's philosophy is, that we are already full enough, and that an addition to our numbers can but add to our misery.

Political economists, social reformers, and practical philanthropists of the highest stamp have thought that the growth of population is unduly pressing upon the nation's means, and there can be no doubt that the problem is one of somewhat difficult solution. For a series of years the national expenditure for food has gone on increasing simultaneously with a diminishing receipt from the sale of the manufactures which our producing power enables us to send to the countries with which we trade.

Since 1872 each year has been worse in this respect than its predecessor, and the present year promises to be the worst of all that have yet passed. Every succeeding year the home resources afford a less amount of food per head of its population, and every year the money value of our exports is also less per head. There are those amongst us, whose judgment is entitled to respect, who view this state of things without anxiety, believing either that the growth of our income abroad advances at least in proportion to our draughts upon it; or that the present depression of trade is but temporary, and will soon give place to returning prosperity. There are some too who really believe that, despite all adverse tokens, the profits in our manufacturing and trading operations are really greater, and so compensate for the larger supplies we draw from abroad. With the soundness or fallacy of these different views it is not the business of this paper to deal; but we have to consider what bearing these circumstances have upon the continued increase of the mouths we have to fill, the wants we have to supply.

Let it be granted again, that there is a real evil to be overcome, what does it mean? that we must interfere with nature's laws, or natural results? or that we must learn the lessons these results are designed to teach; that we must obey the other laws which nature enacts? Is it impossible to bring increased supplies to our people? And if it be so, is it out of our power to carry our people where they may find scope for the employment of their productive power, in making provision for their wants, and securing possession of comforts and luxuries?

When Abraham and Lot found the land too small to pasture their flocks, they agreed to extend the borders they occupied. When Solomon wanted the wood of Lebanon, and the gold of Ophir, he exchanged the surplus products of his own land for those of others. We in times past have done both, and we must still do both in larger degree; for we have this advantage, that the two go hand in hand— the one helps the other, and thus lessens the strain on both. Every family which goes forth to cultivate an unoccupied space, to render the earth productive where it has never hitherto yielded fruits, or to make two blades grow where only one grew before, furnishes additional customers for our industrial class at home, and enables our land in comfort to hold increasing numbers.

It is probable that there never was a time when colonization was so easy as it might be now. We have capitalists who can prevent our emigrants going out empty-handed, and can prepare the way for them with the certainty that the investment will pay. We have ships that can carry them with speed, safety, and economy. We have broad acres under our own sovereign's sway where we may plant or consolidate our laws, our customs, our principles of justice and religion; or we have peaceful relations with other nations who will only be too glad to receive our people. We have scientific means for lessening the hardships incident to a new life, and we have still brave hearts and true to go up and possess the lands. We have, then, mechanical skill, industrious workers, rich capitalists and manufacturers at home to receive the products of industry abroad, to cheaply convert them into articles of utility and luxury, to speedily return them in their useful forms to those who have raised the raw materials; and we have facility of intercourse to prevent the entire rupture of family ties, to cement old friendships, and to create new tastes and inclinations in those who are in reality less separated in time and distance than were our forefathers when actually within the borders of our own little island.

Again, colonization in the present day may be different in its character from that of previous times. We then went forth to conquer, rob, oppress, and exterminate the aboriginal inhabitants of the settlements we chose. We now go, or ought to go, to them with the open hand of friendship, teach them our laws, instruct their ignorance, help their weakness, carry to them the blessings of civilization and Christianity, and thus make them at once our friends and our customers.

In all these several ways a small exodus from home may serve to restore the balance and to furnish the means of subsistence for the many who remain behind. By so doing a redundancy of population will become the means of producing redundant food, health, happiness, and wealth.

VII. Away then with the false economy and cold expediency which would stifle all the finer feelings of our nature, cramp all the expansive powers of our minds, rob us of all the warmer desires of our hearts, which would check the progress of the world in all that can constitute real greatness, by selfishly refusing to convey to the dark regions of the earth the light which art, science, and religion have permitted us to enjoy. Away still more with the impure philosophy which would degrade us to mere machines for the gratification of the inclinations given us for wise and noble ends—creatures of the flesh rather than of the mind and spirit, wallowers in the filth of this world rather than aspirants for the purity of heaven.

Whether therefore we examine into the present resources and demands of the population, or whether we look to the economy of the vegetable or the animal world, the experience of human history, the record of human progress, the constitution of the human frame, the objects of human existence, or the prospects of our race in the future of this world and the eternity of the next, we shall find that the law of increase is of natural and divine enactment. Let us honestly strive to discover wherein lies the secret of our strength, the security for our happiness, and we shall realize the conviction that it is to be found in fulfilling the terms of the charter whereby we hold possession of the earth and dominance over the lower creatures : " Be fruitful, and multiply, and replenish the earth."

VII.

THE DUTIES ON WINE.

[October, 1877.]

THERE can be little doubt that it is both expedient and necessary to make some considerable alterations in the existing duties on wines. The Spanish growers, and with them those of Portugal and Australia, complain that their products are unduly weighted in the competition with those of France and the Rhine. The French producers, on the other hand, are anxious for the introduction of their commoner vintages on such terms as may enable them to appeal to the tastes of those in our country who are now consumers of beer. Again, the distillers complain that the stronger fortified wines are used for the adulteration of spirits, and likewise that the alcohol in wine is admitted at so much lower a rate than that contained in spirits proper. These two last considerations are not unworthy of attention in the interests of the revenue. It is broadly asserted that Hamburg sherry enters largely into the composition of the lower kinds of Irish whiskey as sold by the retailers; and that by a large class of customers it is used more as a dram than a beverage. Thus used, it may extensively supplant both the home and foreign manufactured brandy, gin, and whiskey.

An examination into the several rates of duty charged upon liquors containing spirit, shows that the alcohol they carry is charged with duty at very different rates,—that in

beer and ale being the lowest of all. Adopting the Excise
estimate that two bushels of malt will make a barrel of ordinary beer, and assuming that such beer contains from
8 to 9 degrees of proof spirit, we have somewhere about
three gallons for 5s. 5d. duty, equal to about 1s. 10d. per
gallon. Next in order come the wines that are admitted as
under 26 degrees, but as many of these do not nearly come
up to this strength, we may take the average at 22, which
at 1s. would give 4s. 6d. per gallon. The higher rating at
2s. 6d. up to 42 degrees may probably average 40 degrees,
and thus give a charge of 6s. 3d. per gallon. Lastly come
spirits paying, if of home manufacture, 10s., and if of foreign
production, 10s. 5d., for each gallon of proof spirit they contain. This order of progression is quite sound in principle,
but it may be doubted whether the present ratings for wine
are altogether the most advisable. Those for beer and
spirits are not likely to be altered unless a plethoric state of
revenue should permit a response to the appeals of the agriculturists for a remission of the malt duties; or a necessity
for sustaining the national income, on the one hand, or a
desire for the advancement of temperance on the other,
should induce an additional charge on spirits. Looking at
wine as what it really is, a distinct article from spirits, it is
right that those kinds which contain little alcohol should
pay a small duty, and that just in proportion as the other
descriptions approach to the character of spirits, the alcohol
in them should bear a corresponding charge. This object
may probably be more fully attained by a rating different to
that at present existing.

It is understood that the Spanish Government desires a
substitution of 34 degrees for that of the lower limit of
rating at 26, and with this many of the home merchants
agree. It would be better that 34 should take the place
of the higher limit (that of 42) as the extreme range of
strength allowed for wine proper. This proportion of
alcohol is quite sufficient for the preservation of any well
fermented and pure wine. It is not beyond that which the

natural fermentation of a rich juice from the grape will often-times reach. Its adoption would lead to an abandonment of the practice of stopping fermentation by the addition of spirit, and thus tend to produce a sounder, more wholesome, and altogether higher class of wine.

At the other end of the scale, it would be expedient to admit wines below, say, 16 degrees, at a rate more analogous to that charged upon beer; thus affording opportunity for testing the taste of those who prefer the weaker beverage, and, even if not availed of, satisfying the claims of the French exporters.

Although wine may not be charged at the same duty as it would pay if treated as diluted spirit, it should still be dealt with upon an alcoholic basis, both in fairness to the dis-tiller and for the security of the revenue. No rating, either by quantity of liquid or by value, would effect this end, nor would it be promoted by yielding to the clamour for the admission of all wine, or of that up to 34 degrees, at the uniform duty of 1s.; but with due regard to the interests of all parties,—producer, consumer, and Exchequer alike,—2s. would be a fitting charge for the highest limit, that of 34, and a 6d. rate for all below 16, with intermediate charges upon those between, say 1s. up to 24, 1s. 6d. up to 30. In assessing strengths beyond 34, it would then be right to adjust the charge upon the same principle, that of increasing the alcoholic impost with a greater strength, until the spirit duty is reached. This might be done by putting an addi-tional 3d. upon every two degrees up to 42, which would then pay 3s., and upon every single degree beyond, so that at 50 degrees it would amount to 5s., equivalent to the 10s. on proof spirit at which all beyond 50 would be taken.

One rather serious objection to these proposals presents itself in the necessity they involve of subjecting, if not all, yet nearly all the importations to the test of strength, a process involving some measure of expense and delay. Under the present rating it is only those samples which come near the limits of 26 and 42, and those beyond the latter, which demand more than observation and tasting. When first the duties were levied according to strength there were four distinct rates, 18, 26, 40, and 45 degrees, and some difficulties arose in affixing the proper charges, but since then the process of testing is very much simplified. It is now adopted by several wine merchants upon wines in their own cellars merely for their own guidance. It could not be an insuperable obstacle to a method which seems to possess many advantages, and to be based on the only principle which, at the same time dealing fairly with the several sorts, yet serves to protect the spirit duties.

To obviate the inconvenience attendant upon sampling and testing wines in bottle, it would be well that these should all pay at the same rate, say 2s. This would include the stronger champagnes, some of which there is reason to believe now obtain entrance at 1s. duty, although over 26 degrees. The higher value of most case wines would enable them to bear the somewhat greater charge, and it might not be inappropriate to extend it even beyond 2s. [The objections raised to this charge as since proposed by Mr. Gladstone, would be obviated were it left open to the importer to claim the privilege of having his wines tested and rated according to their alcoholic strength. This would prevent an undue charge on those of inferior quality imported in large parcels, whilst for those of higher quality and in smaller quantity, the testing would seldom be claimed.]

The precise stages at which it is proposed to increase the rate may possibly admit of some adjustment on the experience of the practical officers, and possibly it would not be unacceptable to the trade to have threepenny instead of sixpenny rises by introducing the limits of say 21, 28, 32. Should any alteration at all be made it would be but just to admit sweetened spirits, which now pay a fixed duty without reference to strength, to the privilege of being tested in the same manner as wine, and charged as spirits upon the proof quantity they contain.

There are many objections to the suggested plan for an

ad valorem rating, whether as an alternative charge to that now levied, or as a supplementary one to remedy existing inequalities. The most obvious of these is that it would involve a complete reversal of the policy of late years, which has been entirely opposed to any charge depending upon value. Also, that of all the several articles contributing to the revenue, wine is the one whose value it is the most difficult correctly to appraise. The variations in quality are so great, the diversities in taste so delicate, the caprices of fashion and the supplies from special vintages so varying, that the most experienced judges will be sure to differ widely as to the merits of particular importations. There is thus a certainty of such frequent conflicts of opinion between the officers and the importers as to prevent a correct standard of value ever being adopted.

It would further lie open to the objection that the same method is not applied to other articles, such as tea, where the commonest congou is taxed as highly as the choicest pekoe; or spirits, where the oldest cognac pays no more than the newest potato spirit. This would inevitably lead to demands from the dealers in those articles for a like consideration being given to differences of quality and price in tea, tobacco, spirits, &c.

But the chief difficulty lies in the absolute cheapness of spirit when compared with wine, which destroys altogether the relation of value to strength. The spirit manufactured in Germany averages on importation here little more than 1s. 6d. per gallon, whilst the value of wine from the same country is nearly 5s. Brandy from France averages 6s. 6d., and wine 8s. per gallon. Thus the addition of alcohol actually renders the mixture of less pecuniary value than before, and the more nearly wine can be made to resemble spirits, the less would it pay if value, not quantity or strength, were made the basis of rating.

VIII.

Excess of Imports and Depression of Trade.

[January, 1878.]

POLITICAL economists are puzzled to reconcile the growing preponderance of imports over exports in the present depressed condition of trade and commerce, with the generally received opinion that a nation's prosperity may be fairly measured by the excess of value which it obtains in goods received over the value of those with which it parts. It is still true that a nation which barters its produce and manufactures for less value from other countries cannot be prospering, but there are those amongst us who, without reviving the exploded theory that there should be an excess of exports, yet believe that the continuous increase in our imports, combined with a corresponding decrease in our exports, cannot be indicative of satisfactory progress. Hence the discussions in the daily and weekly journals of such questions as, " Are we consuming our capital ? " " Has England become a spendthrift ? " The immediate occasion of recent attention being given to the subject is to be found in a letter addressed by Mr. Rathbone, M.P., to a journal of high financial repute,[1] which led to such a demand for copies of the issue in which it was published as to necessitate its re-issue as a supplement to the succeeding number. Prior to this, the reading of two papers before the Statistical

---

[1] " Economist," Nov. 24th, and Dec. 7th, 1877.

Societies of London [1] and Manchester [2] had placed the facts of the case as figured in the official returns issued from the Custom House before the public, and laid the basis for argument as to the causes and effects of the condition of affairs thus disclosed. The progress of these since then has not been in any way such as to lessen anxiety, or to render further investigation unnecessary. The case for inquiry may be thus stated.

For a long series of years, with but little more than an occasional trifling fluctuation, the growth of our trade, both inwards and outwards, has been largely and steadily increasing. Going back to the earliest year in which the official records were compiled upon such a system as to admit of fair comparison, we find that the value of the imports has risen from £153,000,000 in 1854 to £354,000,000 in 1872; or, deducting those articles exported to other countries (£19,000,000 and £58,000,000 respectively), there were retained for home use, £134,000,000 in the former, and £296,000,000 in the latter year, showing an increase of 121 per cent. Taking the same period, the exports were, in 1854, £116,000,000, in 1872, £315,000,000, which, again deducting the values of foreign goods as above, gives £97,000,000 in the former year, and £256,000,000 in the latter, being an increase of British produce and manufactures to the extent of 162 per cent. From that year, which was the one in which our exports attained the highest recorded value, down to the one just expired, the imports have gone on increasing, but the exports have steadily declined, as will be seen from the following figures taken from the published official accounts : —

[1] Ante, page 55.   [2] Ante, page 77.

	Total Imports.	Again Exported.	Retained for Home Use.	British Produce and Manufactures Exported.	Total.	Excess of Imports.
1872	354	58	296	256	314	40
'73	371	56	315	255	311	60
'74	370	58	312	240	298	72
'75	374	58	316	224	282	92
'76	375	56	319	201	257	118
'77	394	53	341	199	252	142

The figures as given in the Twenty-first Report of the Commissioners of Customs vary somewhat from these—the difference arising from bullion and specie—which are published separately in the ordinary returns, being here incorporated with the merchandise. They are as follows, stated in millions of pounds only :—

	Imports.	Exports.			Excess of Imports over Exports.	
		British.	Foreign.	Total.	British.	Foreign.
1872	384	287	58	345	97	39
'73	405	284	56	340	121	65
'74	400	262	58	320	138	80
'75	407	251	58	309	156	98
'76	412	230	56	286	182	126

The two sets of figures are here given, because, in discussing the subject, writers appeal sometimes to the one and sometimes to the other. It is as well that the apparent divergence, and yet the real agreement of the statistics, should be rightly understood.

The preliminary question, however, is thus raised—whether in estimating the trade of either this country or those with which we deal, it is proper to mingle goods and bullion together? This depends entirely upon the purpose for which the figures are used. In stating the volume of our trade there can be no doubt that the gold and silver extracted from the earth in Australia or Nevada stand in the same category as the coal and iron raised from our own pits. Both are really goods in which we trade. Nor is the case altered when the mints of Sydney or Japan, for convenience, convert the precious ore into coin. The manipulation does not make it cease to be the produce of the country any more than the manufacture with us of iron into rails or hardware makes that metal less an article of export. When, however, the ingots or specie are once transferred from the country of production to that of use, they cease to be goods in which trade is carried on, and become circulating medium, or the representative of value in the settlement of accounts. The coin goes and comes in the same manner as bank notes or bills of exchange; and to reckon it again in the exports and imports is to double the extent of trade. For instance, Bank of England notes frequently cross the Channel, and, when used in that way, they as effectually cancel a debt or purchase an article as the sovereigns they represent would do; and the bullion just as fully performs its office when lying in the bank cellars as when actually transported abroad. The true method of compiling the trade figures would be to include all production as first produced, and afterwards to exclude everything that passes from hand to hand simply as a means of payment; but, as matter of fact, there is no means of separating the one from the other, and, therefore, it is perhaps best to leave both out.

When, however, we are dealing with the balance of trade, the surplus of import over export, or *vice versâ*, becomes an important element. Still, for reasons which will be shown hereafter, it would seem well to consider remittances of specie to and fro as one of the means by which the balance is adjusted, and, in the first instance, to endeavour to get at the real difference which arises in bartering the goods received and delivered. There are some other considerations to which attention must be given before we can strike a proper balance between the two.

Were our trading operations now conducted upon the

simple conditions which prevailed in earlier years, there would be little difficulty in balancing the incomings and outgoings, and so ascertaining the extent of profit or loss which they yielded. Then, a venturer, either owning a vessel himself, or working in conjunction with others, would purchase goods at home to be sent abroad. There he would dispose of them by sale or barter for other articles for which a demand existed at home, and, on completing the return voyage, turn these into cash. The difference between his first outlay and the sum finally received would show the exact result of the transaction. The aggregate of these operations would constitute the gain to the nation. Now there are many modifications of this system. A large proportion of the trade is carried on for the benefit of those abroad, who may be Englishmen or foreigners, and a commission only accrues to those who earn it at home. As capitalists we are investing and lending money all over the world. As bankers we are exchanging large sums with other nations which at best but yield a percentage of profit. We have large sums remitted here for investment or expenditure, some belonging to foreigners, but most to our own countrymen living abroad. Now all these various transactions, however large or complicated, must find a balance in the goods or bullion which we import and export; and it becomes necessary, in the first instance, to have a clear idea of what the figures on which arguments must be based really mean.

Putting aside, then, for the present the question of how the balance is to be provided for, it will be well to treat the question as one of simple barter, and see if it be possible at some given point to fix what is the real difference between the two values. The official figures being the only ones from which information can be obtained, and these being taken at our own shores, the object to be kept in view is to ascertain how far the goods we export will go in liquidation of the claims against us for those we import; and what, supposing the difference had to be discharged in actual money, would be the sum needed to balance the account. How or when that balance is actually settled is a further branch of the inquiry. It may not be possible to get at this balance for any given year with absolute certainty; but that is not so much a point of importance as it is to be assured that the calculations for several years are relatively correct, and in doing this there is little difficulty.

First take the imports. The value given should be the "wholesale market price at the time and place of arrival," and, therefore, includes freight, which, being paid in this country, does not need to be met by a corresponding export of goods, and must, therefore, be deducted from the official values. Then, on the export side, the value given represents the cost of the goods at the time they leave the country. But there are several items, such as the value of ships built for foreigners, coals shipped for use of steamers, victualling stores, &c., none of which are included in the account, though, in fact, they should be added to the amount.

Without entering into the details shown in the statistical paper before alluded to, we may say that the several corrections, the necessity of which we have just specified, are estimated to alter the apparent excess of imports in the undermentioned years, as follows :—

1872 from	£40	millions to	—£3	
1873	,,	60	,,	14
1874	,,	72	,,	27
1875	,,	92	,,	48
1876	,,	118	,,	75
1877	,,	142	,,	97

We thus arrive at the conclusion that, supposing all the goods imported were paid for on their arrival here, and all those exported exchanged for money at the time of exportation, the cash balance which in 1872 would have been £3,000,000 in our favour, was in 1877 £97,000,000 against us; and that so much money or money's worth has to be provided from some source or other out of the country, for if we add the bullion and specie it would not materially alter the figures. In 1872 the excess would be about £700,000 more; in the four next years the figures are respectively 5, 2, 6, and 8 millions of increase, and in 1877 they show 2 millions of pounds less. These are not serious amounts, but deserve to be stated for the sake of accuracy.

The figures thus assumed as showing the balances which have had to be provided for are not put forward with any pretension to absolute accuracy, although they are believed to fairly represent the actual results of each year's trade, and the calculations on which they are based having been some time before the statisticians of the country have not been impugned. It follows then, we repeat, that in 1872 this balance was in favour of the exports by about £3,000,000, but that it had turned against us in 1877 to the extent of £97,000,000, the intervening years also showing an excess of imports of 14, 27, 48, and 75 millions respectively. These are the sums which, after setting off the whole value of the goods we have sold out of the country against those we have bought into it, remain to be paid or adjusted with our co-traders and producers abroad; and the subjects for inquiry are in what way these claims have been liquidated, how they are to be met in future years, and what effects they indicate or are likely to produce upon our national prosperity. On these points the greatest difference of opinion prevails, arising from the difficulty there is in disentangling in very complicated business transactions the one detail from the other, and the greatest confusion of ideas exists for want of attention to the several relations subsisting between this country and the rest of the world.

Now there are but three sources from which the above-specified obligations can be discharged: the transmission of bullion, the diversion of income accruing abroad, or the absorption of capital invested and debts owing to us in other countries.

The first method has certainly not been adopted, for the

balance of bullion and specie transmitted is very inconsiderable, and only in the first and last of the years of which we are speaking have they been on the export side. If we include these figures, the balances will be changed to 3·6, 18·5, 28·5, 54·2, 83·, and 95· millions of pounds sterling.

The main source of supply is doubtless the income arising or accruing abroad, which is in fact remitted here in goods rather than in money, and, so far as this goes, the higher the amount it may reach, the greater the prosperity it evidences. Whatever it may be, it is won for the country, by the labour, the intellect, and the capital operating beyond our own shores; whether of those actually living abroad, or of those directing and supporting such operations by their talent and their credit whilst remaining at home. What the whole of such income may be, it is perhaps impossible to ascertain. Such an investigation would expand this paper far beyond the limits of space within which it must be confined. All that can be here done is briefly to mention the various channels through which it may flow.

There are, first, the profits derived from the purchase and sale of goods abroad on account of those residing at home and those who remit such gains to this country. Whatever is spent or invested before it comes here clearly cannot be applied in payment for goods sent here, neither can any increase of price obtained after they arrive be so applied without its forming part of the goods or bullion sent away; and both these values have been already applied to prevent the balance accruing. The difference between the price paid for wheat or sugar in the countries of produce and that which the article fetches on arrival here is so much to the good as against the balance only when it is retained here, and not when it has to be remitted to the sender. In like manner, the difference between the sum paid for goods shipped outwards, and that they may realize on arriving at their destination is only to the credit of this country when it is received by the shipper here. On what may be bought or sold here on behalf of speculators abroad, commission and interest on advances are all that accrue. Probably this, at any rate in depressed times like the present, is a surer and better return than the profit made in the trading; and considering the large proportion of business which is done on commission, five per cent. on the total imports will be an ample estimate. Commission obtained on the exports must not be reckoned, having been already included in the value.

Next to these, there must be a considerable sum derived from the salaries and earnings of *employés* and labourers in foreign countries, the surplus of which comes to this country for the support of their families and for investment.

Again, there will be the net earnings of British shipping on that portion of the work they do which is paid for abroad. That portion which is paid at home constitutes a charge on the imports after, and on exports before, their valuation, and consequently does not enter into the account.

Then we have the remittances from the Indian Government in repayment of moneys expended on its account in England; also the dividends on foreign loans, including commission on their raising and management at home; and the profits on manufacturing operations for which the capital and some of the working expenses are provided here.

In short, whatever income may be receivable in this country from any source out of it will come here in the shape of goods, oftentimes not directly, but in the end, in the ultimate settlement of accounts between individuals and nations; and, if it be equivalent to the balance which has to be provided, the magnitude of our imports is a cause for congratulation—a proof of wealth and prosperity.

Against these items, however, must be set off the value of whatever goods we send abroad, the proceeds of which are not actually realized in this country. If we lend money to foreigners, invest it in commercial or manufacturing concerns abroad, or send out machinery and plant to be worked, not paid for, it will all appear in the shape of exports, which have been already set off against the imports.

There is no doubt that in the earlier years of the period embraced in the figures of which we are treating, the exports were swollen largely by the foreign loans and investments we were then embarking in, and that now these are not being repeated ; but it is well known that English capital is still being invested in trading, agricultural, manufacturing, and mining concerns abroad. All this must be either so much diverted from remittances home or be transported abroad in the shape of goods.

The simple enumeration of the various sources—actual, probable, possible—from which the means may be obtained of liquidating the cost of our imports is sufficient to show how very uncertain any estimate of their total produce must be. Yet the question is of the utmost importance, for on its answer depends whether we are indeed only arrested in our national prosperity—simply ceasing to accumulate our savings—or are actually parting with our investments in other lands. Mr. Rathbone, M.P., and other writers boldly assert that we are doing the latter, and even cautious authorities are ready to admit the probability that we are reducing the amount in which the world is indebted to ourselves. *For this is the only remaining way in which our obligations can be discharged.* Nor are there wanting indications that the case really stands in that way. No one of any weight seriously asserts that our foreign income, great as it may be, is equal to so heavy a demand. The public are known to have become distrustful of many foreign securities ; and the plethora of unemployed capital enhances the price of those that are of undoubted stability, so that seekers for high-paying stocks or shares are fain to hold back for better times.

But whatever be the true state of the case as regards our power to pay without withdrawing capital from paying investments or occupations, it is perfectly clear that we must now be worse off by a hundred millions—unless indeed it can be shown that our income has grown to that extent since 1872—and, moreover, the figures are very suggestive of a further decline. The descent has been constant, 17, 13, 21,

27, and 22 millions in successive years, without any prospect yet that the downward limit has been reached. The amounts in the last published account show that December improved slightly over the same month of last year in the exports, but there is nothing like so great an increase as is shown in the imports.

Looking forward to the future, it will be well now to consider whether there is a probability of an improvement setting in. As regards an increase of income from our present investments abroad, there is little room for hope. The borrowing States which have proved defaulters, either in whole or part, seem more likely to become utterly bankrupt than to be able to pay up the lapsed dividends. Some of the public undertakings, such as railways, &c., may possibly improve in their dividends, but others will probably fall off; so that the total yield is not likely to be greater than hitherto. There is more hope that the recent investments in private undertakings, manufacturing and mining, may give better returns; but the incomes derived from trade, besides the fact that the return is not so lucrative as before, manifest a growing tendency to fall into the hands of permanent residents abroad. With the extension of capital, of experience, and of intelligence on the part of those who in their own countries devote themselves to these pursuits, a greater proportion of the business transacted falls into their hands, and less comes to the share of those who remit the surplus profits home. Then economical considerations are reducing the salaries of officials and the gains of professional men, part of which they were in the habit of sending home. Even shipping, which is now in so depressed a condition, will probably become owned to a greater extent by foreigners, although with the growth of commerce it is not improbable that we, who have been for so long the masters of the seas, may still monopolize the greater share of the carrying trade, and may perform it on more remunerative rates. Thus the conclusion is that there is no well grounded expectations of a speedy enlargement of the sources from which the claims upon us can be met from foreign receipts.

Can we, in the next place, hope to increase our exports? It is often asserted that the diminished value of these arises from the fall in price rather than in quantity. Let us take the three great branches of exporting industry, which together contributed last year 110 millions out of the 199 millions of total exports.

In 1872 we exported Cotton   3,537 million yards, in 1877,   3,836.
    „   „   Iron   3,383   „   tons,   „   2,345.
    „   „   Woollens 412   „   yards,   „   262.

It thus appears that iron has actually fallen off 77 per cent. and woollen goods 58 per cent.; although cottons have increased 8 per cent. Thus extraordinarily low prices, such as really leave but little if any room for profit on the manufacture, have failed really to stimulate demand; though it is well understood that a large portion of the shipments are owing to the reduction in price, but for which they would not have taken place at all. The truth seems to be that supply has outstripped demand. The extraordinary sales of 1871-3 raised expectations which led to a vast increase in the means of production at home, and prompted the creation of such means in other countries, whose competition forces down prices to the detriment of ourselves and them. It is the fashion in some quarters to decry foreign competition and to point to the failure of works carried on in other countries to realize profitable returns, but the reality of such competition is too well known to those who are best informed. The foreigners have had to struggle with all the difficulties incident to starting in new undertakings, we have had all the advantages of long established concerns; and yet the lower cost at which labour can be procured assures that under present conditions they will first feel the benefit of a revived demand whenever such shall arrive. So long as coal and iron were more accessible to us at home than those abroad, we might be said to be masters of the situation. These we no longer retain in almost exclusive possession, and our manufacturing population feels the result in diminished wages and shorter hours.

This question of foreign competition is worthy of the closest investigation. It has recently been asserted[1] that compared with our home trade, the foreign is of so little importance that its extinction would be borne without much injury. To support this opinion it is alleged that after deducting the cost of raw material imported and used in the manufacture of the £200,000,000 of value exported, there may be left at the most £140,000,000 of income derived from our foreign trade, whilst the aggregate income of the country is estimated at £1,200,000,000; and supposing some other use to be made of the machines and tools now employed in producing what we send to foreigners,—were the whole of our foreign custom to be lost,—it would not deprive us of more than a tenth or twelfth of our whole income. The estimate of 1,200 millions sterling is arrived at by considering that the gross annual value charged to the Income Tax being 500 millions, to which another hundred millions may be added for exemptions and incomes under Schedule D, which escape payment, "the net incomes of the Income Tax paying classes," it is said, "must be somewhere about 600 millions sterling," and it is added that "the incomes of the wage-receiving and nonpaying section can hardly be taken as less than another 600 millions." Is it, however, correct to take assessment to the income tax as a basis, seeing that the same income is charged over and over again as it passes through different hands? It is charged at its first inception and at many of its subsequent distributions, and hence arises one very cogent argument against the fairness of the tax at all.

This may be illustrated by supposing the case of two individuals deriving incomes of equal amounts, either from the cultivation of the soil, investments in the funds, or from the profits of any manufacture. Each pays the same amount of tax. The one spends all in the maintenance of his

[1] "Times," 19th Nov., 1877, "Foreign Competition."

family at home and the employment of labour on his estate. The other pays a clergyman to teach the adults on his property, a schoolmaster to teach the children, he sends his daughters to school and educates his sons for a profession, and the amounts he pays for each of these objects on passing into the hands of other persons are again assessed, being reckoned in their respective incomes. Again, all these persons pay the butcher and the baker, the physician and the lawyer, and in every one of these cases another charge is raised. Yet all the while the total income, so far as the country is concerned, remains actually the same. Indeed, the incomes of the wage-receiving classes become indirectly assessed, for their earnings pass into the hands of the tradesmen with whom they deal, whose profits become chargeable. The error consists in supposing that the aggregate of individual incomes and the income of the country are one and the same. That only is true income which is created, and none of those who are non-producers adds anything to the national income, although they may have to contribute to its taxes. They are simply agents in this sense of distributing that which has been produced by others.

But a still graver error exists in the supposition that any amount of money passing between individuals at home can have any effect upon that which is required for transmission abroad. In relation to the rest of the world our only income is that which we have power to spend with it. So long as A fattens sheep and B weaves cloth, they may with advantage exchange their respective produce, but neither is one step nearer to obtaining the sugar or the fur he requires from abroad. If the producer of these will not take the wool of the one or the cloth of the other, both A and B must go without. Nor is the real nature of the transaction at all altered because C and D come between them, buying from the one and selling to the other. Let the money, which is simply the medium of exchange, be but sent out of the country to pay the sugar-planter in Jamaica or the hunter in North America, and neither A nor B will long have any. Suppose the 140 millions assumed to be the profits of our foreign trade to be lost, then we should necessarily have by so much to reduce our imports, for if we attempted to pay for them in bullion, national bankruptcy must speedily ensue. Do away with our foreign trade, or let it be taken from us by foreign competition, and we must be content to exist only on that which we can raise within our home boundaries, excepting always that which our investments and earnings abroad provide the means of paying for.

This brings us to the consideration of what probability there may be of our being able to lessen the extent of our imports, the value of which for each of the last six years has already been given. An analysis of these figures in one of the papers already alluded to [1] shows the following distribution under the various headings of Food, Raw Material, and Manufactured Goods in million pounds sterling for the ten years, 1867-76.

	Food.	Raw Material.	Manufactured Material.	Total.
1867	101	100	29	230
'68	105	110	32	247
'69	106	108	34	248
'70	100	119	40	259
'71	118	117	36	271
'72	136	125	35	296
'73	147	133	35	315
'74	143	130	39	312
'75	157	118	41	316
'76	159	119	41	319

The returns for 1877 are not yet completed, when they are it will probably be found that the whole increase of 22 millions has been on articles of food. If so, the growth of consumption during these last ten years has been 80 per cent. on food, 20 per cent. on raw materials, and 40 per cent. on

[1] Manchester Statistical Transactions.

manufactured articles; and that our present demands in these ways require 180, 120, and 40 millions respectively. It will be observed that the increase has been least in the raw materials used in manufacture, which fact corresponds with the falling off of our exports, the bulk of which are manufactured out of imported material. These scarcely admit of reduction unless our manufacturing industries are to be still further crippled, which would imply, as is already apparent, a diminished power of purchase on the part of our artisans and labourers. Neither can we wish any material reduction in manufactured articles, excepting in so far as those of foreign manufacture are superseding the work of our own operatives. It is to be feared that a considerable portion of the increase is due to this cause. We may be well content to avail ourselves of the skill and industry of other nations in rendering natural products fit for use or ornament, so long as we can persuade them to take the works of our hands in exchange; but surely foreign competition is to be dreaded when it is directed against our own manufactures.

Nor would any well-wisher of our own people desire to see any diminution in the supplies of food, but rather he would seek a constant addition to the quantity, excepting indeed in the case of those articles falling under this head which minister to the national vice of intemperance. These, for 1876, are valued in the paper we have quoted from at £11,000,000 of imports in the form of drink, and £14,000,000 for the materials converted in our own breweries and distilleries. Amounts such as these under this head, even if saved, as is to be hoped, will only for a short time prevail in the face of the larger increase which must arise in necessary articles of food for our ever-increasing population. It is calculated that though we have 33 million inhabitants in the United Kingdom, the home growth of food is only sufficient to maintain 18 millions, leaving 15 millions of our people dependent on foreign supplies. The natural increase of population is not quite one per cent. per annum, far less than it should be if life and health were properly cared for ; but at this rate we have every year from a quarter to one-third of a million more to provide for. We are not increasing in home growth of food, and therefore the whole supply for this addition to population must come from abroad. This alone will require an annual addition on our imports to the value of from 3 to 4 millions, sufficient in a very few years to swallow up any savings from the abandonment of useless or vicious expenditure in food.

From all these and some other considerations we are forced to the conclusion before stated, namely, that we need to have an income drawn from sources entirely outside the United Kingdom of at least 100 millions sterling per annum to pay our way with the other nations of the world, and that, unless there be some radical amendment or alteration in our trading and manufacturing condition, there is no prospect for some time to come of this necessity being lessened. To this point, then, it will be well that those who have the means of investigating or discovering the real amount of the world's annual indebtedness to this country should apply their researches. If our receipts in that way be just the 100 millions, we are consuming it all in food, to say nothing of other perishable purchases, leaving nothing for saving or accumulation. If the sum exceed that amount we may be adding to our investments in other countries, and so providing for the growing enlargement of demands on our foreign resources by as much as the excess may be. But if, on the other hand, the receipts fall short of the sum named, we must be calling in our credits, parting with our securities, or creating debts for future liquidation. Whichever way we look at it, we see that we are less prosperous than we were six years ago, and it may be that our present position is one of actual or coming adversity,—that we are now, or soon shall be, really living upon our capital.

It is, however, asserted that we cannot be doing this, because we are making constant accumulations at home.[1] The

[1] "Times," 7th Dec., 1877, "Excess of Imports."

same fallacy pervades this argument as the cognate one regarding home income. Accumulations at home may add to our comfort, but cannot avail us in our dealings with foreign countries, unless the accumulations be of moveable wealth which we transport abroad; and even this will be of no avail if we cannot persuade foreigners to take it in exchange for those products of their lands which we need or desire. We may cover our own land with buildings, increase our rent-rolls to any extent, fill our houses with costly furniture, and adorn them with works of art; we may drain our marshes and embank our rivers; we may extend our railway system, multiply horses and chariots; we may dress in fine linen and fare sumptuously every day;—but not one morsel of foreign food will any of these things bring to our shores, if we cannot barter them with other nations. If we are stocking our warehouses with goods in the expectation of revived demand; if we are erecting factories and machinery which may enable us to produce those goods when that demand shall arise; if we are building ships to carry them away, or laying down railroads to facilitate their transport; we may be laying the foundation for a future accession of wealth, but we are not, in doing this now, accumulating that wealth, we are only preparing for its acquisition, and the wisdom or the folly of such procedure must remain in doubt until subsequent events may justify or condemn our forecast.

Another course of reasoning is constantly to be met with, namely, it is argued that an excess of imports cannot really be at all injurious, since other nations with whom there is an excess of exports are suffering from the same depression of trade. The error here lies in coupling together circumstances which happen to exist at the same time, but which do not necessarily stand in the relation of cause and effect. Trade is depressed both in England and the United States, and from the same cause,—the producers are more than are needed to produce the quantities of goods consumed. But there the parallel ends;—we produce more than we can find buyers for, the Americans owing to maintaining a protective policy produce at a greater cost than consumers are willing to pay. Again, with us, agriculture is barely, if at all, profitable, because we produce at high cost; with them agriculture is flourishing, because they raise their produce at such rates as induce buyers. We buy because we have not enough food at home to support our population ; they sell because they have more than enough. We can sustain doing this for a time, because in former times we have lent them money, the securities for which we can exchange for their food. They from the produce of their fields are paying off the debts incurred in warfare ; we are receiving payment of their obligations and eating it up as fast as we get it. But what would be the position of each country were all trade suddenly to cease, and each people were thrown upon its own resources? We should have empty bellies ; the Americans might have bare backs. They, finding no market for their surplus food, would devote their labour to turning their cotton and their wool into clothing ; we should with difficulty, perhaps by costly methods, strive to increase the produce of the soil, and having exhausted our stores, become destitute of clothing, and whilst the corn was growing, the would-be eaters would starve. In short, we, losing our past gains and consuming our accumulated savings, should fall into decrepitude ; they, husbanding their resources, and unable to spend their means in foreign extravagances, would be prepared, when circumstances altered, to step into the place from whence we had fallen. To them the stoppage of trade would be painful; to us it would be absolutely fatal. More than one-half of our population will soon be absolutely dependent upon foreign supplies for their daily food ; and but two methods of supplying their wants lie open—either to make our land produce double crops, or to maintain the trade by which we exchange our manufactures for food and other necessaries. A third course is, indeed, open, and that is to transport our population to places where food may be grown more cheaply, where those who grow it would be thereby enabled, not only to support themselves, but to become purchasers of our manufactures.

If these things be true the nation is passing through a crisis of greater severity than most of us are aware, and until a radical change take place in our manufacturing and trading relations, we must look for a still greater disparity between its expenditure and its receipts, for the supplies it obtains and renders. By some it is considered that foreign manufacturers having, like our own, been over-producing, are recklessly selling at unremunerative prices their accumulated stocks, and that we, being possessed of more capital than they, will be able to hold out longer, and sooner be able to obtain higher prices for larger quantities. By others the cause of depression is sought in the disturbances occasioned by the war now raging, and they argue that when this is settled there will be an immediate revival of trade. By others the reason of the existing state of things is found in the unfavourable harvests in this country of the last few years, and, believing that the seasons run in cycles, they predict that the turn will soon come for years of abundant yield. Others, again, lay the blame at the door of Free Trade and long for some modification of our treaty arrangements, which shall secure reciprocity, if not exactly a return to the old days of Protection. Once more, it is affirmed by others, that the evil arises from over-population, and that were measures taken to repress our increase in numbers, a different state of things would result.

Now all these several causes and reasons, though in some degree they throw light on the condition in which we stand, appear to be insufficient to explain why the excess of imports should be so large and trade so depressed as it is. Nor does there seem to be any well-grounded hope that the existing evils will be speedily removed. It is with no desire to excite undue alarm that these conclusions are dwelt upon, but solely from the conviction that, when disease exists, a correct diagnosis is the first step towards effecting a cure.

Without this, the true remedies cannot be applied, nor even effectual palliatives be prescribed. The patient whose physician fails to comprehend the true nature of the attack will suffer loss of strength till the sickness becomes chronic, and all anticipations of recovery become hopeless.

Where, then, is the remedy to be found ? In discontinuing the deep-rooted extravagance and want of economy which characterize the present age—extravagance in the expenditure of means, want of economy in the employment of time and strength. It is not that we have too many people, for, as the figures are capable of showing, even with our present consumption of food and other products, the proportion of the population employed in producing these leaves an ample number for producing what are not articles of necessity. With the wages our labouring classes have been receiving, there ought not, until very recently, to have been destitution or poverty amongst them, and, but for their lavish expenditure, comfort might have universally prevailed. It is high wages which enhance the cost of our manufactures, and so drive trade from the country; it is the misemployment of those wages which causes privation, and leads to suffering. Were abstinence from drink, or even moderation in the use of alcoholic liquors, universal, there is no need, or at least there was none until recently, why hunger or nakedness should be undergone by so many. Look at what has been spent in this way. The 25 millions sterling mentioned before is simply the cost of the materials from which spirituous liquors are made. The heavy duties so properly levied on these beverages come to at least treble the cost of the material, and the labour employed in their manufacture must more than quadruple the price to the consumer. Let us add to these items the interest of capital devoted to their manufacture and sale, and we shall see how vast is the cost to the consumer. It is a low estimate which would put this sum down at an amount equalling the balance against our trade. Thus the whole difficulty would be solved could we effect a reformation in the drinking habits of the people. To find so many labourers on an average spending more than half their earnings on this one gratification, leaves no room for surprise that labour is dear and distress so general.

The labouring class, however, are not alone to blame in this matter of extravagant expenditure—the middle and higher classes set the example. To outvie each other in the magnificence of their entertainments, equipments, and dress, seems to be the chief object in life to many; and whilst this feeling exists as it does in the upper classes, we must not be too hard on those lower in position who manifest an equal degree of folly. These may appear harsh words, but they are not too strong. The contrast which is manifested between the splendour of the rich and the squalor of the poor is utterly wrong,—it disgraces both our Christianity and our boasted civilization. We load our tables with course after course, whilst there are thousands whose vital power is impaired for want of proper nourishment; we cover our persons with clothing which we cannot wear out, whilst women and children are perishing for want of necessary protection against the inclemency of our climate; we furnish our houses with gilded finery, whilst the homes of hundreds are loathsome with filth. Nay, more than this, we carry the same principle into our religion, lavishly spending in meretricious ornament the wealth which would provide the means of decent worship for the masses who never enter the places now set apart for religion, and we spend the time of our clergy in multiplying those neglected services rather than in sending them to meet with the outcasts of society who herd in the back streets of our cities and towns, whilst our charities are too many of them so bestowed that the importunate rather than the unfortunate become the recipients. Let it not be thought that this is condemnatory of genuine hospitality and honest social intercourse, of refined taste and liberal expenditure in adorning our homes or our persons, of elegance and grandeur in the erection of churches and chapels, or of frequent invitations to the services in our sanctuaries—for all these there is ample room, without waste of wealth and time. It will not do to say that the owners of wealth may spend it as they please,—consuming much and producing nothing. They are but stewards and trustees for the general welfare, as happily so many of our nobility and capitalists are acknowledging in increasing numbers; but until this truth is universally admitted, there will never be the needed economy in the use of wealth, time, and influence.

It will perhaps, however, be said that if all our people were to become frugal, industrious, and sober, we should increase the products for which there is no demand. Well, then, we must create the demand,—not by competing with other nations in their own markets, or bolstering up effete and decaying peoples who will never be satisfactory customers,—but by seeking out fresh fields, and sending our capital to the newly discovered regions which we may colonize, so finding customers amongst the many natives and the comparatively few of our own population whom we should need to send. Whilst such large portions of the globe are ready to yield their food productions to labour, and teem with multitudes who, with civilization, will bestow that labour, and for that which it raises will take our manufactures in exchange, it cannot be a necessity that there be starvation and misery at home.

It was remarked in one of the papers to which allusion has been made, that " Britain now stands tottering on the eminence to which she has attained." Since that was said, her stability has not become more assured. She still stands tottering,—not from the instability of the foundation on which she rests, or from the want of strength to grasp the supports which may insure her safety,—but simply from the intoxication of success, the excitement of overstrained nerves, the difficulty of breathing in the elevated region she has reached. We have gained so much that we are living too fast. Let us check our progress in this direction, and we shall regain the means of still further progress in higher ends, and shall attain yet more glorious results.   If Xerxes wept that he had no more worlds to conquer, so, now, let us rejoice that there are new worlds to subdue peacefully to the cause of civilization and Christianity.

IX.

On the True Relation in which Imports and Exports should stand to each other in the Trade of a Prosperous Country.[1]

SO much has been written and spoken of late on the question of Imports and Exports in their relation to the Balance of Trade, that it may seem superfluous to tender any further facts or opinions upon this question, but it is only necessary to refer to the proceedings of the Statistical Societies of London and Dublin as well as that of this city during the past year, to show that the subject is by no means exhausted. It may however be doubted whether there would have been so many utterances had there been anything like a thorough understanding or general consensus of opinion as to the principles by which our judgment should be guided in deciding on the evidence which these facts afford as to the prosperity or otherwise of a trading community such as that of the United Kingdom. The keen discussions which have arisen whenever these subjects have been under consideration, and the number of able papers which were read during the course of the last session in London, bear testimony to the wide interest which has arisen regarding these matters. It may not therefore be out of place to take this as the subject of the paper which your secretary has done me the honour to ask at my hands for this evening's meeting.

Trade in its earliest form must have consisted in the

[1] Read November 20th, 1878, before the Manchester Statistical Society.

mutual exchange or barter of articles of consumption possessed by one and needed or desired by another; and
would probably take place first in supplies of food. It
would early be discovered that a concentration of time and
strength on the production of one class of articles would
yield greater results than if each individual attempted to
raise or procure everything that he needed, whilst diversity
of taste as well as circumstance would fix the pursuits in
which each would engage. One being a tiller of the soil
would obtain the animal food he required by giving up a
portion of the grain or fruit which he either found or raised
by his labour and skill. At first, and in the absence of
any imperishable substance as a medium of exchange, the
transaction would be one of simple barter, and the standard
of value or rate of exchange be determined by the time employed in the production of each of the articles in which
they dealt. This would be truly payment in kind, and so
long as the produce of a day's labour was given for that
which bore a similar charge, perfect equality of bargains
would exist, each party gaining more than he could obtain at
the same cost, but neither more than he gave to his neighbour. Soon however, disparity in bodily strength, in skill or
disposition, together with the advent of seasons and other
circumstances favouring one occupation more than another,
would produce inequality, and though for a time the balance
might fluctuate, ultimately prosperity would probably attend
the one and adversity overtake the other. Then would
come the necessity of the weaker to submit to the one in a
stronger position, who, such is human nature, would not be
slow to take advantage of the opportunities afforded by the
other's need to exact unequal terms; and thus the element
of profit and loss would be introduced. At the outset, this
would probably be confined to dealings in food or other
articles of prime necessity in which the buyer would be
more or less at the mercy of the seller, but in those of
more durable character and less indispensable to existence
or comfort, the buyer would have the advantage. Since he

need not purchase unless he willed, he would refrain until
he got or thought he got the best of the bargain,—but so
soon as through custom, habit or overpowering inclination,
the objects of desire became as good as real necessities, the
one who sought to possess them would be led to yield to
the demands of their owner ; and thus the most laborious
or skilled whether of body or mind, as well as the least
scrupulous would cause every exchange to be to his
advantage.

Then in process of time the most durable and the least
easily obtained articles would become the representatives or
standard of value. When jewels and the precious metals
were discovered, these as being the most attractive lasting
and portable of known substances would naturally become
the medium of exchange, the recognized tokens of value;
and payment in kind would be transformed into what was
equivalent to our present cash payments, more distinctly
such, when metals being stamped as coin had a definite
nominal worth attached to each.

Proceeding onward, the necessity real or fancied for one
party to secure the food, clothing, or articles of utility and
desire, although at the time destitute of the proper medium
in which to make payment ; and on the other hand the wish
of the possessor to part with his goods, on the belief that
deferred payment would yield him a greater return than a
present exchange; would lead to his acceptance of a promise
to be fulfilled at a future time, and thus purchasing on
credit would take its rise.

Advancing a step farther, the owner of wealth accumulated
beyond the power of personal employment, seeing those who
desired advances—either under the pressure of poverty, or
the belief that the temporary possession of what they had not
themselves might gain for them more than they would have
to repay—would be led to trust such persons with the use
of his means on being secured a share in the profits arising
from its application to purposes of manufacture or trade,
and thus investment on loan or security would come about.

Another form of this would be where undertakings were started too large for one or a few individuals to compass with their own labour or substance; these would join their powers to those of others in like positions, employing partners or agents to carry on operations for their joint benefit, and in this manner partnerships and public companies would come into existence.

Now just as it is with individuals so is it with nations; and this sketch of the various stages of progress, which must be familiar to all who have devoted thought or study to the subject, has been introduced to bring to view distinctly that which happens in the processes by which commerce is carried on.   To see clearly the true bearing which imports and exports have to each other, we must personify each country, gathering all individual traders as it were into units, and, disregarding all internal interchange of wealth or goods, just as we would the transfer of our purse from one pocket to the other, consider only that which takes place to or from the shores of each nation.

Looking at it in this aspect, we shall see that all the several processes we have described are being carried on at one and the same time in the business of each trading nation, or at any rate in that of our own; and that the true meaning or effect of the apparent balance between imports and exports depends upon the degree or extent in which either or all of these several methods prevail.   In the infancy of trade, such for instance as exists in Africa —so many pounds of beads, or so many yards of calico are sent out to be exchanged for as much ivory or oil as the untutored natives will part with.   Here, although no money passes between the sellers or buyers, the money value of the goods sent out, together with that expended in transporting them from the place of production to that of barter, being set off against the price obtained for those brought back, less the expense of bringing them home, will show the true amount of profit; and were all trade of this description the excess of imports over exports would be the exact measure of the nation's gain. In like manner, although in the first instance the goods may be sold for money, and others purchased with the proceeds brought back, or where one or more exchanges of goods or money may take place on the way; wherever that which comes home is wholly procured by that which goes out, the difference between the money value of the two will be the nation's gain or loss, and if the trade be profitable there must be an excess of import. These are in truth payments in kind between the nations engaged in the transactions.

Again, supposing money to be sent home for goods exported, or money to be sent out for goods imported, the difference between the value of the goods on exportation and the money received in the one case, or in the other, between the value of the goods when imported and the money with which they were purchased, is to the advantage of the country; and if the amount of money in each instance is the same, the difference of value in the goods parted with and the goods received will be the exact gain or otherwise resulting to the trader. Imports must exceed exports in value if the trading has been successful; but the amount of money thus used may not be the same on each occasion, and then the difference between the two will be a cash payment to the advantage of whichever has parted with the most goods.

These are truths so simple and elementary as scarcely to need expression, were it not for the fallacy which pervades so many statements in which it is assumed that because imports exceed exports it necessarily follows that the one *must* have been purchased with the other, and that the difference is wholly gain ; at least so much of it as is not absolutely the produce of earnings or dividends abroad, turned from money into goods, and sent home in this state, instead of bullion or cash. Such writers appear to forget that in the present day the bulk of the trade carried on is not by means of either payment in kind or by cash payments, but on credit. It is true that the individual credits are of short duration, and must be speedily balanced; but they may be, and are, balanced by other credits, not perhaps between the same parties, but between the nations thus trading together; and it is utterly impossible to say as between these, how long or to what extent such credit may be given or taken.

Once more, it does not follow that the goods thus transferred from one country to another are even paid for by credit. Of course, so far as each trader is concerned, they will be settled in one way or at one time or another; but the nations to which these traders belong may by means of other individuals be entrusting money to borrowers or be investing money in property or joint-stock undertakings; and if so, all these must be taken into account before a true balance of profit or loss can be struck; and therefore the apparent balance may in truth represent only temporary or permanent investments, or the calling in of those made at times long since gone by.

It follows, then, that an excess of imports is satisfactory whenever it results :—

1. From a direct exchange of goods, those arriving being of greater value than those sent out to be bartered.

2. From money realized by the sale of exports, instead of being remitted in payment, being exchanged for goods which acquire additional value from transport home; always supposing that their value on arrival is beyond that of those whose proceeds procured their purchase. This, though somewhat differing in form, is really the same as the previous case.

3. From the money with which they are paid for being so much income accruing abroad, whether as earnings from labour, profits in trade, or dividends on investments.

Under all these conditions there may be a constant and growing excess of imports, the extent of which is the indication and measure of national trading prosperity. To these must be added :—

4. When the excesses of goods imported are stored up for

employment in the production of articles for export, such excesses being only temporary, and balanced by an excess of exports at a future time.

On the other hand, an even amount or an excess of exports will be satisfactory when the money they realize is beyond their value on leaving, and is :—

1. Remitted home in cash.

2. Lent on good security abroad.

3. Invested in profitable undertakings or the acquisition of property in other countries.

Applying now these principles to the past and present history of our own country's trade, let us seek to discover the true import of the changes in its condition which the official accounts record and proclaim.

In tracing the earlier history of British commerce, many difficulties stand in the way of arriving at any definite conclusions. It is very uncertain whether full or accurate information was supplied, or the records kept with sufficient care; and the mode adopted for reducing the quantities of the several articles of trade to their equivalent in money was by no means satisfactory. For reasons more fully explained in two papers read before the Statistical Society (London)[1] this, known as *official* value, however correct in the outset, failed as time went on to give anything like a fair representation of the respective worth of goods passing inwards and outwards. It consisted of fixed prices assigned to each then known article of trade, to the list of which new goods were from time to time added, at the market rates attached to them at the period when they came to be of sufficient importance to be specially noted ; and this continued to be adopted in the official returns down to 1854. The values were also thus compiled for the purposes of comparison so late as the year 1869, when this method of computation finally ceased to be adopted. As regards the exports of British produce and manufacture so early as

[1] "Statistical Journals," Vol. xxxv., June, 1872, pp. 207-8 ; Vol. xxxviii., June, 1878, pp. 215-16 ; Vol. xl., March, 1877, pp. 19-22.

1798, for the purpose of levying a war tax under the name
of "Convoy duty," shippers were called upon to make a
declaration of the actual value. This obligation still rests
upon exporters, and we have thus an unbroken record of
declared values down to the present day. For the imports
a system was introduced in 1854, whereby the "official
values" were discarded, and "computed" ones made by
officials at the current market prices were substituted.
These gave place in 1871 to values declared by the importers on each entry for the landing of their goods, and thus
the values now shown in the official returns for both imports
and exports are derived from similar sources,—the owner's
declaration, scrutinized by the officials who supervise the
landing and shipment of the goods, and the Statistical
Department of the Customs from whence the published
returns emanate.

The following table gives an epitome of the trade from
1699, the earliest date of which there are any sufficient
records, to the close of the last century, with the addition
of the first fifteen years of the present one, showing the
annual growth in value of the goods imported and exported,
and the annual increase per cent. of each period over its
immediate predecessor. For the first eighty years the particulars are for England alone, from thence to the end of the
century Scotland is included, and from thence forward the
whole of the United Kingdom. The values on both sides
of the account are the "official" ones, none other being
obtainable for imports during the whole period ; and though
the "declared values" might have been given for the last
portion of the export account, those corresponding to the
import have been retained.

TABLE I.—*Showing the Annual Average Amount (in Official value) of the Imports into and Exports from England, in each decennial period from 1699 to 1778 inclusive, and those into and from Great Britain from 1779 to 1800 inclusive, together with the Average Annual Increase per cent. in each successive period.*

[In million £'s to two decimals.]

Period.	Imports.		Exports.	
	Annual Average.	Increase per cent.	Annual Average.	Increase per cent.
Into England :	£		£	
1699—1708	4·58	—	5·85	—
1709—1718	5·03	10	6·50	11
'19— '28	6·23	24	7·18	10
'29— '38	7·09	14	8·35	16
'39— '48	6·71	—5	8·97	7
'49— '58	7·58	13	11·02	23
'59— '68	9·56	26	12·98	18
'69— '78	10·86	14	12·44	—4
Into Great Britain :				
1779—1788	12·35	14	12·58	1
'89— '98	18·61	51	21·55	71
2 years, 1799—1800...	26·16	41	31·97	48

The same into the United Kingdom from 1801 to 1815 in quinquennial periods :—

Into United Kingdom:				
1801—1805	28·92	11	33·01	3
'06— '10	30·29	5	37·02	12
'11— '15	29·85	1	45·08	22

For the reasons already alluded to, absolute dependence cannot be placed upon these figures, and it would be rash to conclude either that they afford a trustworthy record of the whole value of the goods on either side, or that the difference between the two is certainly the balance for any or all of the years included in the table. There is, however, no reason to doubt that relatively to each other, and comparatively one year with another, they may be taken as fair evidence of the condition of our trade. Having values for later years for both imports and exports on the two systems for the same year, it is quite possible with justice to arrive at the conclusion that however insufficient or erroneous the system may have been, the probabilities of error on either side of the accounts are equal. We know that for the first few years of declared export value, it was in excess of the official; and, therefore, that the figures given above were below the truth. That the same variation, though in less degree, attached to the import figures may be inferred from a comparison of the two rates given in later years. Again, the import values include the cost of bringing the articles hither, and the profit obtained on their trading, whilst the export prices exclude the charges and profit realized upon their sale abroad. These, in the earlier days of commerce, were proportionately heavier than at present, hence the real proceeds of our exports as applied towards the payment for imports would be much larger than they now are. The apparent balance in our favour would fail to adequately represent the gain to the country upon the exchange of its produce for the commodities of other lands.

It will be observed on an inspection of the table, that we started with a balance in favour of exports, and not only maintained this through the whole of the 117 years over which it ranges, but progressively increased it, the imports for the last of the series being $6\frac{1}{4}$ times greater than in the first, whilst the exports were multiplied $7\frac{1}{4}$ times. Taking into consideration the causes of disparity it is safe to conclude that in 1818 the purchases we made could not have absorbed one-half the proceeds of the sales we effected. Now this is just what might have been expected. England was then laying the foundation of her trade, settling her colonies, and starting her connections in foreign countries. To both of these she was sending her sons, not empty-handed, but carrying with them the products of home industry, wherewith to supply the capital necessary for establishing her settlements and businesses in their new homes.

Not idle, or wasteful, but earning money, and employing their savings for future profit abroad, rather than remitting them home. In the first instance trade would take the form of simple barter, inexpensive articles of home production being exchanged for those of foreign growth and manufacture, which as articles of luxury would fetch high prices when brought hither. But the necessity of supporting life and the growing stability of the colonist and settler would also ensure the conversion of the goods from home into the food and other necessaries for the use of those whose labour and skill produced or acquired property abroad.

Again, it must be remembered that excepting with gold or silver-producing countries, there are no means of remitting money from one place to another, and no way unless to a very limited amount, for one country to obtain property in another, but by first sending it there in some tangible shape, when it must appear as an export from the place of origin to that of occupation. That England has become possessed of large holdings in land, merchandise, and securities all over the world no one will dispute. She can only have done this by first sending it forth either as goods exported, or as living beings to produce and earn, first maintenance, and then property. Under such circumstances it is utterly fallacious to say that she could benefit only to the extent of her imports—an excess of exports was necessary to the creation and continuance of her wealth outside her own shores.

The next table continues the account onwards from 1816 to the present year. It differs from the previous one in showing, not the total imports, but only those retained in the country for home use, and the exports of British produce and manufacture only. These quantities afford an easier basis for comparison than when burdened on both sides of the account with those merely passing through our hands to foreign customers. The import values are still "official" up to 1854, therefore not quite accurate for comparison with the actual export values. The double valuation in 1854 showed that at that date the " official " were short of the " computed" by something like 25 per cent., the result of the assumed prices on which they were founded being fixed; whilst increase of population in numbers and wealth had gradually added to the cost of almost all articles of consumption. It is probable, however, that this change was more rapid after the gold discoveries had begun to tell upon prices, and that in the earlier years, say some 10 per cent. would up to 1825 or 1830 represent the departure from accuracy. To this extent and more, allowance must be made in comparing the totals with those of the exports. For the first fifty years the annual amount is the average of quinquennial periods, after that the actual sums for each year are shown. From 1850 to 1870 the values are " computed," and as already explained they may be accepted as equivalent to the declared ones in use since the latter date up to the present time.

TABLE II.—*Showing the Annual Average Amount of Imports of Foreign and Colonial Merchandise retained for Home use, and of Exports of Produce and Manufactures of the United Kingdom in each quinquennial period from 1816 to 1865, and in each year from thence to 1879, with the Annual Increase per cent. in each successive period.*

[In million £'s to two decimals.]

Year.	Imports.		Exports.	
	Value.	Increase per cent.	Value.	Increase per cent.
1816 to 1820	20·66	21	40·31	—6
'21 to '25	26·20	27	37·25	—7
'26 to '30	33·83	23	35·93	—4
'31 to '35	36·53	8	40·46	13
'36 to '40	47·59	30	50·01	24
'41 to '45	57·54	21	54·00	8
'46 to '50	72·92	26	60·89	13
'51 to '55	89·70	23	88·86	46
'56 to '60	158·01	23	124·16	40
'61 to '65	201·18	27	144·40	16
'66	245·30	22	188·92	31
'67	230·34	—6	180·96	—4
'68	246·60	7	179·68	—1
'69	248·40	1	189·95	6
'70	258·76	4	199·59	5
'71	270·51	5	223·07	12
'72	296·36	10	256·26	15
'73	315·45	6	255·17	—
'74	311·99	—1	239·56	—6
'75	315·79	1	223·47	—7
'76	319·01	1	200·64	—10
'77	340·96	7	198·89	—1
'78	316·14	—7	192·85	—3
'79	305·74	—3	191·53	—1

It will be observed that, as in the former table, there is a progressive increase on both sides of the account, although not in the same ratio as before, the imports advancing far more rapidly up to about 1825 than the exports do. So much so, that on making allowance for deficient import value, the two were nearly equal, and they continued so up to about 1845.   From this time, under the influence of free trade, both sides progressed with great rapidity, the imports, however, outstripping the exports up to 1870.   We had then two years, 1871-2, of excessive exports, since when these have rapidly declined, whilst until the present year the imports continued to increase.

Bearing in mind that the import values are loaded with charges for freight, &c., which are *not* paid to the foreigner, and the export values are subject to the like additions accruing *before* they are paid for, it must be understood that to this extent a difference in the amounts here shown does not actually represent the sum to be paid by this country to its customers. Mr. Newmarch considers that to make the comparison just, the imports must be diminished by five and the exports increased by ten per cent.   My own calculations, made upon a different basis,[1] do not when spread over a period embracing the last twenty years, materially differ from his, and this close concurrence in results of the two estimates goes far to prove them correct. Both methods would place the amounts for 1872 almost on a level, thus leaving no balance either way.   Since then the preponderance of imports has been so remarkable as to justify special attention to the calculated figures for the few years preceding and succeeding 1872, as having the most important bearing upon questions arising out of the present depressed conditions of trade and manufacture. The actual balances to be provided for may be thus stated :—

1872........................*nil.*

1871	£15,000,000	1873	£19,000,000
1870	34,000,000	1874	29,000,000
1869	30,000,000	1875	54,000,000
1868	37,000,000	1876	83,000,000
1867	27,000,000	1877	94,000,000
1866	36,000,000	1878	84,000,000

To sum up these observations,—From the earliest periods

---

[1] "Statistical Journals," June, 1877, and September, 1878.

up to about 1825 (growing annually up to 1818, thence declining) the exports of home produce largely exceeded the imports of foreign. From 1825 to 1872, although the imports exceeded the exports, it was not to an extent difficult to be accounted for. From 1872, when there was again if anything a slight excess of exports, the excess of imports has most rapidly increased, until now it must have reached the sum of £94,000,000 per annum. In the first period we were settling our colonies and cultivating trading relations with the world, and by this means accumulating property abroad. In the second, we were proceeding in the same direction, but also enjoying some of the benefits arising from previous outlay, and at its close reached the height of our manufacturing and trading prosperity. In the third we have been declining from this height, and are now experiencing the greatest depression in every branch of commerce and industry both at home and abroad. The causes, effects, and remedies of and for this state of things deserve the closest investigation, but it may be well previously to see what has been the recent progress of some other nations, selecting for this purpose as representative countries Russia, France, and the United States; extracting from official sources[1] the particulars so far as they can be ascertained. It is to be regretted that these tables do not go back farther than the year 1860. The period, however, which they do cover is sufficiently long to present a fair estimate of the recent progress of the trade.

[1] "Statistical Abstract for Foreign Countries." Board of Trade, 1877-8.

TABLE III.—*Imports and Exports of Merchandise into and from the Russian Empire from 1861 to 1876, with the annual increase per cent. of each successive year over its predecessor; also the balance of Bullion thence exported in each year.*

[In million £'s to two decimals.]

| Year. | Imports. | | Exports. | | |
| | | | Merchandise. | | Bullion. |
	Amount.	Increase per cent.	Amount.	Increase per cent.	Balance exported.
1861	25·13	—	27·13	—	1·34
'62	22·72	—10	27·69	2	5·16
'63	22·95	1	28·68	4	9·86
'64	25·84	13	28·53	—1	3·70
'65	24·57	—5	32·13	12	3·21
'66	31·00	26	33·58	4	4·06
'67	39·97	29	36·13	8	—3·05
'68	41·31	4	35·88	—1	—5·30
'69	54·14	31	41·87	17	2·06
'70	53·19	—2	56·99	36	3·35
'71	58·35	10	58·47	3	1·62
'72	68·91	18	51·78	—11	—·81
'73	70·14	2	57·70	11	—·93
'74	74·65	6	68·37	19	·15
'75	84·09	12	60·47	—12	3·41
'76	75·62	—10	63·47	5	15·49

The trade of Russia in common with that of other countries manifests a continuous increase from year to year. It is not large considering the number of its people, imports and exports together not averaging more than 38/- per head, whereas that of France is 184/-, United States 112/-, and the United Kingdom 382/-, but is increasing more rapidly than either of these other countries. In the earlier of the years under review, the exports would seem to have exceeded the imports, not however to any great extent even when the bullion and specie are added, for being a gold-producing country, the quantity exported is a source of income just the same as any other product; though in countries like ours it is merely the circulating medium, ebbing and

N

flowing and not properly included in the produce of the country. In recent years, say from 1872, the general imports have exceeded the exports, though never more than about ten per cent., which is to be accounted for by the known fact that she is improving her internal resources, especially in starting manufactories; although at the same time she has been incurring debts abroad, besides the heavy ones rendered necessary to meet the outlay incurred by war. Under these circumstances there is nothing to indicate waning prosperity in the fact that she is buying more than she is selling, laying out her money on the increase of property. She, but for her wasteful war, her expenditure of money and life, would be a growing and improving country, and even in spite of this is really advancing in manufacturing and trading progress.

TABLE IV.—*The like Imports and Exports of Merchandise into and from France for each year from* 1860 *to* 1877.

[In million £'s to two decimals.]

Year.	Imports.		Exports. Merchandise.	
	Amount.	Increase per cent.	Amount.	Increase per cent.
1860	75·89	—	91·08	—
'61	97·69	26	97·05	7
'62	87·94	—10	89·71	—8
'63	97·06	10	105·70	18
'64	101·13	4	116·97	11
'65	105·67	4	123·54	6
'66	111·74	6	127·22	3
'67	121·06	8	113·04	—11
'68	132·15	9	111·60	—1
'69	126·12	—5	123·00	10
'70	114·70	—9	112·09	—9
'71	142·67	24	114·90	2
'72	142·81	—	150·47	31
'73	142·19	—	151·50	1
'74	140·31	—1	148·04	—2
'75	141·47	1	154·90	5
'76	159·54	13	143·02	—8
'77	146·79	—8	137·45	—4

France is of all the European nations, the one of most growing prosperity. We saw her wealth in the ease with which she provided for the German indemnity and the war expenditure, and in the rapidity with which she is recovering from disasters enough to have paralyzed and destroyed nations even stronger than she. Her trade too is not large, though with a population less than half that of Russia she has double her trade; but exceeding in numbers that of the United Kingdom, her trade is less than half of ours. This she owes in great part to the fact that her soil and climate enable her to produce most of the food and other necessaries she consumes, and that she has not, as we have, to seek her supplies in other countries. External trade is often spoken of as to be valued for its magnitude, forgetting that this altogether depends upon the circumstances of the country carrying it on, since internal trade may render external unnecessary, and yet be every whit as advantageous as the other. Like Russia and England, the excess of exports in the earlier years has given place to a deficiency in the later ones, yet not to an extent to cause any anxiety, seeing that she too has had to repair the losses by war, and will be fully equal to liquidating the external obligations she may have contracted. At present and indeed for some time past she seems to be accumulating bullion largely; she is sharing in the profits from discounting our mercantile bills; and, notwithstanding that she does import more than she exports, manifests a steady growth in wealth and power.

TABLE V.—*The like Imports and Exports of Merchandise and Bullion into and from the United States for each year (ending 30th June) from 1860 to 1878.*

[In million £'s to two decimals.]

| Years. | Imports. | | Exports. | | |
| | | | Merchandise. | | Bullion. |
	Amount.	Increase per cent.	Amount.	Increase per cent.	Balance Exported.
1860	70·06	—	65·88	—	8·70
'61	57·22	18	42·69	—35	·86
'62	37·15	—35	37·43	—12	4·25
'63	46·85	26	38·75	4	11·36
'64	62·73	34	29·90	—23	19·22
'65	43·69	—30	28·52	—5	12·05
'66	88·22	102	27·60	—3	15·69
'67	79·38	—10	57·84	110	8·08
'68	71·85	—9	56·12	—3	16·58
'69	84·70	18	57·33	2	7·78
'70	87·46	3	78·46	37	6·61
'71	105·29	20	89·25	14	16·07
'72	127·27	21	89·27	—	13·78
'73	130·14	2	105·22	18	13·15
'74	114·70	—12	118·63	13	7·95
'75	108·09	—6	104·02	—12	14·84
'76	92·90	—14	109·50	5	8·45
'77	91·34	—2	122·85	12	3·21
'78	88·10	—4	141·81	15	·32
Total...	1587·14		1401·07		188·95

The United States shows for the earlier years a continuously increasing preponderance of imports, and for the later, a rapidly growing excess of exports, its trade thus standing in direct contrast to that of the countries this side of the Atlantic. From 1860 to 1873, its purchases must have exceeded its sales by nearly 300 millions, of which not more than the half would have been met by the exports of bullion. Since that year, in exact opposition to the condition of our own trade, its imports have regularly fallen, and its exports risen in a greater ratio. In 1872, the imports were some 40 millions above the exports (not including bullion), in the twelve months ending last June more than 50 millions below them. During the first period she was paying for her imports in bonds, and securities, which we on this side were ready to take; and putting her purchases to such good use that now she is able to redeem her obligations, and has already almost if not quite balanced the account, with every prospect of its continuing to be greatly in her favour. But for the exhausting influence of her internal warfare, this change would doubtless have taken place earlier, and been even more complete than it now is. Nothing could more clearly demonstrate the fallacy of supposing that prosperity cannot be the occasion of an excess of exports. The following table of the trade between this country and the United States, affords equally conclusive proof that an excess of imports is not necessarily an evidence of the nations' well-being.

TABLE VI.—*Trade between the United Kingdom and the United States from 1860 to 1878* [1879 *added*].

[In million £'s to two decimals.]

Year.	Imports into United Kingdom.	Exports to United States.			Excess of Imports into the United Kingdom.
		British Produce and Manufactures.	Foreign and Colonial Merchandise.	Total.	
	£	£	£	£	£
1860	44·73	21·67	1·26	22·91	21·82
'61	49·39	9·07	1·96	11·03	38·36
'62	27·72	14·33	4·84	19·17	8·55
'63	19·57	15·35	4·35	19·70	—·13
'64	17·92	16·71	3·46	20·17	—2·25
'65	21·62	21·23	3·94	25·17	—3·55
'66	46·85	28·50	3·34	31·84	15·01
'67	41·05	21·83	2·29	24·12	16·93
'68	43·06	21·43	2·37	23·80	19·26
'69	42·57	24·62	2·16	26·78	15·79
'70	49·80	28·33	2·98	31·31	18·49
'71	61·13	34·24	4·45	38·69	22·44
'72	54·66	40·74	5·17	45·91	8·75
'73	71·47	33·57	3·12	36·70	34·77
'74	73·90	28·24	4·00	32·24	41·66
'75	69·59	21·86	3·20	25·06	44·53
'76	75·90	16·83	3·39	20·22	55·68
'77	77·83	16·38	3·51	19·89	57·94
'78	89·15	14·55	2·98	17·53	71·62
	977·91	429·48	62·76	492·24	485·67
1879	91·84	20·32	5·20	25·52	66·32

It will be observed that with the exception of the few years of the war, there has been a constant growth in our receipts from the United States, and since 1872 an equal decay in the supplies she has required from us. In 1860, we took from thence only twice as much as we sent. During the present year we shall take at least six times the amount she draws from us. It would appear that our purchases from her at the present time actually exceed the amount of hers from the whole world.

It needs but a cursory examination of the foregoing tables and explanations to show that since 1872 a rapid change has been taking place in the trading condition of the United Kingdom, one so marked as to account for the monetary crisis through which we have been passing, and the financial anxieties with which we are at present surrounded. The apparent difference between imports and exports in that year was £40,000,000; in 1877 it was £142,000,000. The real balance to be provided for in settlement of our accounts with the rest of the world was last year some hundred millions of money; in 1872 it was nothing, or some four millions less than nothing.   It is not for a moment assumed that we have actually to pay the whole of this sum; a large portion of it is met by the retention abroad of interests on loans, dividends on shares, earnings of civil and military servants, freights in the carriage of goods, profits on trade, &c.   These have been variously estimated at from fifty to a hundred millions per annum—the exact amount it is not possible to obtain, nor with any certainty to assume, but various circumstances concur in placing it nearer to fifty than a hundred.   The point for consideration, however, is not so much the exact amount as wherein it varies from that which existed in the former year, and it is impossible to believe that there is any difference at all approaching to the increased demands we have to meet.   Many of our creditors have failed to fulfil their engagements; many companies and speculations have come to grief.   The story of the Glasgow Bank shows us how business has been carried on without profit, and altogether it is very doubtful whether, taking all the sources of income accruing abroad together, the supply now applicable to remittance home or retention abroad is as great as it was in 1872.

Beyond this we have positive proof that this country is transferring securities largely to foreign owners, and is not making corresponding investments with the proceeds. This is one reason why the process of payment which has been going on has failed to excite observation,—has not until now adversely affected the foreign exchanges with this country. The war with Turkey, before its outbreak, excited distrust in Russian Bonds, of which some twenty millions are known, and double that value are supposed, to have changed hands from home to foreign owners. Every mail from America tells of remittances in her Bonds from this country, and some fifty millions of these, formerly held here, are now possessed on the other side of the Atlantic. The Bank of France, and discount houses in Paris, Frankfort, Berlin, Vienna, and Holland compete with our own money-lenders for the discount of mercantile bills and our own Treasury notes. A very competent authority considers that the amount of British paper in foreign portfolios at the present moment cannot be less than thirty millions of pounds, and that five years back five millions would have more than covered the whole. The German Government is known to have considerable sums deposited in England, to meet its contemplated purchase of gold, and there is reason to believe that foreign holdings in the English Funds and various stocks have been greatly added to.

Now, what is all this but an actual transferral of capital from this country to America and Europe, not as in the days when we were contracting foreign loans, and supporting foreign enterprises, but in exchange for the excess of imports we are drawing from foreign sources? This is clearly shown by the difference in the value of money in London and, for instance, in Paris. It would never pay to send money from here, where it cannot be obtained at less than six per cent., to there, where it is only worth three; but it does pay to send securities instead of money. This is the very object which the Bank of England seeks to effect by its high rate—for there is no competition for money for home use which could send it up—to prevent gold being sent abroad, as it otherwise must, to pay for the goods we import. And this process must go on until relief is obtained. The high rate for money here lowers the price of stocks and shares, until it suits the purpose of foreign holders to buy back their own, or to purchase ours. But the inevitable result is a diminution of capital in English hands, a lessening of the indebtedness of the world to this country, and a permanent loss on the income arising from our foreign holdings. It must be admitted that this coincides with a period in which imports largely preponderate. Is it untrue to assert that it is the natural result of such preponderance, and therefore affords proof that an adverse balance of trade is not always to be deemed a sign of prosperity?

If now we turn to the United States what do we find there? A state of things exactly opposed in this respect to that which is existing here. Money is not plentiful, because in times past she contracted obligations which she is now discharging; trade may not be prosperous because it is contracted, and prices are low—manufactures are not profitable because they are forced, in opposition to the principles of free trade—of this more hereafter, but amidst it all she is buying back her bonds with the excess of her exports. Just as England is diminishing her monetary claims upon the world, so America is diminishing her indebtedness to the mother country. It is somewhat curious to note, without saying that they are the counterpart of each other, that the fifty millions which we may be supposed to be parting with is just about the difference between our imports from, and exports to America.

England, it may be believed, is in the position of a capitalist, who, having invested his money on mortgages upon the shops and plant of his butcher and baker, and finding his annual outlay increasing whilst his income is at the same time lessening, cancels his Christmas bills for meat and bread by writing off portions of the mortgage debt. The United States is the butcher and baker who, gaining more than she wants to spend, is glad to lessen the incumbrances on her properties. The capitalist may thus retain a good balance at his bankers, the tradesmen may still have overdrawn accounts, but the one is inevitably growing poorer, the others are surely gaining in wealth. Here again an excess of exports is no token of adversity.

But we must pursue this question a step farther. Even though it be true that all this monetary derangement and interchange of property and indebtedness result from the state of our imports and exports, these conditions of trade and manufacture are not the causes but only the effects of something more real and lasting which it is of paramount importance to us to discover. The balance of trade in any country may be the result of growth or decay in either imports or exports, or of an opposite condition in the one and the other existing at the same time. With the trade of the United Kingdom there was from 1872 until the present year, when both are decreasing, a constantly increasing amount of arrivals inwards and a like decrease of departures outwards, intensifying the evil, if such it be, and rapidly swelling the adverse balance. As the causes of this double movement were totally diverse, each requires its own consideration. To go fully into the question would require larger space than it is possible now to occupy, but the main causes may be briefly stated as an increased consumption of food at home, and a decreased or at least stationary use of our manufactures abroad.

The natural growth of population has something to do with the increased importations of food, but is not the sole or principal cause, for as was shown in a paper on this special subject, which I had the honour of reading on a former occasion,[1] in the ten years 1867-76 the addition to the population was barely nine per cent.—while the consumption of food (including alcoholic and other beverages and tobacco), was fifty-eight per cent. on the value; in 1877 it was fully seventeen per cent. more, and if there be any falling-off for this year, it will be in price only, and not in quantity. It is not meant by this that the average consumption of food per head has increased in this degree, for

[1] "Transactions Manchester Statistical Society," 1877. Pp. 156-181.

our home produce having remained stationary, the fresh mouths would have to be fed entirely from foreign supplies, which would likewise have to bear the charge of better quality as well as of quantity.   During the same ten years the increase of raw materials for manufacture, both for home use and foreign sale, had only risen nineteen per cent. It cannot be questioned that there was great room for improvement in the quantity and character of the food supplies for our labouring population, and that even now a better supply of wholesale nutriment for many would be a decided gain in the health and strength which it would yield; but it may be doubted whether the change has been in all respects necessary or advantageous, whether there has not been too much, especially in drink and tobacco, which has brought evils with it other than the great increase of expenditure it has occasioned, an expenditure far beyond the increase in productive power by which it has been accompanied.   Nor have the evils been confined to the lower classes, those of the middle and upper have in a far greater degree adopted a style of living, which in addition to the direct cost for articles of consumption, has also absorbed the labour of many consumers besides, and thus both enhanced the cost, and lessened the quantity of the disposable products of that labour.   The higher wages granted to the labouring class, higher not only in nominal amount, but also in the hours' service for which they have been given, combined with the power of lavish expenditure the higher classes have attained, have been very far from unmixed blessings, since to them in a great degree must be attributed the inconvenient increase of our imports.   The nation altogether has been living too fast.

On the other hand the very prosperity which has for a time furnished the means of undue expenditure, has in several ways led to the loss of the power to continue it. It has increased the cost of labour, thus neutralizing the advantages of labour-saving machinery; it has led to an extension of means of production at a greater pace than our foreign customers have been disposed to advance, and it has stimulated other nations to compete with us in producing for their own necessities and the markets of the world. Hence the prices of our manufactures have fallen below those which yield a profit, and in many branches of industry the quantities taken from us are greatly reduced.

Now this is just what we as a nation cannot possibly afford. Our country only grows half the food which our people consume, and therefore for our continued existence it is absolutely essential that we should produce something else wherewith we may purchase or take in exchange from other nations the food we cannot, or do not raise for ourselves. Herein again we stand in decided contrast to the United States, she grows more food than she can consume. Were she blockaded or shut out from access to the products of other nations, the prices of provisions would fall, and her people might be all of them better fed than even now they are. Were England isolated, the cost of everything would rapidly rise, and so soon as the accumulated stores were exhausted half her inhabitants would starve. Again, we may say that the necessity which compels imports to exceed exports is the very reverse of prosperity; the ability which permits exports to exceed imports is an exactly opposite condition to one of adversity.

If, then, these be truths, and that they are so it seems impossible to deny, is it wise to hide them from view, or to cavil as some do at those who strive to invite public attention to their existence? Like the ostrich who hides her head in the sand, we may fancy that they are best put out of sight, but the very attempt to deny their existence only serves to magnify their importance to others, and to arrest remedial attempts by ourselves. The patient who will not admit that he is ailing, and the physician who ignores the fact that his disorder is serious, are alike answerable if recovery is protracted or rendered impossible, whilst those who are not afraid to acknowledge the presence of disease, and boldly adopt the most likely measures for restoration, are those who also manifest the greatest confidence in the strength of the sufferer's constitution, and thus help best to maintain it unimpaired. We believe that England is seriously sick, but by no means irrecoverably so. Let us then consider what are the steps to be taken for her preservation and the renewal of her vigour.

Considering the important bearing which a right understanding of this question must have upon the measures necessary for the preservation or restoration of our national life and prosperity, it is not surprising that some thoughtful minds have been driven to a consideration of the best means for the attainment of these objects. Rather, is it to be wondered at that so few appear to think it of due importance or are disposed to see that a very decided course of action is needed. It would seem as though the influx of prosperity in former years had so intoxicated all those who were drinking in its copious draughts that they could not dream of reverses or listen with patience to any who raised the voice of warning. Even now there are those who deem the present depression a thing of passing note, and who look to a revival of confidence, the settlement of the Eastern question, or the briskness of a war, as destined to restore trade and encourage manufactures to an extent beyond any former experience. It may be that some sudden and unexpected events will arise to dissipate our fears and restore prosperity; but true wisdom would dictate a recourse to such remedies as it may be possible to discover and apply. Before, however, suggesting anything in this direction it may be well to allude to a few of the plans which have been suggested, especially to the three methods which find favour with many, viz., reciprocity, protection, and the curtailment of production.

Wherein the adoption of reciprocity consists has never been distinctly stated, but it may be taken to mean either the removal of some duties or restrictions on our part, in

response to the abandonment by other countries of those
which restrict our trade—or the imposition by us of duties
or prohibitions in retaliation for those which most impede
our trade already—in other words, a system of " limited
protection." The first of these plans was that on which
Mr. Cobden acted in the treaty he negotiated with France ;
but apart from any question as to the soundness of such a
policy, it would seem that the wholesale removal of all hin-
drances to foreign trade with us, which took place years
ago, has left us little or nothing to offer in exchange for
such privileges as other countries might be induced to offer.
All the Customs duties which we levy are imposed strictly
for revenue purposes. Those upon alcoholic liquors fall quite
as heavily on home production, and their diminution would
entail a loss to the Chancellor of the Exchequer, which no
increase of consumption could repay. Any advantage which
a freer exchange of these commodities from abroad for home
manufactures might procure, would certainly be purchased
at a cost to health and morality which no philanthropist
could possibly desire. The same may be said of tobacco ;
and as regards tea, coffee, and cocoa, the increased trade
which a remission of these duties would bring would be
wholly insufficient, for many years to come, to compensate for
the additional taxation which would have to be imposed on
our own people. The re-enactment of the former, or the
imposition of fresh duties, would in nowise differ from " protection," and as such must be approved or condemned.

A recurrence to " protection" has many advocates in the
present day, and there is no little reason to fear that the
specious arguments by which it is supported may meet with
such acceptance as to induce an attempt to reverse the free
trade policy under which we have had so many years of
prosperity. It is useless to contend that the protective
policy of other countries—notably that of America—does
not in fact most materially injure our trade and restrict our
manufacturing industry, but its success in promoting the
welfare of the countries in which it is adopted is not so

marked as to offer any inducements for its restoration in
ours. Even the protected industries abroad are few of them
in a prosperous condition, and whatever prosperity they do
enjoy is at the expense of the other members of their own
communities. It is true that France injures our sugar
refiners, but the injury is paid for by the consumers in her
own country. The United States, by protective duties on
our iron and cottons, deprives our home workers of the
employment they might obtain; but the growers of wheat
and the feeders of stock there are doubly losers, from
the enhanced price they pay for the articles they buy, and
the loss of sale for the articles which they might exchange
for our manufactures. When we slacken—as we must do
before long—in the demand we make upon their agricultural produce, her farmers will learn that they have much
to gain from us, both as purchasers of their produce and
sellers of the goods we can produce cheaper than their own
manufacturers. At present both France and America can
afford to be protectionists, because they have within themselves all that is necessary for existence. England cannot
afford to be so, because she is dependent upon other lands
for a large portion of her daily supplies of food, and for
these she can only make payment in the produce and manufactures she can sell.

Let us see how protective duties if imposed on imports
from abroad would work. There is no denying that such
as were levied on articles which we ourselves manufacture
would enhance the cost of importation, and so the price of
those made at home. The first effect of this would be to
restore and quicken extinct or languishing industries here,
and so far as these were in articles of luxury no harm would
be done to the purchasers, although possibly it would
restrict the sale and so soon defeat its own ends. But with
articles of necessity for the labouring class any increase in
price would really be ultimately paid in the higher wages
they would have to receive. If duties were levied on
articles of food, the same beneficial effect would at the out-

set bo experienced by the growers at home. But this would in like manner raise tho wages of those who manufacture for foreign markets, and thus still farther enhance the cost of those things in which we have to compete with foreign producers. Few persons seem to be aware how small an amount of manufactured goods for home use are supplied by foreign competitors when compared with tho large amount of others which we manufacture for sale abroad. Of imports to the value of £319 millions in 1876, only £41 millions were manufactured goods; whilst of our own produce, tho cost of which must be enhanced if protection be restored, we exported £200 millions. Now, supposing the half of the £41 millions were articles of the kind which enter into competition for home use with those we manufacture for ourselves, any benefit accruing from protection would only affect a value one-tenth of that on which suffering would be inflicted. Competition with foreigners in our own markets, however seriously it may affect many branches of our industry, is insignificant when compared with competition in foreign markets, where protection would not possibly benefit us at all, but must assuredly be of serious injury. We must have food for our population. We can only pay for that food by the products of our industry. Our present difficulty is that we cannot sell sufficient of these to meet our payments for food, and that difficulty protection would inevitably enhance.

The third of these supposed corrections—that of curtailing production by running short time—is the least likely of all to lead to a satisfactory result. Had we been wise enough when the demand was greatest to see that it would not go on increasing, and have abstained from extending the means of production, tho suffering caused by its stoppage would have been less than it now is. But having sunk our mines, erected our mills and furnaces, and gathered together the labourers to work them; to lessen their productiveness now would be to increase the cost of their produce. Could we indeed turn part of the plant to other purposes, and employ the workers in other pursuits, the remainder might still go on producing at a limited cost; but to sacrifice capital and labour by partial idleness, whilst the interest of money and the support of the labourers must necessarily continue, would encourage the rivalry of competitors abroad, whose chief advantage already lies in the cheapness with which they are able to manufacture. If we possessed a monopoly in the production of any article of necessary but limited use, the lessening of stocks at home might enable us to raise the price; but when other nations make as well as we, and are prepared to go on making, prices would be little affected by our ceasing to produce in the same quantity; and in the end those who made the most and the cheapest would be sure to secure what custom was to be had. Inability to continue producing, and the abandonment of the manufacture by some, would doubtless be to the advantage of those who held on, but the national loss from the sacrifice would be the same whether centred in few or distributed among many. The true policy would seem to be to abstain from adding to the means of production, but at the same time to employ those at present in existence to their utmost capacity for good and cheap manufacture. With the hearty co-operation of all concerned, a quiet endurance of the consequent privation, and a patient waiting for better times, we ought to be able to maintain our supremacy in those industries of which we have so long been masters, and to beat all others in the neutral markets of the world.

These observations have extended to an altogether unintended length, and but little space remains for further remark. Yet the subject must not be left shrouded in the gloom of the picture they present, without at least an attempt to illumine it with some rays of hope. It cannot be that the enterprise, the skill, and the industry which have created the position to which we have reached, will fail us in the present time of distress. These national attributes will, if still maintained and rightly exercised, sustain and guide us until the darkness shall pass away, and the sunshine of prosperity again overspread the land. But before that can happen we have much patient endurance and active exertion to pass through. It will no longer do to act upon the maxim—"Take care of the imports and let the exports care for themselves." This did well enough when the world was pressing upon us to supply its wants—not now, when we have to press our wares upon the world.

The first effort we have to make is one that scarcely needs to be suggested, for it will be forced upon us by stern necessity. Shortened wages for the labouring classes, and too often the absence of any wages at all, will enforce economy in the use of the necessaries of life, and entire abstinence from many of the luxuries and enjoyments which have gone far to swell the amount of our imports. Diminished profits in trade and want of employment for many will teach the same lesson to the middle-classes, whilst failing incomes and smaller returns for the use of capital will place the upper ranks in a similar position of necessity. Thus shall we lessen the payments we have to make for our imports, and also reduce the price of many articles of consumption for which, under the influence of extravagant expenditure, we have raised the charges to an unwarrantable height. It will also be impossible to maintain the shortened hours of service which have been introduced into many employments, or to be satisfied with the insufficient amount of work performed in the hours thus shortened.

There is the unavoidable evil attendant upon all measures of retrenchment, and the concentration of labour amongst fewer hands, that they throw many persons in all ranks out of employment, and also bring many to seek for profitable occupation of their time who have heretofore had little to think of but spending time, money and strength in the mere enjoyment of life. This consideration brings us face to face with the special conditions which have had more to do in producing the present state of affairs than any other cause of which we know.

Productive labour and capital have been over-weighted

with the unproductive members of the community, whom
they have had to support. We have had too few producers
and too many consumers.   In the lower ranks of life this
has led to the diffusion of work over too large a space of
time, or the abstraction of too many days for enjoyment or
relaxation, rather than to the entire idleness of many individuals.   In the ranks of tradesmen, men of business, and
professional men, and their assistants or servants, it has
manifested itself in the crowding of too many into the different occupations, and the unnecessary multiplication of employments.   Competition, so far as it stimulates industry
and develops skill, or the talents which produce something
that shall add to the general stock, is highly beneficial;
but competition which has for its object the obtaining the
largest share of that which has been already produced is
baneful in the extreme.   Now this, in truth, has been the
curse of our land.   Is there any article of consumption to
be sold, two shops for its sale are opened where one would
suffice; extravagant adornment and show are resorted to,
to tempt customers from one to the other.   Traveller after
traveller waits upon the shopkeeper to gain orders for the
manufacturer or importer; advertisements, placards, mes-
sengers are all employed to induce support to each of the
rivals.   The wholesale producer expends upon making his
wares attractive, rather than good; upon outwitting his
rivals in trade, or satisfying the fancies of the consumer,
rather than meeting his legitimate wants.   Is a railway to
be made, or some public undertaking to be started? pro-
moters, stockbrokers, solicitors, secretaries, first; then
landowners, contractors, manufacturers, all rush to the front
endeavouring to secure the greatest share of the money to
be expended, rather than to diminish the outlay by the
shareholders.   Is a public office to be filled or a charity
to be bestowed? a crowd of competitors waste their time in
struggling who shall obtain the prize.   Thus has it come
to pass that the cost of everything has been swelled, the
expense of division increased, until the difference between

the outlay, whether of time or money, on the first production, has been far below what it ought to have been from
the price paid by the ultimate consumer or person who has
enjoyed the benefit. Notwithstanding all our contrivances
for saving labour, all our intense devotion to business, all
our exercise of skill, scarce any object is attained or accomplished which has not occasioned greater outlay between its
first and final stages than was really needed. Too many
hands have been employed upon it, to each of which it has
paid toll rather than received help, and a feeling has per-
vaded a large portion of all classes of society that they were
to subsist upon appropriating that which others had produced, rather than that which their own efforts had created.
There is everywhere a superabundance of producing power
which needs to find employment. Its wasteful expenditure
has had much to do with enhancing the cost or lessening the
produce of our exports, and thus in diminishing rather than
enlarging our foreign trade. This might be borne so long
as we were increasing in exports, for its weight fell largely
upon the foreign consumer—but with rivals running us so
closely in the race, he will no longer consent to help us in
bearing it.

In the previous tables (I. and II.) the trade shown is
that of the United Kingdom, not only with foreign countries,
but also with her colonies, which are there classified with
foreigners, in both the imports and exports. Had the
Colonies been left out, the balance would have been greater,
for the traffic between us and them is more nearly balanced
than it is with other places. Take for instance the year
1877, of £394 millions gross imports, £305 were from
foreign countries, and £89 from British possessions, and of
exports to the extent of £252 millions, the amounts were
respectively £176 and £75. The excess of the former being
at the rate of 72 per cent. in the one case and 18 in the other,
showing how much better customers are our own kindred
than foreigners. Had we gone a step further and shown
not the trade of the United Kingdom, but that of the

British Empire, including with our own all the regions which go to make up that mighty whole, the total figures would have been much larger, but the balance not very different. But in truth when speaking of our own country we ought not to confine our thoughts simply to the two islands of Great Britain and Ireland—rather extend them to all the continents and islands which own our Sovereign's sway. Geographically they may be distant from us, but with steam and telegraphic communication they are really more closely connected with us than the remote parts of Scotland and Ireland were in the last century. So are they in heart and soul, at least those who are of the same blood. The tendency of all our efforts ought to be to bind together mother and children more firmly than they have ever been before; and if we mistake not herein is to be found the only solid and lasting relief from the depression and anxiety we now experience. Economy in the consumption of our imports and in the production of our exports will do much to prevent the outflow of capital. The revival of a demand for our manufactures by our old and present customers may do still more. Somewhat better prices for the goods we sell, without a corresponding increase in those we pay, it may not be unreasonable to expect, and we may naturally look for new markets to spring up amongst the people not yet civilized enough to manufacture for themselves; but it is futile to expect that the mining and manufacturing industries brought into existence in other countries will be destroyed—and we must anticipate that every year will strengthen their efforts to provide for their own wants. All that we may hope for is that they will learn the folly of fettering industry by protective duties and bounties, and recognize the truth that in promoting the interests of mankind at large, by removing all restrictions or regulations which prevent each country making the most of its natural advantages, they will in fact be most advancing their own welfare. Yet economy in the use of our substance, and therefore in the labour which creates it, together with the better preservation of existing life and its natural multiplication, will sooner or later force large numbers to seek new homes. We must bridge over the intervening seas, and extend our borders till we fill the territories which are placed in our charge. We hear much in these times of over-production—there is one branch of it we have never fully tried—that is the over-production of consumers for our products. Yet every life which is sacrificed by crowded dwellings, by neglect of sanitary laws, by the consumption of intoxicating liquors, by insufficient food, by actual starvation, might and ought to be made a source of wealth. The Registrar-General estimates the average money value of each labourer's life, that is, the difference between the wages he may earn and the cost of his sustenance between birth and death, at £150, and that of every man, woman, and child at £159; and it would be difficult to impugn the accuracy of Dr. Farr's calculations. My own researches, as detailed last year to the British Association,[1] seem to prove that even at present the productive power of one is able to support eight; and since the producer has an average of but three persons to provide for, there must be at least one-half free for luxury, enjoyment, or the cultivation of higher pursuits. There is surely something very wrong in the administration of affairs which permits the want of food here, and the want of food-producers elsewhere. The coming leader of the State will have a problem to solve of far higher moment than the support of dynasties, the maintenance of the balance of power, the rectification of frontiers, however important these may be. He must find out how to feed the people at home, how to people our possessions abroad. The man who shall thus rectify this balance of trade and of population, will be the greatest benefactor with which England, her colonies, and possessions, the united British Empire, has ever been blessed.

[1] " Report of British Association, Plymouth," 1878.

X.

On Some Phases of the Silver Question.[1]

IT is with much diffidence that I approach the very difficult question which stands for discussion on the present occasion. At other times when it has been my lot either to introduce or take part in the subject of debate, the matters under consideration have generally been those upon which official experience had qualified me for the expression of opinions that might be held with some confidence; and though those opinions have sometimes been at variance with generally received views, the course of events has shown them to have been of some value in directing the course of inquiry, and eliciting information on topics of great national importance. In the present instance the inducement to investigate the question has been the belief that it was fitting that this Society should discuss it, that coming to the inquiry without any preconceived notions or special theory to support, and bringing to bear upon it the habit of careful observation and comparison, it might be possible for me to bring together facts and figures such as might serve to call forth the knowledge and experience of those whose judgment on the various points at issue would be of greater value than my own. Assured that whatever may be adduced will meet with kind attention, I shall feel happy if the effort now to be made should succeed in throwing any light on the sub-

[1] Read before the Statistical Society, 1st April, 1879. Journal, Vol. xlii.

ject, or of drawing out the intelligent thoughts of those to
whom it has been an object of interest or study. In thus
doing I must disclaim any intention of taking a comprehensive grasp of that which in all its bearings and results
is too wide for me to attempt, and I have therefore limited
the title of this paper to that of " *Some* Phases of the Silver
Question."

I.—*Connection of Gold with Silver.*

It is obviously impossible to treat of silver apart from
gold. The two metals have in common not only that they
belong to the same class, and as articles of consumption
subserve much the same purposes ; but that they have by
universal consent been selected for use as a medium of
exchange—the representatives of value for other articles—
and thus as money have an employment distinct from all
other substances (excepting the limited use of copper or
bronze as coins). In our country when we speak of the
depreciation of silver, we mean that a definite weight of it
will pass in exchange for a lesser weight of gold than it
did ; that the pound sterling will purchase more of it than
was formerly the case—that is, that an alteration has taken
place in the relative value which it and gold bear to each
other. That whereas in July, 1859, when the highest
price was reached, $62\frac{3}{4}d.$ per standard ounce, 15 grs. of
pure silver were exchangeable for 1 gr. of pure gold ; in
the same month of 1876, when it fell as low as $46\frac{3}{4}d.$, it
took 20 grs. of the former to purchase one of the latter,
the extreme fall being $25\frac{1}{4}$ per cent. Practically, however, we have to deal with a fall from $60\frac{1}{4}d.$—the average
for 1871, and also for the whole period from 1833 to 1871
—to $49\frac{3}{4}d.$, the average price of the last eight weeks, being
a depreciation in value as compared with gold to the extent
of 18 per cent.

We are so accustomed to speak and think of gold as
having a fixed value because a certain weight of it, stamped

with the Queen's image and named a sovereign, is the legal
and tangible representative of the pound sterling in which
all our contracts or engagements are expressed, that we
forget that gold too varies in price. For unless we have
it in possession we can only obtain it by parting with something else we possess, or promising to pay so many pounds
for it at some future time, and to thus obtain it we must
accept the purchasers' terms for the goods, or the promise,
we choose to sell. Whenever we try thus to sell, we find
that the number of sovereigns to be received varies with
the current value of other articles or the rate of interest on
loans. Thus gold measured with other standards alters its
relative worth, and it is always difficult to say whether the
variation is in the gold or the article, or in both together.
The only real fixture in value is the pound sterling, which,
though in itself an imaginary standard, becomes a very real
one when practically applied.[1] Now there can be no doubt
that for many years succeeding the gold discoveries in
California and Australia the purchasing power of the
sovereign became lessened—gold was said, and truly so, to
be depreciated in value; now again the purchasing power
of the sovereign is rising, and gold is said to be undergoing
an appreciation. That is, it goes further in the purchase
of articles, though not in the payment of debts; but
whether this is due to the increased value of gold in itself,
or to a decrease of value in the articles it procures, is a
point not easy to determine, and yet in relation to silver it
is one of vital moment. It may be remarked here, though
this point must be treated afterwards, that during the whole
course of the plentifulness of gold, silver never varied more
than from 58⅞d. per oz. in May, 1845 (the lowest point
until recently), to 62¼d. in July, 1859, a range of 6½ per
cent. as opposed to the present fall of 18 per cent.

The arguments on which this assumed appreciation of
gold is stated to rest, are: 1st, That the production being
diminished, it becomes scarcer, and therefore must increase

<hr />

[1] See "Postscript," p. 237.

in value. 2nd, That there is so general a fall in prices as could only have arisen from the gold with which they are paid having actually become more valuable. A little inquiry into the accuracy of these views is absolutely necessary before we can consider the relative worth of silver and gold. Let us first of all see what are the actual facts as to the quantity of gold in circulation, and the work it has to perform. It will scarcely be contended that so far as our home trade is concerned, there is any want of sovereigns for all the transactions of daily life. If there be scarcity it must be found in impediments to the discharge of international obligations, or the conduct of the larger operations of home trade ; and in neither of these does the difficulty seem to exist.

II.—*Relation of Production and Quantity of Precious Metals to State of Trade.*

There would seem to be the greatest difficulty in obtaining any estimate of the total quantity of the precious metals in existence, either at the present or any former period. As regards the production since 1849 or 1852, there is not much difference of opinion. Messrs. Tooke and Newmarch, followed by the "Economist," consider that between the former year and 1875 the world's production of gold has been £573,652,000; whilst Sir Hector Hay[1] gives £572,195,000 from 1852, and during the same period £241,890,000 of silver, together £814,085,000. The same authorities would set down the consumption in the arts and manufactures and wear and tear of coin at about £2,000,000 per annum of each metal; thus if we accept either estimate, leaving something more than 500 million pounds sterling to have been added to the stock of gold, and something less than 200 millions to that of silver. Prior to 1849 it is supposed by Tooke and Newmarch that

---

[1] H. C. Com. on Depreciation of Silver, 1876.

560 millions' worth of gold was in existence—about an equal quantity to that since produced. If so, there must at the present time be more than 1,100 millions diffused amongst the various countries in which it is used. Mr. Seyd's[1] opinion is that in 1849 there was about 400 millions, that 500 was raised between that year and 1875, but only 350 millions of this was added to stock, the difference having been absorbed in various uses ; so that there was then but 750 millions in circulation, which, brought down to this year, would be about 800 millions only. Thus both estimates assume that there is now, as near as may be, double the quantity there was thirty years ago. Our concern, however, is not so much with the actual amount, as the rate at which it has increased, and the necessity or opportunity for its employment has arisen. These are points on which great diversity of opinion is sure to be found, and anything like certainty is scarcely to be expected ; but in the following table I have endeavoured to place in juxtaposition some information which may help towards the formation of a tolerably accurate judgment.

The first section sets forth the assumed production of both gold and silver since 1849. It is taken from the Appendix to the Report of the House of Commons Committee on the depreciation of silver, and, excepting for the first and last three years, the figures are those given by Sir Hector Hay.[2] Our present purpose is with gold alone. During the first twelve years, that is up to and including 1860, the amount is 278 millions ; deducting 24 millions as used up, and adding the remainder to the 560 in existence prior to 1849, it may be assumed that 814 millions were available for circulation as coin or in bullion in 1860.

---

[1] Committee of House of Commons Report.

[2] The figures from 1870 onwards are altered from those originally read, Sir H. Hay having kindly supplied them with the latest corrections, so that the whole of the series, 1852-78, now rests upon the same authority. Other estimates for recent years are somewhat higher.

TABLE I.—*Showing the Estimated Production of Gold and Silver in each Year from 1849 to 1877; with the Imports and Exports of Bullion and Coin, as well as Merchandise, into and from the Principal Countries, since 1860.*

[In million £'s to two decimals.]

Year.	Production of Precious Metals.			Bullion and Coin.			Merchandise.		
	Gold.	Silver.	Total.	Imports.	Exports.	Total.	Imports.	Exports.	Total.
1849 ..	5·42	8·12	13·54	—	—	—	—	—	—
'50 ..	8·89	8·12	17·01	—'	—	—	—	—	—
'51 ..	13·52	8·12	21·64	—	—	—	—	—	—
'52 ..	36·55	8·12	44·67	—	—	—	—	—	—
'53 ..	31·09	8·12	39·21	—	—	—	—	—	—
'54 ..	25·49	8·12	33·61	—	—	—	—	—	—
'55 ..	27·02	8·12	35·14	—	—	—	—	—	—
'56 ..	29·52	8·13	37·65	—	—	—	—	—	—
'57 ..	26·66	8·13	34·79	—	—	—	—	—	—
'58 ..	24·93	8·13	33·06	—	—	—	—	—	—
'59 ..	24·97	8·15	33·12	—	—	—	—	—	—
'60 ..	23·85	8·16	32·01	83·72	83·30	167·02	677·87	530·69	1,258·56
'61 ..	22·76	8·54	31·30	71·71	73·79	145·50	692·81	540·56	1,233·37
'62 ..	21·59	9·04	30·63	91·98	89·02	181·00	681·01	570·84	1,251·85
'63 ..	21·39	9·84	31·23	97·68	96·14	193·82	745·87	654·57	1,400·44
'64 ..	22·60	10·34	32·94	108·62	109·75	218·37	829·78	702·77	1,532·55
'65 ..	24·04	10·39	34·43	93·22	72·85	166·07	810·25	729·26	1,539·51
'66 ..	24·22	10·14	34·36	131·59	96·61	228·20	892·27	757·85	1,650·12
'67 ..	22·80	10·85	33·65	101·61	64·41	166·02	891·76	749·47	1,641·23
'68 ..	21·95	10·04	31·99	94·62	80·19	174·81	949·90	773·61	1,723·51
'69 ..	21·24	9·50	30·74	86·28	68·36	154·64	983·89	807·84	1,791·73
'70 ..	19·90	10·90	30·80	90·57	70·67	161·24	969·18	831·43	1,800·61
'71 ..	21·10	11·00	32·10	105·29	108·32	213·61	1,127·78	954·68	2,082·46
'72 ..	20·60	11·20	31·80	104·57	89·61	194·18	1,226·25	1,028·73	2,254·98
'73 ..	21·30	12·20	32·50	152·58	145·80	298·38	1,273·72	1,056·88	2,330·60
'74 ..	19·40	12·90	32·30	106·45	69·26	175·71	1,251·97	1,055·54	2,307·51
'75 ..	19·50	13·40	32·90	121·30	82·32	203·62	1,272·37	1,042·72	2,315·09
'76 ..	19·00	14·80	33·80	105·47	87·03	192·50	1,267·28	1,025·04	2,292·32
'77 ..	19·40	16·10	35·50	119·89	99·77	219·66	1,236·26	1,011·85	2,248·11
'78 ..	17·80	14·70	32·50	—	—	—	—	—	—

In the second section there are collected together the imports and exports of coin and bullion in both metals between the principal countries for each year from 1860 to 1877. The countries embraced in this collection are Russia, Hamburg, Holland, Belgium, France, Italy, Austria, United States, with the United Kingdom and her possessions in India and elsewhere, constituting probably five-sixths of the world's traffic. The particulars are taken from the several official "Statistical Abstracts" for the United Kingdom, foreign countries, and our colonies. The latter two do not go back further than 1860. With the exception of the quantities received from or sent to countries not named, it is evident that the return will be double, the import of one country being in each case the export of another, but by adding the two together and taking the mean amount we may obtain a tolerably correct idea of the movements to and fro in each year. It is not practicable to obtain the separate quantities of gold and silver from all countries, nor to rely implicitly on the division in those in which it is recorded, but Mr. Giffen in a table laid before the Committee has shown that for the United Kingdom the proportion of silver to gold stood for the years—

1858—61 as .... 0·57 to 1
'62—66 „ .... 0.63 „ 1
'67—71 „ .... 0·63 „ 1
'72—75 „ .... 0·59 „ 1

the average of the whole period being 0·61 to 1.

For reasons which it is not necessary to explain, I am induced to think that the proportion of silver for the middle period, 1862-72, was overstated in the official tables, possibly so for other years, and that 0·50 or 0·55 to 1 would be a better ratio. Allowing then that between other countries there is more frequent transport of silver, it will not be far wrong to roughly estimate that altogether there would be twice as much gold as silver, and therefore that two-thirds of the movements are in the superior metal. This would show that the quantity of gold carried backwards and forwards in 1860 was 56, and in 1877 73 millions.

In the third section a like collection has been made of the imports and exports of merchandise, giving a tolerable representation of the trade of perhaps five-sixths of the whole world. Taking, as before, the mean between the two, we get goods to the value of more than 600 millions in 1860, and 1,100 millions in 1877 internationally exchanged, and having to be paid for in specie or by some other mode of settlement.

III.—*Sufficiency of Gold Supply.*

The connection of this information with the subject may not at first sight be apparent, but its purport is to show that the trade of the world has not increased in an undue proportion to the stock of gold available for the purposes of the settlement of accounts between the different countries.

This will appear on comparing the progress made from year to year, thus—

	Existing Gold.	Moving Bullion.	Moving Merchandise.
	Mlns.	Mlns.	Mlns.
1860	814	84=10 per cent.	629= 77 per cent.
'61—66 average	876	94=11 ,,	717= 82 ,,
'67—72 ,,	996	89= 9 ,,	941= 94 ,,
'73..............	1,072	149=14 ,,	1,165=109 ,,
'74..............	1,089	88= 8 ,,	1,154=106 ,,
'75..............	1,106	102= 9 ,,	1,158=105 ,,
'76..............	1,125	96= 9 ,,	1,146=102 ,,
'77..............	1,145	110=10 ,,	1,124= 98 ,,

From 1860 up to 1873, the year in which the trade of the world reached its highest point, whilst there was a continuous addition to the stock of gold, and a corresponding activity in the movements of the precious metals, there was a still greater increase in the interchanging of goods. Yet the gold in existence was ample for conducting the necessary exchanges. From 1873 to the present time there has been a steady decline in trade, and all the while an accession of gold, which forbids the supposition that there is an insufficient quantity for the purposes of international exchanges. There are no data for determining in what degree the home trade of the various nations has advanced, but it is pretty certain n ot to have done so to a greater extent in the several nations than their foreign has done. Nor are there any indications, so far at least as our own country is concerned, that the supplies of gold have been below our needs. The records of the London Clearing House are generally taken to show the magnitude of the business being transacted, and in these the highest point was reached in the same year, 1875, when the amount of clearing was 6,013 millions; having risen from 3,257 in 1868, and now fallen again to 4,885 in 1879. The amount of bullion which the Bank of England was enabled to retain and consequently the extent of its note circulation, as shown in Table II.,[1] together with the same particulars for the Bank of France, would seem to show that there was no lack of gold to meet the uses to which it had to be applied.

Beyond this, there can be no question that every ounce of gold is at the present moment capable of doing more duty than at any former period. In proof of this it is sufficient to allude to a few of the alterations which have taken place. The opening of the Suez Canal has halved the time occupied in transmitting bullion to and from the East and Australia; and in like degree abridged the interval between the despatch of goods from hence, and the realization of their value in the countries of sale. An almost equal increase in the rapidity and frequency of communication by steam between other parts of the world, and especially in the use of telegraphic intercourse, has produced much the same result in other directions. Then the extension of banking facilities has rendered unnecessary and unusual the storing up of any quantity of coin by traders or private individuals, and occasioned the vast majority of receipts and payments to be made with the use of very little money; how little will appear from the following analysis of "the total payments to credit of customers" kindly furnished by a banker, whose business may be taken as a sample of the general usage :—

	Per cent.
Bills of exchange	8·6
Cheques	88·5
Bank notes	2·6
Coin	0·3
	100·0

[1] Published in "Statistical Journal" for June, 1879.

Do not these several observations justify the conclusion, that though at particular times and places there may be a temporary deficiency of supply ; so far from there being any scarcity of gold, there never was a period in the world's commercial history when the existing quantity was so large as it is at present, in proportion to the necessity for its use or the purposes it has to serve ?

IV.—*Fall in Prices.*

Much stress has been laid upon the general fall in the price of commodities as an evidence that gold has become appreciated, and hence the inference drawn, particularly by Mr. Giffen in his paper read not long ago before this society,[1] that "very likely gold and silver have both changed." This opinion is so important as to deserve a close investigation into its validity.

Mr. Giffen puts " the average *fall* of prices between 1873 and 1877 at more than 20 per cent., exclusive, of course, of the additional fall in 1878." The " Economist," writing on 28th December last, referring to a letter from Professor Jevons in its number of 8th May, 1869, " reasserting with the utmost confidence that a real *rise* in prices to the extent of 18 per cent. had been established since 1849," endeavours to show " that a real *fall* in prices to the extent of 16 per cent. has been established since 1869." Each of these three authorities measures the fluctuations which have taken place by a system of index numbers, in which the average prices of a number of articles (twenty-two in one case, fifty in another), ascertained in the years 1845-50, are each represented by 100, and the variations in every subsequent year by a corresponding addition or otherwise to this number. The aggregate of these several ratios becomes then the " index number," representing the value of all commodities, and consequently the general rise or fall which prices have sustained in each successive year for which

---

[1] " Statistical Journal," vol. xlii. pp. 57 *et seq.*

the calculations have been made. Dividing this number by as many articles as have been employed, the average is ascertained.

This system appears so well adapted to attain the desired results, that I have followed it in constructing tables, showing not only the prices prevailing in this country, but likewise of some staple articles in the places of their production; taking as the price the average of the year's transactions shown in the "Statistical Abstracts for Foreign Countries and for Colonial Possessions," issued from the Board of Trade. I am unable, however, to adopt the "Economist" figures as they stand, for they seem to me to err, inasmuch as of the twenty-two articles four are for different descriptions of cotton goods; and as this commodity is subject to unusual fluctuations, the alterations in price affect the "index number" in a fourfold degree. I have, therefore, corrected the figures by including only one value for cotton (the average of the four), and have added coal,[1] as an article too important to be left out; thus obtaining an average of twenty instead of twenty-two articles. Professor Jevons's figures differ somewhat in principle. I should have preferred using them, but that they are not carried forward further than 1869, and the subsequent years are essential to the question under consideration.

The "Economist" numbers, together with the same as I have ventured to alter them, and those of Professor Jevons, will thus compare together:—

---

[1] The exceptionally high prices to which coal, together with iron and other articles in the manufacture of which coal is consumed, rose in 1872 and following years, unduly raises the index numbers. But for this cause those for 1872 to 1875 would probably have been 125, 132, 127, 124, rather than 133, 142, 136, 130, as shown in column 3 of next page.

Year.	"Economist."	Same corrected.	Jevons.
1847	—	—	122
'48	—	—	106
'49	—	—	100
'50	—	—	101
'51	104	103	103
'52	—	—	101
'53	107	114	116
'54	—	—	130
'55	—	—	125
'56	—	—	129
'57	136	140	132
'58	119	123	118
'59	115	118	120
'60	122	123	124
'61	124	124	123
'62	131	125	124
'63	158	144	123
'64	172	151	122
'65	162	138	121
'66	162	141	128
'67	137	128	118
'68	122	122	120
'69	121	118	119
'70	122	119	—
'71	118	118	—
'72	129	133	—
'73	134	142 *Vide note on previous page.*	—
'74	131	136	—
'75	126	130	—
'76	123	123	—
'77	123	126	—
'78	116	118	—
'79 (1st January)	101	106	—

Note—Average 1845-50, for each series, 100.

It will be noticed that all the foregoing numbers relate
solely to prices in this country. In dealing with those in
other countries it becomes necessary to adopt a different
point of comparison or datum line, because there are not
within my reach any available records earlier than 1861
from which to ascertain the average of the six years 1845-50,

that would be represented by 100. I have therefore formed a new index number, in which 100 stands for the average of each article for the six years 1877-72, thus working backwards and showing each of the specified articles for each year in its relation to that number. In this manner it becomes practicable to compare to some extent the prices in other countries with our own. The following table shows these in detail :—

TABLE II.—*Index Numbers for Prices of certain Articles in the Country of Production. The Average of Six Years, 1872-77, being represented by 100.*

Year.	Wheat.			Cotton.		Wine, France.	Silk, France.	Rice, India.	Opium, India.	Tea, China.
	England.	United States.	France.	United States.	India.					
1849	83	—	—	—	—	—	—	—	—	—
'50	75	—	—	—	53	—	—	—	87	—
'51	72	—	—	—	61	—	—	—	77	—
'52	76	—	—	—	57	—	—	—	79	—
'53	100	—	—	—	55	—	—	—	87	—
'54	136	—	—	—	56	—	—	—	72	—
'55	141	—	—	—	55	—	—	—	61	—
'56	131	—	—	—	55	—	—	—	70	—
'57	106	—	—	—	55	—	—	—	74	—
'58	83	—	—	—	50	—	—	—	92	—
'59	82	—	—	—	74	—	—	—	108	—
'60	100	—	—	—	53	—	—	—	116	—
'61	104	95	122	71	—	118	123	120	121	—
'62	104	88	82	150	103	156	111	126	123	—
'63	84	100	63	376	157	155	106	124	115	—
'64	75	103	74	529	258	141	108	105	115	—
'65	78	140	78	554	283	128	145	83	89	—
'66	94	109	96	277	175	113	139	71	93	—
'67	121	98	93	195	153	114	114	89	107	—
'68	119	117	82	125	129	110	129	100	103	—
'69	92	108	78	161	114	121	134	86	108	—
'70	88	100	82	152	136	111	136	97	101	—
'71	107	102	82	96	133	100	121	110	95	—
'72	107	113	92	124	104	112	112	104	108	—
'73	110	102	108	121	111	101	99	102	105	—
'74	104	111	104	99	104	100	85	90	96	—
'75	85	88	96	97	96	91	89	101	95	—
'76	87	96	93	83	94	91	119	94	96	—
'77	107	90	107	76	91	101	96	107	98	—
'78	87	—	—	—	—	—	—	—	—	—
Average 1872-77 }	100	100	100	100	100	100	100	100	100	100

The mean number of these nine articles, compared with those previously shown as altered from the "Economist," and converted to the datum line of the preceding table, will then stand thus running backwards :—

	Home Prices.	World Prices.		Home Prices.	World Prices.
1879......	80	—	1869......	90	111
'78......	90	—	'68..	93	116
'77......	96	97	'67......	98	120
'76......	94	95	'66......	107	132
'75......	99	94	'65......	105	175
'74......	103	99	'64......	115	170
'73......	108	107	'63......	109	143
'72......	101	108	'62......	95	116
'71......	90	105	'61......	94	113
'70......	91	111	'60......	94	—

It is obvious that these foreign prices are too limited in number and in range of articles to form an adequate basis for comparison, but so far as they go they indicate—more especially in the earlier years—a great difference from those at home. The later years approach much nearer to each other, a proof how much rapid transit, more especially the speed of telegraphic communication, does towards equalizing prices in the most distant places.

Many curious questions may arise out of these comparisons, which it would be unfitting at present to discuss, but the figures having been collected at considerable labour are set forth in much greater detail than is perhaps necessary, in the hope that they may be available for other objects than the one we are now pursuing. It is important, however, to notice their great irregularity and the absence of any steady sequence of rise or fall which would establish the fact that prices are affected wholly or even mainly by the existing quantities of gold or silver.

V.—*Purchasing Power of Gold.*

There can be no question that with the gold discoveries and the sudden influx of money thus produced, there was a great increase in prices, giving evidence of a diminution in the purchasing power of gold, and there has lately been a lessening of price which materially adds to that purchasing power; but it may fairly bo questioned whether this is rightly attributed to a depreciation at one time, or appreciation at another of the metal itself, rather than to the influence of other causes, appreciating and depreciating at different periods the commodities which gold is employed to purchase. If I may be allowed the expression of an opinion differing from that of so many great authorities, I would venture to assert that the influence of gold in raising or reducing prices depends not so much upon the quantity of it available for use, as on the circumstances attending its production, and the facilities offered for its employment. Wealth of any description easily and rapidly acquired has a tendency to an equally easy and rapid dispersion. The sudden acquisition of money by those who rushed into gold mining, combined with the abstraction of so much labour from other pursuits, and the employment of so much more labour in ministering to the wants of those who ceased to become producers, could not do otherwise than raise the demand for the necessaries and luxuries of life beyond the supply, and thus enhance their cost. Almost exactly the same thing has happened with other commodities than gold; at one time iron, at another coal, at another something else, has brought about the same result. These have been real additions to the wealth of the world, because they have been articles of real utility, but their influence has been less enduring because of their destructibility, whilst gold as money is almost indestructible. The stone thrown into the pond, partly by its bulk and partly by its imparted force, raises the level of the water with which it comes in contact, but each succeeding ripple becomes lower and lower, till no elevation is perceptible; so the masses of gold thrown amongst the moving multitude of purchasers, raised the level of prices; but with each succeeding transmission from hand to hand its elevating power became less, and notwithstanding the mass still remains, its influence on prices ceases. Were it otherwise, with the ever-increasing stock of gold in the world, and the constant growth of realized property, which in the securities by which it is represented answers the purpose of gold for exchanges, there should be an ever-increasing rise in prices; and at the present moment, with the store of gold in this country, prices should be higher than ever. We must look then for other causes for the recent fall of prices. They are to be found in the condition of the manufacturers for foreign markets, who, unable as before to effect profitable exchanges of the goods wherewith to obtain possession of gold to purchase articles of consumption, cannot give high prices, which thus perforce must sink.

A striking confirmation of the previously expressed views that the alteration in prices must be attributed to other causes than the influence of gold, may be derived from the study of some tables furnished to the "Economist" in July of last, and January of this year, comparing the imports and exports of 1872 with those of 1877, and 1877 with 1878 (a similar comparison of 1872 with 1873 having appeared in "Lloyd's List" of June, 1873). These tables I have combined into one contrasting the import trade of 1878 with 1872, and another the exports for the same periods. They will be found in the Appendix (D and E);[1] but the results are not so marked as in the originals, because of the rise in many articles which took place between 1872 and 1877, being balanced or varied by the fall which was experienced in the following year. A few extracts showing the actual increases and decreases in prices on the values of certain classes of articles will make this apparent.

In the face of such irregularities of growth and decay in value as are here manifested, it is impossible to ascribe the changes wholly or chiefly to any assumed alteration in the valuation of the gold in which the values are expressed. These tables were compiled in the first instance to determine how far the diminution of our trade was due to the quantities as they rose and fell, or to the progressive alterations of prices. They have an important bearing upon the present

[1] Vide "Statistical Journal," June, 1879.

question from the disparity they show between imports and exports; the one for several years manifesting a tendency to increase in price, the other to a fall; most incontrovertibly demonstrating that these changes were in the goods themselves and the circumstances of the buyers and sellers, *not* in the value of gold. Thus—

[In million £'s to two decimals.]

	Year.	Value.	Increase or Decrease on 1872.	Increase or Decrease on 1877.
		£	£	£
Imports—				
Animal food...........................	1877	36·34	+ 3·50	—
,, ...	'78	40·29	—	— 3·75
Vegetable food.......................	'77	102·18	— 1·04	—
,, ...	'78	89·28	—	— 10·17
Cocoa, coffee, and tea..............	'77	20·82	+ 1·52	—
,, ...	'78	19·80	—	— 0·71
Textile materials.....................	'77	74·92	— 17·58	—
,, ...	'78	70·43	—	— 3·34
Total food consumption	'77	183·77	+ 2·38	—
,, ...	'78	172·67	—	— 15·74
Total materials for manufacture...	'77	128·12	— 22·98	—
,, ...	'78	122·34	—	— 8·21
Exports—				
Textile manufactures................	1877	100·55	— 25·12	—
,, ...	'78	98·65	—	— 2·70
Total British produce	'77	142·36	— 39·19	—
,, ...	'78	138·46	—	— 5·31
Total foreign and colonial goods...	'77	36·63	— 2·22	—
,, ...	'78	37·76	—	— 1·61

VI.—*Variations in the Value of Gold.*

But apart from the variations in the value of gold, as measured by its power to purchase other commodities, some consideration is due to the alterations in its value for use as money, not for expenditure in consumption but in production. Although absolutely inert in itself, and unable to increase as natural products do, or as the products of labour, whether bodily or mental, do; it yet has a power to increase in the hands of its holders by drawing to itself that which other means have produced. In this sense it may be said to have two values—permanent and temporary—according

as it is devoted to stationary or fluctuating investment.
The one value is to be seen in the price of the public Funds;
the other in the price of short-lived employment, as represented by the Bank rate. The following table [1] shows the
price for thirty years of English Consols and French Rentes,
each paying 3 per cent. interest, and for the same period
the minimum Bank rates in England, France, and Germany.

In this country and in others having a gold standard,
whereby there is a fixed relation between the ounce of
metal and the pound sterling or other unit, having no other
term whereby to express value than this same sovereign,
we are apt to forget that gold really does fluctuate in value
almost as greatly as other commodities ; or at least we are
in the habit of thinking of depreciation or appreciation, as
a gradual process so slow and steady as to escape notice,
except by the occasional comparison of one period with
another, whereas in truth an ounce or pound is worth much
more at one time than another and in different places at the
same time. The average price of Consols during thirty
years is shown to be $93\frac{1}{8}$, yielding thus an annual interest
of £3·24. Now, looking to the facts that there is a probability of having to sell or buy at a different price, and that the
transfer occasions some small expense, we may strike off
the odd ·24, and say that in England gold lying absolutely
secure without chance of loss or gain is valued at 3 per
cent. In France the average price has been 66·03, yielding 4·64 per cent., a difference due doubtless to the unsettled
state of government and other causes rendering it of some
risk to hold such securities. But taking 3 per cent. as the
absolute value of gold because the value of its representative, we find that during this period its price has varied as
much as from 88 to $99\frac{3}{8}$; that is, a person parting with
ninety-nine sovereigns at one time would only receive back
eighty-eight at another, or *vice versâ*. A somewhat start-
ling variation in a value which is thought to be fixed and
unalterable. In France the range has been still greater,

[1] Vide " Statistical Journal," as before.

tho samo interest-bearing security being at ono timo 53·65, at another, 79·52.

Then for temporary use—not dwelling upon the rise onco or twico for a few days to 10 per cent.—tho yearly averages havo varied as much as from 2·15 to 7·50 in England, and from 2·25 to 6·50 in France, although for tho wholo period tho averago has been almost identical, 3·91 here, 4·04 there. Yet it has happened moro than onco that at tho samo timo gold would purchaso in tho ono placo tho samo or equally good securities at prices yielding double tho interest it would in tho other. The variations in tho German rates do not appear to havo been so great, although they by no means show a constant value attaching to either gold or silver.

The causes of theso fluctuations in value it would bo out of placo to consider on this occasion. All that is necessary to tho argument as regards silver, is to show that tho prico of gold itself is so greatly subject to change that it never can bo said to havo any natural fixed value in relation to either tho pound, silver, or any other commodity.

VII.—*Production and Depreciation of Silver.*

So largo a space has been devoted to tho consideration of tho gold question, for the simplo reason that having to deal with two elements, either of which or both together may bo unstable, it is quito necessary to determino with somo precision with which of tho two tho wholo or tho greater part of tho instability rests. That it is not with gold to anything liko such an extent as tho very great depreciation in tho gold-value of silver would point, seems to bo pretty clearly established by the evidence already adduced. Tho way is thus prepared for considering tho actual position in which silver now stands.

TABLE III.—*Estimated Production of Silver in Each Year from* 1849 *to* 1878, *with Average Prices in London Market; Imports and Exports of United Kingdom; Exports to the East; and Bills Drawn on Indian Government for same Period.*

[In million £'s to two decimals.]

Years.	Silver Produced.	Price, London.	United Kingdom.		India.	
			Imports.	Exports.	Exports to East.	Bills on Indian Government.
		d.				
1849...	8·12	$59\frac{3}{4}$	—	7·72	3·81	1·89
'50...	8·12	$60\frac{1}{16}$	—	4·37	5·05	2·94
'51...	8·12	61	—	5·08	1·72	3·24
'52...	8·12	$60\frac{1}{2}$	—	5·97	2·45	2·78
'53...	8·12	$61\frac{1}{2}$	—	6·15	3·12	3·32
'54...	8·12	$61\frac{1}{2}$	—	6·03	3·10	3·85
'55...	8·12	$61\frac{5}{16}$	—	6·98	6·43	3·67
'56...	8·13	$61\frac{5}{16}$	—	12·81	12·11	1·48
'57...	8·13	$61\frac{3}{4}$	—	18·51	16·73	2·82
'58...	8·13	$61\frac{5}{16}$	6·70	7·06	4·75	·63
'59...	8·15	$62\frac{1}{16}$	14·77	17·61	14·83	·03
'60...	8·16	$61\frac{11}{16}$	10·39	9·89	8·48	—
'61...	8·54	$60\frac{13}{16}$	6·58	9·57	6·82	—
'62...	9·04	$61\frac{7}{16}$	11·75	13·31	10·10	1·19
'63...	9·84	$61\frac{3}{8}$	10·89	11·24	8·26	6·64
'64...	10·34	$61\frac{3}{8}$	10·83	9·85	6·25	8·98
'65...	10·39	$61\frac{1}{16}$	6·98	6·60	3·60	6·79
'66...	10·14	$61\frac{1}{8}$	10·78	8·90	2·37	7·00
'67...	10·85	$60\frac{9}{16}$	8·02	6·44	·64	5·61
'68...	10·04	$60\frac{1}{2}$	7·72	7·51	1·64	4·14
'69...	9·50	$60\frac{7}{16}$	6·73	7·90	2·36	3·71
'70...	10·90	$60\frac{9}{16}$	10·65	8·91	1·58	6·98
'71...	11·00	$60\frac{1}{2}$	16·52	13·06	3·71	8·44
'72...	11·20	$60\frac{5}{16}$	11·14	10·59	5·65	10·31
'73...	12·20	$59\frac{1}{4}$	12·99	9·83	2·50	13·94
'74...	12·90	$58\frac{5}{16}$	12·30	12·21	7·09	13·29
'75...	13·40	$56\frac{7}{8}$	10·12	8·98	3·71	10·84
'76...	14·80	$52\frac{3}{4}$	13·58	12·95	10·91	11·51
'77...	16·10	$54\frac{13}{16}$	21·71	19·44	17·00	8.64
'78...	14·70	$52\frac{9}{16}$	11·55	11·72	5·84	13·97

The annexed table shows the production of silver since 1852, as estimated by Sir Hector Hay, commencing with a yearly produce of about 8 millions, and ending with more than double that amount in the last few years, giving an average of some 10 millions per annum. If from this we deduct 2 millions as absorbed in the arts, wear and tear, &c., the existing silver must have been increasing for the last

thirty years at the rate of about 8 millions per annum.
There seems to be great difficulty, more so than with gold,
in arriving at anything like an accurate notion of the
quantity of silver in coin or bullion which the world possessed, either in 1848 or 1879, and so to see what ratio
the annual additions bear to the previous accumulation.
Mr. Seyd estimates the amount in 1848 as 600 millions;
but then allows for an increase of 50 millions only up to
1875, which is quite incompatible with the estimate of the
successive additions of 8 millions in every year. For our
present purpose, however, the actual amount dispersed
amongst the various nations by whom it is used is not so
important as the progressive growth in that quantity whatever it may be. Perhaps we are safe in setting the former
amount at something like 500 millions, and if so the total
increase must be about one half of that sum.

The same table shows the average prices in London, per
ounce of standard silver, for each of the last thirty years,
beginning with $59\frac{1}{4}d$. in 1849, and ending with $52\frac{9}{16}d$. for
1878. Since then there has been a further reduction, until
the last price quoted to-day is $50\frac{1}{8}d$. Side by side with
these will be found the silver imports and exports to and
from the United Kingdom, the exports to the East, and the
amount of bills drawn at home on the Indian Government,
all of which particulars present features of interest, although
their sequence is not so regular or so closely following
either production or price as to establish any law of intimate
connection with either the one or the other. The column
of price shows that between 1849 and 1872 there was no
very great variation from $59\frac{1}{4}d$.; in the earlier years it rose
by slow degrees as high as $62\frac{1}{16}d$., in 1859, having in the
months of March and July been $62\frac{1}{4}d$. (the highest price
ever quoted), and then by almost equally regular descent
reached $60\frac{5}{16}d$. in the latter years, the average of the whole
period having been $61d$. It is evident, therefore, that
neither the increasing rate of production, nor the varying
rates of movement to and fro, nor yet the absorption by the

East, have exercised any regular or constant effect upon the price. All these and many other causes must have each had their specific influence, but want of uniformity in their occurrence neutralizing each other, no marked result followed. We must look then for some other cause or causes to account for the marked and rapid decline which has been going on since then. In six years, without reckoning the further changes of the present year, the fall has been from $60\frac{5}{8}$—$61\frac{1}{8}$ in January, 1872, to $49\frac{1}{2}$—$50\frac{11}{16}$ in December, 1878, equal to $10\frac{1}{4}$ in seven years, or an average of $1\frac{1}{4}$ per annum, being 21 per cent. altogether, or 3 per cent. yearly.

In the opinion of the committee of the House of Commons, this fall is due to three principal causes :—

1st. " The greatly increased yield from the new mines in Nevada," to which all the increase in production since 1870 is to be attributed.

2nd. " To the introduction of a gold currency into Germany," which commenced at the end of 1871. The total amount of silver which it is estimated has thus to be withdrawn, when the operation is complete, is £48,000,000, of which probably 30 to 35 millions has been already sold.

3rd. "To the decreased demand for silver for export to India." From a paper laid before the committee by Mr. Waterfield, it would appear that the surplus of imports of silver into India in periods of ten years have been :—

			£
1835-36	to	1844-45	20,534,669
'45-46	„	'54-55	15,327.009
'55-56	„	'64-65	100,202,612
'65-66	„	'74-75	62,400,060
'75-76	„	'77-78	21,873,207
			220,337,557

Comparing the six years 1866-72, with the same number since that, we shall find—

	Average.
1866-72	5,988,860
'72-78	4,945,240
	1,043,620

To these the committee add three other causes:—

1st. The substitution by the Scandinavian Governments of gold for silver in their currency, which is estimated to have caused the withdrawal from employment of £1,800,000 between 1873 and 1876.

2nd. The suspension of silver coinage by the Latin union.

3rd. The temporary prohibition of silver coining in Holland, by which some £4,000,000 of gold has been substituted.

These several causes have been so fully entered into, that it may be sufficient here to state the estimate of their collected amount of silver thrown out of use during the last six years, to be from 40 to 50 millions.

Now giving full weight to this amount, and likewise to the fear of effects yet to be produced by the further sale of German silver, these causes seem insufficient to account for the depreciated value at which silver now stands, and I would venture to add some other results of the altered condition of monetary affairs.

1st. The hoarding of money which was formerly common has very much ceased, both in our own and other countries, especially in France, in consequence of the great increase in banking facilities, and still more in the creation of numerous interest-bearing securities which are available for persons of but limited means. The vast increase in the deposits in our own savings' banks, and the number of small holders of French Government stock which the system of the Emperor Napoleon introduced, are but two instances of this change.

2nd. Here, and doubtless elsewhere, shopkeepers and petty tradesmen as well as the larger dealers and merchants now have banking accounts, to which at short intervals they carry their receipts, and from which they draw by cheques, many of which are interchanged without the use of coin, the sums required for paying their accounts. Everybody now seems anxious to get rid of coin as soon as received, and the saving thus induced must vastly economize the employment of both gold and silver.

3rd. The great accession to the stock of gold in the world cannot fail to have its effect upon the employment of silver also. The greater convenience which the superior metal has for all uses excepting that of small change, must tend very much to circumscribe the use of the inferior. This is greatly enhanced by the extension of postal, telegraph, and railway communications, which render the transport of coin or bank notes so much more rapid and easy, especially of gold or notes, which occupy little space and are easily moved, whilst silver is cumbrous and therefore difficult of transfer from one place to another. Now if it be true, as previously asserted, that the quantity of the precious metals in the world is at present greater in proportion to the uses they have to serve, the weightier and less valuable of the two is sure to be the first to be disused where any option exists. So far from there being any scarcity of gold which should cause an appreciation of its value in relation to silver, there appears to be good ground for believing that a plethora of it exists. It fails to depreciate in value, because it thrusts out silver from use as money and tends more and more to reduce it to the condition of a commodity. Herein probably consists a very potent cause for the overstocking of the silver market, and hence the diminishing price in gold which can be obtained for it.

VIII.—*Depression of Trade.*

It is impossible not to notice the coincidence in point of time of the decay in the value of silver with the earlier stages of that depression in trade of which it is much to be feared we are far from having reached the culminating point. Messrs. Pixley and Abel's circular remarks on the year 1872, "commencement of decline in price of silver," and the remarks at foot will bo found in articles on tho trado of 1873, furnished by myself to "Lloyd's List." [1] [2] It was not till tho latter half of tho year that silver began to fall, nor till tho middle of tho following year that it assumed any serious proportions, and bearing in mind that it is frequently some months before any change becomes manifest in tho official trade accounts, it is clear that silver, tho imports of materials for manufacture, and tho exports of manufactured articles, all began to decline in price or quantity about tho same time. It is to bo noticed, too, that silver depreciation

[1] "The conclusions to bo drawn from tho facts disclosed in these returns, when viewed in connection with the diminution in our exports which has been for some time slowly advancing, aro by no means consolatory or reassuring. It is evident that we have commenced to buy less of tho materials on which our great manufactures depend ; and that as we sell less and less of these we must diminish still further tho imports we can afford to purchase ; also, that just in proportion as we purchase less, the countries from which we take these products will be the less able to buy the articles into which we manufacture the raw materials. Meantime we are largely and continuously adding to our receipts of articles for food, the cost of which is so much loss to the nation if we cannot find employment for the working power which this food sustains ; or if the price at which that labour is obtained be so enhanced as to render its employment unprofitable."—*30th July*, 1873.

[2] "It is barely possible that the conclusions arrived at by a cursory study of these returns may be somewhat modified on more matured consideration of the fuller information to be furnished in the ' Annual Statement of Trade ; ' but thus far there appears nothing to remove the impression—that our extending importation of articles to be consumed as food, unaccompanied by an increased exportation of our own produce and manufacture, cannot be a satisfactory condition of trade. So far as the importations of articles necessary for the sustenance of our population are concerned, unless that food be transformed into some tangible productions of the labour it feeds, with which to pay for its cost, there is to that extent a loss of national wealth : and the same remark may apply in some measure to those articles which, not strictly necessary as food, enter largely into consumption. The increased sale for these may indicate, as doubtless it does, the possession by the labouring classes of greater means for enjoyment and personal gratification, but, unless our producing power is employed as well as maintained, the supply of these means must fail, and our importations as well as our exportations will decline both in quantity and value."—*26th January*, 1874.

preceded its demonetization by the German Government by
some months, although it is probable that the anticipation
of this action may have exercised an influence prior to its
actual performance.   It would be out of place here to go
over the same ground as regards imports and exports that
has been travelled before, but it must be remarked that the
growing balance of trade against us in each year from 1872
to 1877 would prevent silver being sent to us in payment
for other goods.   It would come here either in exchange
for gold procured by the sale of securities, or on consignment for sale, and thus like any other commodity for which
the demand is slack have to suffer in value.

The direct effects of this silver depreciation upon the
trade and financial condition of our own country are not so
serious as its indirect results.   Our own standard being a
gold one, and silver being used only for tokens passing at
an artificial value by legislative enactment, no loss on our
money is sustained ; but the Mint gains on the metal converted into coin to the full extent of the lower price at
which it can be purchased.   There are never very large
stocks in the hands of British holders, and it is probable
that the bullion merchants and speculative dealers have
realized quite as much profit from fluctuations downwards
as they would if the direction had been different.   No doubt
loss ensues wherever contracts exist which have to be met
by receipts of silver, and trade must be impeded in silver-
using countries by the necessity of charging higher for the
goods we sell to meet the difference in exchange ; but as it
does not appear that the prices of articles purchased for the
home market have greatly risen in their silver value, there
would on these be a corresponding gain.

As regards India, up to March, 1877, neither the Viceroy
there, nor the India Office here, seem to think that the purchasing power of the rupee had become less, " The relative
values of gold and silver not having varied in the same proportion as elsewhere ; "[1] and though " the silver prices of

_____
[1] Parliamentary papers relating to silver, 22nd March, 1877.

imported goods had not risen," this may be accounted for by the fall in the price of their first cost. The Indian finances, however, have suffered most grievously from the revenue having to be collected in silver, and so large a portion of it having to be paid in gold or its equivalent in England. The bills drawn last year upon India by the Government to meet the expenditure upon Indian account in this country amounted to £14,000,000, and the fall from $60\frac{1}{2}$ to $52\frac{2}{6}$ represented a depreciation of 13 per cent., making an actual loss to the Indian revenue of nearly £2,000,000 for the one year only, whilst the estimate for the coming year is nearly double that sum. On official or private persons having to remit money either in specie or bills, the same sacrifice is entailed.

So far as concerns internal circulation in countries where the silver standard exists, it matters little what the price of silver in other places may be, but on whatever amounts they have to export to countries having a gold standard, a loss must ensue; and that not only on the actual transmission of the silver, but on all transactions for which it is the standard, or rather upon the balance between the imports and exports. India suffers to the extent that she has to remit money to this country; but it must be remembered that as between the mother country and herself there can be no absolute loss, and India, as a country whose exports exceed its imports (as shown in the following figures), should gain an equivalent for the loss on remittances, and in addition benefit by all payments from this side :—

[In million £'s to two decimals.]

	Imports.	Exports.	Surplus Exports.
	£	£	£
1854-59 (average)......	14·83	23·99	9·16
'60-65 (,,)......	24·67	46·46	21·79
'66-71 (,,)......	32·96	53·18	20·22
'72......................	32·09	63·19	31·10
'73......................	31·87	55·24	23·37
'74......................	33·82	55·00	21·18
'75......................	36·22	56·36	20·14
'76......................	38·89	58·05	19·16
'77......................	37·44	60·96	23·52

Either the rupee has retained its purchasing power or become depreciated. If the former, it will purchase the same quantity of goods which—were no other cause in existence—would sell here for as many sovereigns as before, and purchase a greater number of rupees or weight of silver. If the latter, then labour and produce must obtain more rupees; and taxation being levied in rupees, its burden must be correspondingly lightened. It will be observed that the surplus of exports exceeds the remittances that have to be made. The whole question would thus ultimately resolve itself into an adjustment of wages, prices, and taxes, to fit the altered value of money, were it not for the fact that India seems to be yearly growing poorer and less able to bear the charges for its government and expenditure.

I am aware that far greater evils than these are assigned to this depreciation by a large number of thinkers and writers on this subject. The limits of this paper will not permit a consideration of the various arguments by which it is attempted to be proved that the decline of our exports, the fall in prices, and the general depression of trade, are all due to the altered relation in the value of gold and silver, and to the folly of our Government and others in not agreeing to a fixed and unalterable ratio of value between the two metals. They seem to me to rest upon the fallacy that money, rather than the wants, be they real or artificial, of mankind, creates trade, and that you have but to stamp the one metal with an effigy which shall give it a certain value in another metal, to promote an almost unlimited growth and interchange of the products of industry, and thus enhance the welfare of nations. I cannot but think that whilst a sufficiency of the circulating medium, be it in precious metals, bank notes, or other securities which pass readily from hand to hand, economizes labour, and so adds to the wealth of the world, the real prosperity alike of individuals and nations depends upon the judicious use they make of their productive powers, and the right expenditure or consumption of the products thus created.

IX.—*Bi-metallic and other Theories.*

Did this paper profess to be an exhaustive one, it would be necessary to take up the various propositions which have been made for dealing with the difficulties arising from the existing depreciation, or providing against their aggravation in the future. Pretending, however, only to deal with some portions of a subject far too vast to be disposed of in a short paper, this branch of it might be passed by. Yet a few remarks will probably be expected, and can hardly be omitted. Two classes of suggestions are offered, the one having for its object the restoration of value to silver by fixing its relation to gold at a higher ratio than at present, such a proportion as till recently it enjoyed ; the other, that of obviating the inconveniences of a fluctuating standard and a varying state of the exchanges, by the substitution of one that may be fixed. The views of one side favour the adoption of the bi-metallic standard or even the demonetization of gold ; those of the other, the universal acceptance of a gold standard, or such measures as would lead to its ultimate adoption.

The great objection to the bi-metallic system is that it must rest upon an arbitrary valuation of the two metals, which would with difficulty be maintained in the home cir-

culation, and could not be permanently upheld in the international use of money.   Its establishment requires that
both metals should be a legal tender within the limits of
every State, and therefore renders the choice of metal for
the discharge of obligations dependent upon the will of the
payer, who, in selecting the coin most convenient for himself, might not always choose that most acceptable to the
recipient. The simple difference in bulk—rendering transport difficult—and in the number of coins to be counted or
weighed, would in most circumstances be to the advantage
of gold and ensure a small premium in its favour.   Under
other conditions silver might be preferable, and its holder
be enabled to dictate the terms on which he would part with
its possession.

A striking proof of the impossibility of maintaining any
definite ratio of value between gold and silver is to be seen
in the present accumulations of British silver coin in the
hands of bankers and other holders. Owing to the reduced
expenditure on wages and the lesser amounts required for
the purchase of articles of consumption, it becomes difficult
to dispose of large quantities and a commission is charged
on its transfer.   This is virtually a fall in value, notwithstanding that its worth in relation to the sovereign is unaltered.   It may be said that this results from silver not
being made a legal tender to any amount, but the same
condition would arise whenever the one metal or the other
—almost always silver—was found to be in excess of the
requirements for its employment.

Without entering upon other details or producing illustrations, it must be evident that in a country under such
monetary conditions as ours, the mere possibility of being
forced to transact business in the more cumbrous metal
would be intolerable.   The necessity imposed upon bankers
and others of providing a sufficient supply of both to meet
all demands would be adverse to economy in the use of
money, thus both adding to the expense and raising impediments to the settlement of business transactions.   Here,

practically, no more silver would get into circulation, but much more would have to be kept in reserve at the Bank of England and the Mint, either of which might be called upon to meet large or sudden demands. Nothing can work better than our system of restricting the use of silver by its limited circulation as a token at an artificial value, and making gold, or notes whose convertibility is secure, legal tenders for all but trifling amounts. Other nations, even where the standard is silver, are finding the convenience of our system, and the use of gold in preference to the heavier metal is becoming more desirable every day.

The introduction of such a system into our coinage could only be effected in one of two ways, either by replacing our present coins by others of such a standard value as might be agreed upon with other nations, say 15½ to 1; or by the addition to it of new full value pieces of such a size as would keep them distinct from the token coins now current, say those of four or five shillings—the fifth or fourth of the pound sterling—which should contain the requisite amount of pure metal to make them equivalent to gold in all transactions either at home or abroad. In our present coinage twenty shillings contain 1,614 grs. of pure silver; those proposed would require 1,753, an excess of rather more than 8½ per cent. They would absorb, if the estimate of 20 millions as the amount in circulation be correct, at least a million and a half of money, besides all the expense of re-coinage, should now pieces be substituted for the old. It is difficult to see what advantage as regards internal circulation could arise from either course, or what difference it would make in the exchange with other nations, over the use of bar silver which now passes freely from one country to another. The advancement of the price of silver in the hands of British holders, whether as coin, bullion, or plate would be a decided gain; but for this would be sacrificed the favourable standing given us by the gold standard in the face of the diminishing production of that metal and the increasing supplies of silver. Should these continue or be extended, and we had the double standard, a drain of gold would most certainly ensue, which would prove embarrassing in the extreme.

The great difficulty with which we have to contend is India. Mr. Seyd's proposition, ingenious as it is, to introduce a new silver coin of 350·625 grs. fine, which should be declared equivalent in value to four shillings, or one-fifth of the pound sterling, is avowedly dependent for its success upon a general agreement for a bi-metallic currency on the basis of $15\frac{1}{4}$ to 1. Colonel Smith's plan, of stopping the coinage of rupees until by their scarceness they had attained the artificial value of two shillings, concurrently with the introduction of a ten-rupee gold piece identical with the English sovereign, establishing a still higher ratio of 14·6 to 1 (which is the intrinsic value of our present English silver coins), could never be maintained unless other nations agreed to adopt it; since, however possible it may be to keep a limited amount of token coinage in circulation, as we do here, it would be utterly impossible to maintain it for the whole currency of a nation.

Mr. Hendriks's proposal for the introduction of a ten-rupee gold coin worth $\frac{49}{17}$ths of the sovereign, and an alteration of the silver rupee to 11 per cent. less pure silver than at present, seems hardly practicable in the face of the present reduced price of the metal.

Now all these schemes, as well as the new American dollar, and various other arrangements, seem to be based upon the fallacy that it is possible by any agreement or law to fix an unalterable ratio between two substances the circumstances of whose production and employment are subject to constant variations. We have seen how impossible it is to maintain an equilibrium in the value of gold at different times, or even in different places at the same time. It is, therefore, scarcely too much to assert that the attempt to do so with silver must inevitably fail; for although the internal relation may be enforced by law, the conditions of different countries are so diverse and fluctuating, that each one in its external relations must be subject to ever-changing adaptations, suited to the position of affairs at the moment when the exchanges of commodities, securities, or bullion require to be effected.

The true wisdom would therefore appear to be found in every country having but a single standard. For facility of intercourse with other countries it would be well if that standard were the same for all, and until some other substance of superior fitness be found, everything points to the conclusion that the best standard is gold. It does not, however, at all follow that it would be wise for every nation to imitate the example of the German Government by changing from the one metal to the other. The existing stocks of gold are clearly insufficient to supply the wants of the world should this be done, and at the present price of silver, to say nothing of that to which it would fall if it were everywhere demonetized, such a step would entail heavy and ultimately ruinous loss upon the countries making the change. Sound policy would seem to dictate that each country should, for the present at least, maintain its existing standard, and that all should put up with the inconveniences, and even loss, which the diversity occasions. Least of all would it be wise for England to forego the advantage she herself possesses in her gold standard, her convertible notes, and her subsidiary silver and copper coinage. For India, she should wait her time for the introduction of gold, and meanwhile, hard as it is upon that country to be fettered by engagements to pay in gold, or according to the gold standard, large sums which are collected in silver, it really only amounts to a failure of revenue such as might have arisen from other causes, and is a far lesser difficulty than she will have to cope with when, as it assuredly must be, and that at no distant date, her opium revenue is extinguished.

It will be asked, then, is nothing to be done? Are all the distresses and inconveniences, public and private, pertaining to the present state of things to be unmitigated? Are all the derangements in mercantile affairs to continue

as they are? The answer to such questioners is two-fold.
Firstly: Let us see any remedy proposed which does not
create a disease far worse than the one it professes to cure.
Secondly: Is there any need for action?   Will not time
and patience bring round a recovery?   The depreciation
of silver commenced with the adverse turn in the balance of
our trade, and I firmly believe that when trade recovers
from its present depression, such abundant use will be
found for all the silver as will restore it to its former relation to gold; and then the substitution of a gold for a
silver standard in India, though it will not effect any stable
relation of the one to the other, will obviate much of the
inconvenience resulting from the want of a uniform standard
for every portion of the same empire.   It would be absurd
to say that such a restoration may not be retarded, advanced,
or even defeated altogether by some new discoveries or increased production of either the one metal or the other;
but supposing the supplies to continue at the present rate, or
not greatly to vary from it, either the opening up of new
markets amongst a poor or uncivilized people, or the dispersion of a large number of our population to open up new
colonies or extend the old ones, will call into use quite as
much small change as will absorb all the silver yet available,
and thus correct the evil which is now the source of so
much disquietude.

X.—*Concluding Remarks.*

Shortly to recapitulate the several phases of this question
which have thus passed under observation, we may observe:

1. That basing our calculations upon the best estimates
which can be obtained of the annual production of gold and
silver, and comparing the assumed stock of gold with the
movements of bullion and merchandise throughout the
world, there appears no reason to suppose that the existing
supply is not amply sufficient for all the purposes of trade
as at present carried on.

II. That the general fall of prices in recent years has

neither been so regular nor so closely connected with the supply of gold and silver, as to prove that alterations in the purchasing power of the sovereign have been due wholly or chiefly to an appreciation of gold.

III. That the variations in the value of gold itself, as shown by the fluctuations in the price of the funds, and the rates of interest charged for the use of money, prove that it has no constant or unalterable value.

IV. That, in addition to the well-known effects on the value of silver arising from the growing yield of the American mines and the decrease in its use from its demonetization by Germany, there are others resulting from the increased quantity of gold, the facilities for economizing its use, and its natural superiority to silver, sufficient to account in some measure for the depreciation of the inferior metal.

V. That the coincidence of the fall in the price of silver with the contraction and depression of trade renders it probable that in this is to be found the most potent cause of depreciation, and that the revival of trade will in all probability be accompanied by a restoration of its value.

VI. That it is not likely that any agreement to establish a fixed ratio in the value of silver to gold could ever be permanently maintained, or not be liable to disruption at any moment from causes incapable of regulation or control.

VII. That it is a fallacy to suppose that the extent of trade, and consequently the value of the medium through which its transactions are settled, depends so much upon the quantity of money in existence as upon the assiduous and judicious employment of productive power, the thrift by which its products are accumulated, and the wisdom which governs their consumption or expenditure.

In conclusion, let me say that I offer the foregoing remarks and calculations in thorough consciousness of my own inability to deal with a subject of so much intricacy and so much gravity; but also with the full knowledge that honest labour, however imperfect in its performance, never

fails to be appreciated by the members of this Society, and
the earnest hope that however little there may be in what
I have written to enlighten those who are better informed
than myself, it will be followed by a discussion instructive
and interesting to all who may be present.

POSTSCRIPT.—The point raised by Mr. Giffen in the discussion which followed the reading of this paper, as to the
meaning attached to the value of the pound, will be better
seen if some other standard be assumed wherein to express
the value of gold, say consols; we shall then speak of the
sovereign as worth 1·25 or 1·11 consols, to express what
we now mean by the price of £100 consols being 80 or 90.
The difference between the two prices may result either
from the rising value of the consols or the falling value of
the gold. To which of the two it is due would depend
upon whether the ultimate cause lay with the one or the
other. So with regard to the altered prices of articles : in
practice it matters not how it comes to pass that the
sovereign purchases more or less, but in theory, and therefore in relation to other articles, everything depends upon
which of the two it is that has changed its circumstances so
as to produce the alteration. Political and other causes
influence the value of stocks and shares, but not to the
whole or principal part of the variation in price. This is
oftener due to the present abundance or scarcity of gold,
which really rises or falls in value just as silver or any other
article does. So with the price of goods. The change
may be either with them or with the gold, and to ascertain
in which it has taken place is essential to the discovery of
the cause, the provision of a remedy, or the forecasting of
the future.

Considerable difficulty arose on the consideration of
Mr. Giffen's paper, previously referred to, from the disparity
of results in his comparison between two years and those
which were then stated in brief, and are now shown in
detail.[1] The one set of calculations was between 1873 and

---

[1] Vide "Statistical Journal," as before.

1877, the other between 1872 and 1878, and it so happens that there was a rise of price in many articles in 1873 and a fall in 1878, but in *both* of these years a considerable fall in quantity. It was in the latter part of 1872 that the coal famine set in, producing in 1873 an abnormal price for that article, and the many dependent upon it. Thus comparing the exports for the two years :—

	1873.		Over 1872.		Amount of altered value due.	
	Tons.	Price.	Tons.	Price.	To Quantity.	To Price.
		£		£	£	£
Coals............	12·63	13·21	— 0·57	+ 2·77	— 0·45	+ 3·22
Pig iron.........	1·14	7·08	— 0·19	+ 0·37	— 0·96	+ 1·33
Railway iron...	0·79	10·43	— 0·16	+ 0·20	— 1·72	+ 1·92
	—	30·72	—	+ 3·34	— 3·13	+ 6·47

Thus, when measuring the two years by total value, the increase of price conceals the decrease in quantity, and as these two articles alone represent one-sixth of the whole of the exports dealt with in Mr. Giffen's table, they cover a large portion of the difference. The same cause operated to some extent to throw out the calculations for 1872 in the other table. But for these inflated prices the decrease on "Total British Produce," there shown as £45·26, would have been £10·36 less. Again, for coals and iron, together with the diminished cost of the imported raw material from which many of the articles are manufactured, would cause a shrinkage in value, and thus lessen the total to be brought into comparison with the diminution due to quantity. Making due allowance for these causes, it is proved that of the lower total value of the British exports in 1878 as compared with 1872, two-fifths, if not one-half, represent an absolute falling off in *quantity*, and as this cannot by any possibility indicate an appreciation of gold, it may not be assumed that the falling off in prices proves any alteration to have taken place in the value of gold. That fall in price is amply accounted for by the unwillingness or the inability of other nations to purchase our manufactures to the extent they formerly did, and the necessity under which we are placed of giving a larger quantity for the money in order to effect sales at all.

It should also be remarked, in answer to one of the questions, that in the foreign accounts of the gold and silver production, ounces are converted into dollars at a fixed rate, and dollars into pounds sterling at the nominal value of 4s. each, so that the estimates really present a proper basis for the comparison of quantities. Rupees also into sterling at 10 to the £.

An additional table (see Appendix), in compliance with Mr. Giffen's suggestion, shows the countries whose production is estimated in Table I. (p. 204), whilst Appendices B and C[1] divide in like manner the values of bullion and merchandise in the same table.

[1] Vide " Statistical Journal," as before.

APPENDIX.

Production of Gold and Silver throughout the World (Corrected as regards the United States from the " Financial Review," published in New York, 1879). Sir Hector M. Hay.

[In million £'s to two decimals.]

Years.	Gold.					Silver.		
	Australia.	United States.	Mexico and South America.	Russia.	Other Countries.	United States.	Mexico and South America.	Other Countries.
1852....	20·60	12·00	1·00	2·45	0·50	—	6·00	2·12
'53....	14·14	13·00	1·00	2·45	0·50	—	6·00	2·12
'54....	9·54	12·00	1·00	2·45	0·50	—	6·00	2·12
'55....	12·07	11·00	1·00	2·45	0·50	—	6·00	2·12
'56....	14·27	11·00	1·00	2·75	0·50	—	6·00	2·13
'57....	11·41	11·00	1·00	2·75	0·50	—	6·00	2·13
'58....	10·68	10·00	1·00	2·75	0·50	—	6·00	2·13
'59....	10·82	10·00	0·90	2·75	0·50	0·02	6·00	2·13
1860....	10·50	9·20	0·90	2·75	0·50	0·03	6·00	2·13
'61....	9·76	8·60	0·90	3·00	0·50	0·40	6·00	2·14
'62....	—9·35	7·81	0·90	3·00	0·50	0·90	6·00	2·14
'63....	8·88	8·00	0·90	3·11	0·50	1·70	6·00	2·14
'64....	9·13	9·22	0·80	2·95	0·50	2·20	6·00	2·14
'65....	8·82	10·64	0·80	3·23	0·50	2·25	6·00	2·14
'66....	8·84	10·70	0·80	3·34	0·50	2·00	6·00	2·14
'67....	7·91	10·35	0·70	3·35	0·50	2·70	6·00	2·14
'68....	7·64	9·60	0·60	3·60	0·50	2·40	5·50	2·15
'69....	6·31	9·90	0·50	4·03	0·50	2·40	5·00	2·10
1870....	7·70	6·70	0·50	4·50	0·50	3·40	5·50	2·00
'71....	8·60	6·80	0·70	4·50	0·50	3·80	5·20	2·00
'72....	7·30	7·60	0·70	4·50	0·50	4·00	5·20	2·00
'73....	7·80	7·80	0·70	4·50	0·50	5·40	4·80	2·00
'74....	5·90	7·70	0·80	4·50	0·50	5·90	5·00	2·00
'75....	5·70	8·00	0·80	4·50	0·50	6·40	5·00	2·00
'76....	4·50	8·50	1·00	4·50	0·50	7·80	5·00	2·00
'77....	4·50	8·90	1·00	4·50	0·50	9·10	5·00	2·00
'78....	4·00	7·80	1·00	4·50	0·50	7·70	5·00	2·00
	246·67	253·85	22·90	93·75	13·50	70·50	152·20	56·36

Note.—These amounts make up the totals shown in the table on page 201.

XI

On the Decay in the Export Trade of the United Kingdom.[1]

MUCH attention has been given to the state of our export trade, and the fact that for several years past there has been a progressive decline in its total value. Considerable discussion has taken place as to whether the fall has been in the quantities of the goods we have sold or the prices which they have realized; and a large preponderance of the opinions expressed has been, that it is due to the latter rather than to the former cause. The Prime Minister on two occasions especially, when the subject has been under discussion, has drawn consolation from this conviction. Mr. Bonamy Price has treated it in the same light in the " Contemporary Review," and Mr. Brassey in the " Nineteenth Century," whilst most of the leading journals have adopted the same theory. It cannot, therefore, be unfitting to inquire upon what foundation it rests, or whether the few voices which have been raised on the other side may not have some reason for the view they take.

At first sight it may seem a very easy question to determine whether it be the volume or the value of the exports which has suffered change, and a simple inspection of the figures for any particular article will decide the point so far as that article is concerned. Thus when we see that in 1872 we exported cotton piece goods to the extent of

---

[1] Read before Section F of the British Association, at Sheffield, August, 1879.—" Statist," Sept. 6, 1879.

3,538 million yards at a value of £58,931,000, whilst in 1878 our exports were 3,618 million yards, the value of which was £48,086,000, it is evident that the difference in value is due to a fall in price. Also when there was an export of sheep's wool in the former year of 7,605 million lbs. at a value of £629,000, and in the latter of 6,440 million lbs. at a value of £546,000, it is equally clear that the lesser value is owing to diminished quantity, and an easy calculation will show that the average price per lb. was slightly higher in 1878 than in 1872. Again, with linen piece goods the quantities were 245 million yards in 1872 and 161 millions in 1878, the respective values being £7,700,000 and £4,917,000; it is at once seen that there has been a serious falling off in quantity, whilst the average price has varied but little. In like manner each specific article speaks for itself, but the proportion in which it affects the total result has to be ascertained in combination with that of every other article, before it can be discovered whether on the whole the admitted fall in value received has been occasioned by diminished quantities or reduced prices.

Lord Beaconsfield's statement rested upon the authority of a report made by Mr. Giffen, the head of the Statistical and Commercial Department of the Board of Trade, comparing the quantity and value of the goods exported in 1873 with those in 1877, and showing that, whereas in the former year the total declared value of the exports included in the return was £192,433,000, and in the latter only £147,800,000, the changes in the average prices had been so great that had all the exports of 1877 been valued as those of 1873, the total valuation would have amounted to £191,530,000, or less than a million below that returned for the former year. There are many articles of which the statistical records do not show the quantities, but the values only; these are not included in the above figures, it being impossible to subject them to the same treatment. Those dealt with, however, represented 75·1 per cent. of the total exports of 1873, and 74·6 per cent. of 1877. The calculations are carefully worked out, and the deductions are unimpeachable; yet there is good reason to doubt the correctness of the inference drawn, viz., that the export trade of the country is suffering only in the prices and not in the volume of our transactions.

Tables having the same object, and formed upon a somewhat similar basis, comparing the trade for a portion of 1872 and 1873, were published in " Lloyd's List " in July, 1873, and that of 1872 with 1877, and of 1877 with 1878 in the "Economist" of July, 1878, and January, 1879, and the "Statistical Society's Journal" for June of the present year contains one contrasting 1872 with 1878. These all point to a real deficiency of quantity as well as value, the latter table showing that whereas the total difference on a value of £195,820,000 in the specified articles for the two years was £57,360,000; of this amount £45,260,000 only was due to a difference in price, £12,100,000 to an actual diminution in quantity. That is, articles which in 1878 were valued at but £138,460,000 would at the prices of 1872 have amounted to £183,720,000, or 32·69 per cent. more.

A similar disparity is manifested by a comparison between the exports for the first six months of the present year and the same period of 1872. In these the difference on a value of £83,460,000 was £28,500,000, of which £21,620,000 arose from altered prices, and £6,880,000 from diminished quantity. That is, the articles which in 1879 were valued at but £54,960,000 would at the prices of 1872 have amounted to £76,580,000, or 39·34 per cent. more.

The main sources from which these variations arise will be more clearly seen from the following selection (Table I.) of the seven principal articles of which the foreign export trade consists, and comparing together the three periods already alluded to, that of 1877 with 1873, 1878 with 1872, and the first half of 1879 with the corresponding portion of

1872; showing in each case the total value of the exports in the later year, and the amount wherein it varies from the earlier one, dividing this variation into the respective sums arising from differences in quantity and in price. These seven descriptions of goods embrace between 60 and 70 per cent. of the whole export trade, that is of those which, from being recorded in both quantity and value, permit of being thus analyzed, and are fairly representative of those not thus included. Of goods coming under other denominations, such as apparel, chinaware, machinery, &c., all of which are shown in value only, it may be assumed that they very much follow the same rules as those that are specified,

TABLE I.

[In million £'s to two decimals.]

Goods Exported.		Years.		Total Value in Later Years.	More or less than Earlier Year.	Increase or Decrease in Value due to	
						Quantity.	Price.
				£	£	£	£
Cotton Manfs		1877 with 1873		64·22	— 7·54	+ 6·30	—13·84
		'78 „ '72		63·01	—13·98	+ 5·14	—19·12
	(6 Mo.)...	'79 „ '72		28·27	— 8·34	+ 2·51	- 10·85
Jute „		1877 „ 1873		3·28	— 0·43	+ 0·60	— 1·03
		'78 „ '72		3·33	0·03	+ 1·35	— 1·38
	(6 Mo.)..	'79 „ '72		1·64	+ 0·08	+ 0·85	— 0·77
Linen „		1877 „ 1873		6·59	— 2·12	— 1·64	— 0·18
		'78 „ '72		5·93	— 3·68	— 3·48	— 0·20
	(6 Mo.)...	'79 „ '72		3·22	— 2·01	— 1·61	— 0·40
Woollen „		1877 „ 1873		19·92	— 9·04	5·16	— 3·88
		'78 „ '72		19·52	17·52	—10·90	— 6·62
	(6 Mo.)...	'79 „ '72		8·48	10·02	- 6·44	— 3·58
Coals..............		1877 „ 1873		7·84	— 5·34	+ 2·93	— 8·27
		'78 „ '72		7·32	— 3·12	+ 1·79	— 4·91
	(6 Mo.)...	'79 „ '72		3·34	— 0·63	+ 0·65	— 1·28
Copper		1877 „ 1873		3·06	— 0·22	+ 0·43	— 0·65
		'78 „ '72		3·11	0·14	+ 0·98	— 1·12
	(6 Mo.)...	'79 „ '72		1·50	— 0·09	+ 0·60	— 0·69
Iron		1877 „ 1873		20·11	17·61	— 5·56	- 12·05
		'78 „ '72		18·40	—17·66	— 9·00	— 8·66
	(6 Mo.)...	'79 „ '72		8·51	— 7·49	— 3·44	— 4·05
Totals of specified Articles	(6 Mo.)	1877 „ 1873		125·02	42·30	— 2·10	—40·20
		'78 „ '72		120·62	—56·13	14·12	42·01
		'79 „ '72		54·90	—28·50	6·88	21·62

R

and would not materially alter the result if it were possible to take them into the comparison.

Collecting thus these specified articles, it appears that there was exported of them in 1877 a total value of £125·02 millions, which fell short of the trade in them in 1873 to the extent of £42·30; and that dividing this fall into the amount due respectively to diminished quantities and prices, there was £2·10 of the one, and £40·20 of the other, or at the rate of rather more than 1 to 20. These years of 1877 and 1873 were the two which have been relied on as establishing the fact that the fall in total value has been almost entirely in price; but, as will be shown presently, this conclusion will not bear a close investigation. Extending the comparison to one year further back and another further forward (1878-72), an interval of six years instead of four, and dealing with a total value of £120·62 for the later, it will be seen that the fall from the value of the earlier year was £56·13, of which £14·12 arose from lessened quantities, and £42·01 from lower prices. Upon comparing the first half of the present year with the same months of 1872, the value for this year is £54·96, or £28·50 below that of 1872, divisible into £6·88 and £21·62 for quantity and price, these two periods being in the proportion of about 1 to 3 of quantity to price. But even this relation of the one to the other is subject to large corrections, and would not be supported by a comparison with 1871 instead of 1872. That year has not been selected on account of an alteration in the system of accounts which then took place interposing a difficulty.

It will be remembered by those who have at all watched the market prices of various articles, that in 1872 there set in what may be termed a famine of coal, during which almost fabulous prices were obtained for this article. For the eleven preceding years the export price had averaged 9·64s. per ton; the highest of any year not having exceeded 10·39s., nor the lowest fallen below 9s.; but for 1872 the average was 15·83s., increasing to 20·90s. in 1873, then by successive stages coming down to 9·46s. for last year, and 8.91s. for the first half of the present year. Nor was this rise confined to coal; it necessarily extended to all articles whose cost was increased by that of the fuel employed in their manufacture. To take pig-iron as an example. The average for the years 1860-71 had been 57·76s., the limit of variation between the highest and lowest years having been but 10·75s. It rose, however, in 1872 to 100·85s., and in 1873 to 124·65s., falling again to 57·34s. in 1877, 53·52s. in 1878, and 48·63s. in the present year. The effect of this rise was to raise the percentage which these two articles bore to the whole exports of British and Irish produce exported from the United Kingdom from 3·2 in 1871 to 8·0 in 1873, or, including every description of iron, from 14·3 to 20·0. Now, it is obvious that any comparison based on such inflated prices as these, when contrasted with other articles, might, as in fact it did, when the two descriptions were brought into one common total, conceal an extensive decrease in the quantities of those articles which maintained a more equable price. A grocer who found his gross receipts increased by 20 per cent. might be gaining 25 on his tea, whilst losing 5 on his sugar, without being conscious of the fact until he analyzed the different sources of profit and loss. We must, therefore, before we can arrive at a correct appreciation of the relative influences of the changes in volume and value in the whole of the exports, make large deductions from the value of the earlier years on account of these exceptional prices.

But yet another correction of the figures is needed. Many of our articles of export are manufactured from materials of foreign growth, the cost of which varies considerably at different dates; and any accurate comparison between the values of the finished exports at the two periods requires those values to be reduced by the sums paid for the raw material of which they are composed before the relative rise or fall in price or quantity can be rightly

estimated.   Cotton is a prominent example of this, and it
so happens that its cost varied very much in 1872 and 1873
from what it did in 1877, 1878, and 1879—viz., 84s. 11d.
and 80s. 3d. being the average price of importations in the
former years, 58s. 7d., 56s., and 43s. 1d. in the latter.

In the following table (II.) there are shown, for each of
the three periods which have been already brought into
comparison, the actual effect upon the collected values of
the seven specified classes of articles, of the inflated prices
of coals and iron, and these, together with the estimated
cost of the foreign cotton used, have been deducted from
the earlier years, in order to obtain a fair net value for comparison, the cost of cotton being in like manner deducted
from the later years.   All minor variations in the value of
the articles influenced by the coal and iron employed in
their production, or entering into their composition, have
been disregarded, although in the aggregate these must be
far from inconsiderable.   The influence also of the price of
raw cotton on the values of the many articles of export,
such as wearing apparel, haberdashery, &c., and also the
effect of the lessened cost of other foreign materials used
in the manufacture of other export goods, has not been
reduced to figures.   The total values thus brought into
comparison are for 1873 £113·88, with £98·02 in 1877,
showing a fall of £15·86, or at the rate of 13·9 per cent.
For 1872 £126·41, with £95·62 in 1878, a fall of £30·79,
or at the rate of £24·4 per cent.; and for the first half of
1879 £60·77, with £43·46, a fall of £17·31, or 28·4 per
cent.   We arrive then at this result: that in the first period
a fall of £15·86 must be divided into £13·76 due to price,
and £2·10 to quantity, or in the ratio of very nearly 6 to 1.
In the second period £30·79, into £16·67 to price, and
£14·12 to quantity, or the ratio of 13 to 11.   In the third
period £17·31, into £10·43 to price, and £6·88 to quantity,
a ratio of 17½ to 11.

TABLE II.

[In Millions £'s to two decimals.]

	1873.	1872.	6 Mo. 1872.
Value of Specified Articles	£167·52	£176·75	£83·46
Dedt. Coal.......... £6·47		... £4·06	... £1·07
Iron.......... 13·17		... 9·28	... 4·12
Cotton....... 34·00		... 37·00	... 17·50
	53·64	50·34	22·69
Net value for Comparison ...113·88		126·41	60·77

	1877.	1878.	6 Mo. 1879.
	£125·02	£120·62	£54·96
Less Cotton.......... 27·00		25·00	11·50
	98·02	95·62	43·46
			℞ ct.
Fall in Value........	15·86=13·9 ℞ ct.	30·79=24·4 ℞ ct.	17·31=28·4
Due to Price.........	13·76=12·0 ,,	16·67=13·2 ,,	10·43=17·0
,, Quantity....	2·10= 1·9 ,,	14·12=11·1 ,,	6·88=11·4

Two or three observations on these results may be made in passing. First, that these several deductions from the values of the respective years really account for some considerable portion of the lessened total amounts for which the products of our industry have been sold, or rather at which they have been valued. Thus, still keeping to the specified articles, at first sight it would appear that a trade amounting to £167,000,000 in 1873 had dwindled to £125,000,000 in 1877, or a reduction of £42,000,000, whereas the real difference in value was but £16,000,000. That amounting in 1872 to £177,000,000 had apparently sunk to 121 millions in 1878, a fall of 56 millions, but should only be deemed to be 31 millions; and that of the first half of 1872, amounting to 83 millions, had been lowered to 55 millions in 1879, or 28 millions; whereas 17 millions will represent the real extent of depression. Viewed in this light, the severity of our loss in export trade is considerably mitigated.

In the second place, however, it must be admitted that there is no abatement, but rather an increase, of diminution in the actual net amounts we are receiving from the sale of our commodities.   Sixteen millions in 1877, 31 millions in 1878, and 17 millions for the first half of 1879 afford no indication that the tide is ceasing to ebb.

Thirdly, if the comparison of one year's export trade with that of its predecessor affords no grounds for satisfaction, neither does comparison with our imports give much or any reason for congratulation.   It is true that the balance of trade—or the difference between the sums we have to pay for the things we buy, over and above that we receive for those we sell—is each year lessening, but solely for the reason that our imports are decreasing in value faster than our exports are.   Much of this arises from falling prices, and, happily, in part, from the diminution in the amount of grain we have this year [1878-9] required from abroad; but it is an undeniable fact that we are taking lesser supplies of the raw materials which form the staples of our industries both for home and foreign use.   It is well to practise economy in consumption when the necessity arises, but real prosperity is to be looked for in an increasing sale of our manufactures, leading to an increasing demand for the materials from which they are formed.

Reverting, however, to the main question : these figures, if they have any value at all, demonstrate the fallacy of the too often expressed opinion that the diminished value of the goods exported lies altogether, or almost wholly, in the fall of prices.   They distinctly prove that which the experience of merchants and shipowners has already told them—that there is a very serious lessening in the demand for our produce and manufactures.   It may not be shown in cotton or jute manufactures, but it is in linen and woollen, to an extent which far outweighs any growth in the others. Coals, too, do not diminish in quantity, nor does copper ; but in iron it assumes proportions so alarming that we may well welcome with joy the hopes now expressed that American orders to this town are the heralds of approaching revival.

If, then, it be impossible to deny that the lessened value

of our exports is not confined to a general fall in prices, there are two reasons amongst others with which many seem to be satisfied. The one is that the change is not so much in the real value of the articles as in that of the gold by which that value is estimated—that an appreciation of gold is taking place, in consequence of which its purchasing power is increased. The answer to this assertion is simple. If such were the case, the rise in price would apply to all articles equally, whereas there is no such equable or uniform change of prices as would indicate much alteration in the value of gold. The fluctuations are too great to be due to any such cause, at any rate in any marked degree. The other reason given is that prices are everywhere falling, and must soon rise again in like manner. The reply to this is not so easy; for it is apparent to all that this alteration of prices does not arise from causes so deep-seated as to render a recovery from them very doubtful. One thing is certain, that at the present time we have to part with a much larger quantity of goods for each sovereign we obtain, and that notwithstanding we do this, the number of sovereigns we receive is continually growing less.

It is not the purpose of this paper to enter upon an examination into the causes from which this decay of our trade has arisen, nor to inquire by what methods it may be met or reversed. This has been done to some extent by the writer in papers read before the Statistical Societies of London and Manchester, the discussion on which has been full. Briefly, however, it may be stated that the first step is retrenchment. The country must consume less. It is not one class alone, but all classes who have been inflated by prosperity, and become extravagant in expenditure or waste. It must then strive to produce more, not of those things which foreigners decline to buy, but of those which we at present buy from them, until they learn the folly of shutting out our goods to the detriment of their own producers of the things we are willing to take in exchange. Yet another course is open to us, dependent as we are for

our food upon foreign supplies, and, should the demand for
our manufactures still continue to decline— over-full as we
shall be with population at home—we must occupy the vast
regions we possess abroad, and thus raise up new customers
with whom we may exchange our goods, to their advantage
as well as ours.

But there are not wanting those amongst us who, whether
from their place in Parliament, in the columns of the public
journals, or through the medium of such Associations as
this and others, openly advocate a reversal of the commercial policy under which our country has risen to its late
prosperity.   At one time under the specious claim for reciprocity, at another under the bolder plea for protection,
they seek to bind again the fetters from which trade and
commerce have been emancipated.   To assertions such as
they make, with no little *show* of soundness, we owe much
of the growing desire for either reciprocity or protection,
and these are greatly aided by the injudicious arguments of
free-traders themselves.   These too often forget that free
trade is not an active but a negative principle or policy,
and they claim for it all the success which has followed its
adoption.   Now, free trade confers no advantages or powers
which were not previously existent; it but removes ob-
structions to the development of that which is inherent in
those whom it benefits, and had it not been for the discoveries
of gold and the adaptation of steam, combined with the gifts
of nature and the acquisitions of science, the introduction of
freedom of trade could never have given us the pre-eminence
in manufacture and commerce to which we have attained.
The exclusive possession of these is now contested by other
nations, and will be still more so when they too shake off
the self-imposed bondage of a restrictive policy.   In a
country like ours, which is absolutely dependent upon the
produce of other lands for the maintenance of the life of its
population, and can only obtain the food which that life
needs for its sustenance by the sale of its manufactures
abroad, the fullest and freest expansion is necessary.   The

home trade can never flourish if the foreign be destroyed, for much of the one is but the distribution of the surplus wealth which the other creates. Let protection be accorded to the mechanic who devotes his labour and skill to the production of the articles which he exchanges for the food grown for him at home, and it cannot be denied to the agriculturist who grows that food. Let the food of the man who labours for the foreign market be taxed, and he can no longer compete with the foreigner whose food is untaxed, and thus he will cease to be a customer for the produce of the protected agriculturist.

It is plain, however, that our commercial relations—and with them, too, our political and economic conditions—are being exposed to a severe strain, the continuance of which is probably not yet approaching its end. It is an ungrateful task thus to take the pessimist view, and in so doing to be exposed to suspicion; but the true philanthropist, the real worker for his country's welfare, must not, therefore, shrink from laying bare the actual position in which its trade and commerce stand, if thereby he can arouse attention to the latent sources of evil which lie beneath the surface. Let us but fail to recognize our faults, to unite in learning the lessons which chastisement is designed to teach, to promote that spirit of unity and concord in thought and action which can alone enable us to stem the current of adversity whilst it lasts; and we shall see the nations whom we have hitherto led in the progress of civilization and wealth stepping into our place, and enjoying the supremacy we shall renounce.

XII.

On the Social Aspect of Trade Depression.[1]

THE depression of trade under which the country suffers has continued for so long a time, exists under conditions so different from those of any preceding seasons, and is as yet so unmitigated in its severity, that it may well be said to form an epoch in the commercial history of our country ; the more so that it is now accompanied by an equally serious state of depression in agriculture. Whether this sister form of suffering be the occasion or the result of that which affects trade, or whether it be a fortuitous occurrence that the two should accompany each other ; there can be no question that it complicates the matter greatly, causes it to exercise a greater influence over a wider area than did either exist without the other, and renders the present period a more marked one as it affects the social position in which the country stands. An inquiry into the special facts relating to either trade or agricultural depression falls properly within the province of the statistician, just as the investigation of the causes from which they spring, and the remedies with which they should be met, belongs to those who are versed in the principles and practice of political economy. Although neither of these lines of research lies without the range of subjects which may be followed by a Social Science Congress, it is not with them that it is proposed to deal on this occasion ; but

[1] Read at the Meeting of the Social Science Congress, Manchester, 1879.

rather to take the condition of things as they now stand, and to consider briefly the social state as thus presented to our view.   Some little allusion, however, to the history of the case, and some attention to its special circumstances are absolutely necessary to an understanding of the social condition we have to consider.

It has been noticed by many that crises such as these are of periodic occurrence, inflation being followed by depression, and adversity giving place to prosperity, at intervals of ten or eleven years; and the fact that these periods are coincident with marked appearances on the solar disc has been thought to show that, in some way or other, there is an intimate connection between the spots which darken the sun's visage and the gloom which overspreads the mercantile world.   It has even been started as a theory, by no mean authority, that the abstraction of the sun's heat so lessens the earth's fertility as to diminish the amount of food produced, depriving consumers of their power to purchase our manufactures, and thus deranging the whole course of our trading and manufacturing operations.   But apart from the circumstance that the present depression has been growing for at least half of the supposed cycle, and even if it have yet reached its maximum growth must necessarily occupy some years in the process of passing away—thus filling up the whole or nearly all of the period allotted to both depression and inflation—the character of the present times is so different from that of any which have gone before, as to suggest a different origin, and to predicate a different course towards recovery.   On former occasions some national drain on our resources, or some natural loss of production, has pushed us downwards, or some sudden accession of wealth, or unexpected openings of new channels for trade have borne us upwards, until the force of either being spent, we have been unable to sustain the elevation we had reached.   These have been temporary ebbs and flows of the same tide, but now there seems, besides all these, to be a steady current setting to leeward, which, unless we can find means to resist or to turn it, threatens to strand us amongst the breakers which far-sighted thinkers seem to discover ahead of us.   If this be so, it is surely important to know from whence it comes and whither it is tending; and it may not be useless to inquire whether, paradoxical as it may appear, it is not this : that whereas in former times the streams of production and consumption, though not always flowing with uniform velocity, did yet keep average pace with each other ; of late years consumption has sped faster than production—consumption, I mean, of that which is absolutely essential to continued sustenance of individual and national life.   Hence, amidst all our abounding wealth, we are in no little danger of absolute poverty.   The tenants of a besieged fortress may possess no end of gold or treasure, and yet perish for lack of bread.   The State which consumes more of the necessaries of life than it produces may have accumulated any amount of capital by past industry and trade, and yet be in abject want if that capital be not held in a form which permits of its exchânge for the means of subsistence.

In the earliest stage of the world's history, when, as we believe, but two individuals were in existence, and the earth ceased spontaneously to produce the requisite supplies of food ; it was ordained, " in the sweat of thy face shalt thou eat bread," and the condition on which man's life depended was that he should " till the ground."   When, again, population was reduced to the eight who emerged from the ark to " be fruitful and multiply and replenish the earth," the green herb of the field needed the husbandry of a Noah ; the wild flocks of the plain were to be hunted by a Nimrod and an Esau ; and the cattle of the fold to be tended by a Jacob. The three necessaries of life, food, raiment, and shelter, could only be procured by the bestowal of labour ; and in a barbaric state of life we may well believe that little else resulted from the employment of man's powers.   Each individual family or community had to produce for itself that which it consumed, and could only exist or increase as production was kept up to, or in excess of, consumption. As, however, knowledge and civilization advanced, the economy of labour and the aid of art enabled more to be produced than there was a need to consume, and production took the form in a great measure of that which ministered to comfort, to luxury, to the increase of wealth. The strong, the thrifty, the wise became the possessors of wealth, or devoted themselves to the production of that which they could exchange for the means of sustenance; and so far as the necessaries of life were concerned, mankind became divided into the two great classes of consumers and producers. It mattered not, then, whether each individual or community produced food or other essentials for his or its own consumption, provided he either had or produced that with which these could be purchased. Two things, however, were absolutely requisite—that the necessaries for the whole should be produced by some one or more, and that those who did not produce for themselves should be able to induce or compel the producers to part with their superabundant stores.

Bearing in mind these principles, but not stopping to trace their application to the progress of our country in knowledge, civilization, and wealth, we find that she embraces three classes in her community. Those who produce nothing themselves, but, either by inheritance or the power of ministering to the wants or tastes of others, obtain their share not only of the necessaries but the superfluities of life; those who produce that which they can exchange for what they need; and those who actually produce these necessaries, not only for themselves but for the other members of the community. So long as in any country these three orders can maintain their due relation to each other, and sufficient labour is employed in producing the means of subsistence, it may prosper and increase in wealth, because the labour employed produces more than is consumed, and the surplus goes into accumulation. It

may be that some have too little, and some too much ;
there may be unnatural and unhappy diversities of condition amongst its members, but as a whole it goes on and
prospers without external aid, or such aid as it derives
from abroad in the acquisition of substance is compensated
for by the products of its art or its industry.   Advancing
one step further : just as to the individual it is of no consequence whether that which he produces—be it the product
of the hand or the brain—is suited to his wants, so long as
that which is so suited is produced by others and procured
by exchange ; so to the country it mattered not whether its
products were such as its consumers needed, or such as were
sought by other countries in exchange for that which sup-
·plied these needs.   In such case the producers of that
which procured food and necessaries really stood in the
same position as those who directly produced these essentials; but it was absolutely requisite, not only that the
supplies for consumption could be obtained, but that they
should be obtainable by means of the products of labour
so bestowed as to produce what was disposable in exchange.

Now England, by which is meant the whole United
Kingdom, is just in that position.   For a long series of
years she fed herself, and obtained the further supplies she
needed by exchanging her products for those of other
nations ; and, owing to her capital and power, obtained
them on advantageous terms.   Then, though from the
growth of her population and the increase of individual
consumption she became dependent upon other lands for
her necessary supplies of food and other articles, she was
still independent and prosperous, because those lands required and obtained from her the products they took in
exchange for the supplies they gave.   Now, whether it be
for a time only or in perpetuity, many of the products of
our industry and skill have ceased to be convertible into
those supplies ; and thus the balance has been destroyed.
We are at the present consuming more of that which is

really or conventionally necessary for our subsistence than we are either directly or indirectly producing. Hence the rapid spread of adversity and the deepening cry of distress from all ranks and classes of society.

It is the social aspect of this national condition which forms the proper subject of this Paper, and apology is needed for so long a digression from it. One word more, however, must be pardoned. This statement of the case is fully open to criticism, but to shelve it under the cry of pessimism, anti-free-trade, protectionism or reciprocity-heresy, is as absurd as it is unjust. If the evils exist, and who can deny that they do? let us honestly and carefully try to discover whence they arise and in what manner they may best be dealt with.

It was in the years 1872 and 1873 that our trading prosperity appeared to have reached the greatest elevation it has ever attained, since when to the present time it has been continuously falling. Just as we may best estimate the unknown depth of a mountain valley by comparison with the height of a known hill, so may we best gauge the trading depression by contrasting it with the late elevation. The height of the one we know, for we have been descending rapidly ; whether we have yet touched the lowest depth remains to be seen. There are not wanting grounds for hope that it is so ; but the existence of any solid basis on which to rest a settled belief is not yet clearly visible. During the whole series of years that have elapsed since she entered upon her career as a trading and manufacturing nation, besides accumulating the products of her own surplus labour—the surplus beyond that expended in raising the means of subsistence for her own labourers—England had been drawing to herself a considerable portion of other nations' produce. At one period, by force of arms, conquering peoples weaker or less civilized than herself and taking tribute from them ; not as of old by actual forced contributions to her revenue, but for the support of her officers and servants administering the government, or from

the gains of her trade; both of these to a considerable extent being remitted home in the shape of produce. It is,
however, doubtful whether there is ever any permanent accession of wealth from conquest, for the waste of life, the
outlay of money, and the expenditure of power, really consume more than they obtain. At another, by the discoveries
of the precious metals gaining the power to purchase,
though here again it is more than probable that the labour
expended in searching for—and the lavish waste of—the
gold and silver when found, have really been equal to the
value secured. At other times—and this with varying
seasons of productive or unproductive trade, though, on the
whole, more of the former than the latter—exchanging the
products of her own industry for that of others, or increasing the value of those products by the further employment
of skill in fitting them for use. By all these means there
has been a constant addition to her own wealth. She may
have given ample return to those from whom she drew these
accessions by the introduction of art and science, the establishment of order, the development of resources, and the advancement of civilization, morality, and religion; but there
can be no question that England has, and still does acquire
and retain, by appropriation to the purposes of her own consumption, enjoyment, or accumulation, a large share of the
labouring power of the world. How great a portion it would
be a curious and not uninstructive statistical employment to
estimate and compile. It is to this constant absorption of the
results of other men's labours, as well as to her own internal
progress and appreciation, that England owes the supremacy
she obtained and the social position which so distinctly
marked the period of her inflated prosperity. At first, the
conquerors and the actual residents in, or traders with,
foreign countries or our colonial possessions, were those who
thus became benefited. Then the capitalists and manufacturers through whom were produced the staple articles
of our commerce; then the artisans by whose manual
labour these were created, and the labourers and seamen

employed in their transport, all claimed a share in the profits of our foreign trades. Then followed the owners of land and of the mineral products derived from under the soil, who exacted increased rents and royalties. Following upon these came all those who lived by collecting and distributing what others produced or consumed, and the professional class who ministered to the wants, and lived upon the expenditure of those who thus grew rich. Beyond all these must be named the horde of speculators, many honest and useful in the exercise of their foresight and talents, but many rapacious and dishonest in grasping that which other men had exhausted their bodily and mental powers in producing; swooping into their nets the savings of a lifetime laid by for the support of old age, or the hardly-won provision for those dependent upon the bread-winner whilst living, and that which he left behind him when taken away.

There thus arose a general diffusion of wealth; an almost universal rise of prices; an extravagance of expenditure, not confined to any class; a greed in the race of acquisition, and a recklessness in the means by which it was obtained; an unscrupulousness in the transactions of every-day life which exercised influences of the most unfavourable character upon the conditions in which society existed. Easily acquired wealth was lavishly squandered; dishonest gains were hoarded by the miser, or dissipated by the spendthrift; every form of luxurious living and sensual gratification was adopted, invented, and indulged in. Nor was this all; those who had by the most upright conduct, the most patient exercise of talent, the most assiduous devotion to the lawful employment of their powers become possessed of property or income—and especially those whose fixed incomes admitted of no augmentation—were drawn into an undue expenditure either actually or in desire. Habits were being formed, plans in life pursued, time and substance employed, in methods which, however pleasing and even elevating to the few, were by no means calculated for the real advancement even of those few, still less of the many who form the bulk of the nation.   Just as England herself appropriated more than her fair share of the world's substance, so was her portion of that wealth unequally distributed amongst the different members of her own community.   Extremes of affluence and destitution—the continuance of which are wholly incompatible with any real prosperity—existed side by side.   It would take too long to trace out the relation of cause and effect ; but it is too true, that between the satins of St. James's and the rags of St. Giles's, the luxurious living of Belgravia and Manchester and the squalid misery of the courts and alleys in their immediate proximity, the trifling loungers of Pall Mall and the nightly throngs of the Haymarket, there is a much closer connection than many know or will be disposed to admit.   The social aspect of trade inflation was unsatisfactory in the extreme ; it carried with it the absolute certainty of its own overthrow.

Now the point upon which all this turned was the continued progress of our export trade.   With a constantly increasing population to be fed, and a stationary or retrograde home production of food, our very existence depends upon our ability to produce that which other nations will exchange for food ; and this dependence is the more entire in proportion to the increase of average consumption which has grown up with our growth in wealth.   In like manner with other necessaries, or those things which habit or education lead us to consider to be necessary.   No doubt we have large resources abroad in the shape of debts on which interest is paid, shares in undertakings which may be profitable, earnings and profits remitted by residents abroad ; but there is no reason to think that these have of late years been increasing—rather the reverse.   It is to the results of our export trade that we must look for the means of turning the labour at home which is not employed in producing the necessaries of life into those products to be obtained from abroad. Other conditions may possibly spring up : such a wonderful discovery of new sources of wealth like that of gold in

Australia; some new development of agricultural operations
at home, whereby the labour now employed in other channels
may be diverted to the production of supplies to supersede
imported ones; or some unexpected diminution in our present draughts upon the world's resources. But failing any
such alterations, the decay of our export trade must involve
an entire change in our social condition, and not impro-
bably nor remotely our decadence as a nation. It is with
no intention of maintaining that this decay must necessarily
continue or increase, that on this and on other occasions
the real circumstances are sought out and insisted upon.
Rather is it desired to direct attention to the facts of the
case, so that whatever means can be adopted to alter existing conditions may be taken in hand. What those means
are cannot now be inquired into; but the alterations which
have taken and are taking place in our social condition may
be discussed. A few words, however, as to the way in which
this decay has been brought about.

It would be unreasonable to expect that, however willing
the nations of the world might be in their infancy to depend
upon this country for their manufactured goods and the
articles of luxury they choose to consume, they would continue to purchase them from us by a larger amount of
labour bestowed upon the raising of food and raw materials,
than we bestow upon the finished articles they take in exchange. We have had the honour of being the pioneers
in arts and manufactures, and have had our reward in the
wealth we have acquired. It is now the turn of other
nations to follow in our steps, at least to the extent of supplying their own wants; and this they are sure to do as
they increase in numbers and knowledge. We can have no
hope of retarding this progress, but we may repeat the process by which we have hitherto succeeded in advancing our
own interest—that of civilizing the nations yet existing in
barbarism, of peopling the regions yet uncultivated by
man. We have no right to expect, for instance, that
America will continue to purchase from us the coals and the

iron she has within her own shores, or permit us to fetch
from her the raw cotton her fields produce, and take back
to her the calico or the hosiery to clothe her population;
but we may abstain from exterminating the naked races
who would raise us food in exchange for our clothing. We
may laugh or mourn over the folly to themselves and the
injury to us, of the United States' policy in retarding their
own progress by refusing to take our products in exchange
for their surplus food, until they are able under free trade to
supply their own wants ; but we may not in imitation of this
revert to the suicidal policy of resorting to protection or
reciprocity. It is certainly not in this direction that we
can in any way advance the return of trading prosperity, or
retard the progress of trade decay. It is by the throwing
open of our ports for the reception of whatever the world
will send us, that we have fed our population and enabled
them to cheapen the goods we have to sell; and just in proportion as we stand in need of customers for our manufactured products, must we maintain or extend the facilities
for the interchange of that which each nation can or does
produce in perfection at a low cost.

It is so much easier to affirm the positive than to state
the negative, to observe the object which is displayed in
relief rather than that which is cut in reverse; that it is
hoped what has been said of prosperous trade may, in some
measure, present to view what adverse commerce means.
Yet there are some of the aspects of trade depression which,
in pursuance of the object of this Paper, must be distinctly
set out and briefly enlarged upon.

It would appear that a serious social revolution is im-
pending over us, or rather we may say has already commenced in our midst; and is only not more distinctly visible
because everybody is living in hopes that the present depression is but for a time, and even now gives prospect, as
many think, to a revival of trade. No one can dispute the
vast falling off in the value of our exports. Whether this be
due principally, or only in part, to a diminution of price, and

not of quantity, has been argued elsewhere. Even were it wholly due to the fall of prices, it would still remain true that the nation's resources must be greatly diminished, and the fact that our manufactures can only be sold for so much less money does not alter the state of the case. It is said also that this evil is not confined to England, but has fallen upon other nations as well. Be it so, the effect on their prosperity is not so serious as on ours, because in no other nation is there so large a portion of the community dependent for subsistence upon the proceeds of trade; for none other has to rely so much upon foreign supplies of food. There is also a wide difference in the effect of depressed prices of goods for foreign and for home consumption. The one absolutely lessens the purchasing power of the nation, the other, however it may for a time disturb and afflict the home traders, is really only a question of internal regulation, entailing no loss on the country, though playing an important part in settling or unsettling the social relations of its different members.

The first effect of lesser money return for the same quantity of goods must obviously be felt by the manufacturer, since the standing cost of plant, &c., cannot be materially reduced, and wages do not fall until profits are diminished or altogether cease. It is generally admitted that at the present time few of the manufacturers of our staple exports are keeping up their gains: it is fortunate for many if they are not actually working at a loss. The spending power of this class must thus be greatly lessened. That this is not yet manifested more clearly in their expenditure arises from the vast accumulations of prosperous times having been placed in various investments not yet so completely affected, and that many are actually drawing upon capital to tide over disastrous times. The next in order to suffer are the labouring classes, who are everywhere compelled to accept reduced wages, and thus become able to spend less. These two classes necessarily affect the shopkeepers, from whom they purchase. These, again, the traders and manufacturers from whom they obtain their goods. Then come the landowners, whose largely-increased incomes of late years have been occasioned and sustained by the general desire of those acquiring fortunes to become occupiers of the soil, and the lavish prices which prosperous trade has enabled them to afford. The professional class and all whose receipts come solely out of the incomes of others, having during prosperity been large recipients, must gradually share in the failing wealth of those by whom they have been supported.

So far as actual loss to the nation is concerned, agricultural depression (excepting as it arises from diminished production—and this, owing to the succession of bad harvests, is of immense importance—though not falling within the scope of this Paper) has really nothing to do with it. There can be no ground for believing that for a series of years nature will yield less abundant supplies than formerly ; and so long as on the average equal labour expended upon the soil produces the same return, there is the same amount of sustenance for the population. Not so, however, when our export trade falls off. If it be in quantity, there are fewer hands employed to produce it; and if in price, less return. In fact, the labouring power both employed and unused procures diminished supplies of necessaries, and an actual loss ensues to one or more classes of the community. It is the fewer millions of money which our exports have produced, to be set against the more millions we have expended on imports to meet the growing numbers, and the increased average consumption of those numbers, which makes the real difference between national prosperity or adversity. Should the times recur when the same employment of labour, increasing with the addition to the population, will purchase for us supplies from abroad to a proportionate extent, the social condition of the country may remain unchanged; without such conditions it cannot do so, and even with them such a result is highly improbable.

Let it be supposed that our manufacturers and traders

should have as full employment as before—to secure which there must be an increase in the total amount, not only commensurate with that of the population, but also of the constant ascension from the lower ranks—there is no reason to suppose that it can ever be as profitable as it was. The producing power of the world has been and still is increasing in a higher ratio than the consuming need, and hence producers can never expect to command the same surplus of profit for themselves on the sale of their manufactures or the conduct of their trade. The continuous and probably increasing loss of income to the higher classes will necessarily alter their style of living, and with this their relative social condition. But other causes put in operation by this prime mover will all tend in the same direction. The very largeness of the mercantile and manufacturing firms which have come into existence has led to the formation of companies and the general spirit of co-operation, which distributes incomes amongst larger numbers. Diminished incomes necessitate a resort to employment by many who have hitherto had money to spend without earning it, so that more will press forward to divide the profits earned. All the old methods of making a business are becoming overtasked. The peculiar means this country possessed of drawing to it the trade of other nations are now being shared with them; and amongst ourselves it will rarely happen that any new business will exclusively remain long in the hands of those who first start it. When all were full of employment the special ground which one man or firm occupied, as we have many instances in our large trades, was left to himself; now competitors spring up on every side. The possession of capital gives far less power than it did before the existence of facilities for obtaining money wherewith to manufacture or speculate. It is thus tolerably certain that the enormous fortunes hitherto so frequently made will not arise, nor will our landowners have the same large amounts at their disposal. In every way the social condition of both must thus be changed.

With such materially reduced expenditure must go the means of those who have lived upon the trade of the rich—shopkeepers and other distributors will be lessened in number, and their gains contracted. These then will press upon the working classes, for whom fewer employments will offer and to whom lesser wages will be given. There will be less money to spend and more frugality to be exercised.

Another cause will, it is to be hoped, come into extensive operation. It is impossible not to have seen that in all classes of society the success of those who have prospered in life has in great measure been owing to the ignorance, the folly, or the vice of those who have failed. The advantages and opportunities offered to the many have been embraced by the few; and excepting in instances of exalted genius, rare skill, or extraordinary circumstances, few men would have risen to eminence or fortune but for the indisposition or incapacity of their compeers to divide with them the success they have obtained. If education, morality, and religion are to increase, many more must be qualified to obtain the prizes, and there must be a more equal division of the benefits which man's labour, his own or others', can create. If this be true as regards individuals and families amongst ourselves, it is also true as regards nations. England's prosperity has been owing not only to the industry, the skill, and the energy she has put forth at home and abroad, but very much to the folly of other nations in neglecting the resources they possessed and wasting their substance in war. We too have had our share of this in time past, and are not free from its indulgence now; but since the days which closed with Waterloo, and again with the termination of the Crimean War, all our rivals in manufacture and commerce—America, France, Italy, Germany, Austria, and Russia, as well as every minor State, excepting perhaps Switzerland, whether in the East or the West, or this side of the Atlantic or the other—have retarded their own progress, and thus left room for us to advance, by the wholesale destruction of life and the products of life's labour. It is the peace which France seems determined to enjoy which is enabling her to exercise her powers in supplying so much to our markets, and yet take less from us; whilst the United States, no longer cursed with slavery or dissevered in interests, is able to advance rapidly in furnishing herself with manufactured goods, and to spare us of the food she raises. To these happy causes are owing much of the check which our manufacturing efforts are receiving.

It is not forgotten that with these social changes—should the present promise be realized—there will be a large addition to the present overstocked labour market, and that the problems will have to be solved how that labour is to find employment, and how those who yield it are to find food. But it must be remembered that with less wasteful and luxurious living, whether it be in the destruction or misuse of food, or the awful extravagance in drink which are indulged in by both rich and poor, there will be enough to fill many mouths. There is a certainty that with lesser wages and smaller profits, together with greater honesty in the processes of manufacture and the conduct of trade, we shall find for a time at least many customers, especially amongst the least civilized people, who will be ready to grow food wherewith to purchase our clothing and other productions. It is not impossible that our own soil may be made to yield a larger supply; and if that fail, who shall estimate the countless multitudes for which food can be raised in our colonies when our superabundant labourers go forth to people their fertile valleys and their sun-clad hills ?

To come back to the point from which we started, England has for a long series of years appropriated and expended in consumption and accumulation the proceeds of a larger share of the world's labour than she has herself contributed. This she has been enabled to do through the force of her Anglo-Saxon character, her early discovery of the mineral treasures she possessed, and her power to utilize

them ; her indomitable perseverance in seeking out and
occupying new places for the employment of her energies,
and new markets for the sale of her products. By the maintenance of peace and the cultivation of intercourse with all
the world to a larger extent than any other nation which
ever existed, by shaking off the trammels in which her trade
was fettered, and thus giving the widest expansion to all
her powers.   Possessing, however, no special monopoly of
any of these gifts, her success has induced other nations—
especially those to whom she has herself given birth—to
follow more or less in her footsteps, and thus to become
suppliers of their own wants first, and then competitors for
the custom of the world.   Concurrently with this, the
wealth which has fallen to her share has been unequally
divided amongst her own children ; deservedly so, because
the industrious, the wise, the thrifty, have only done to their
fellows what England has done to the world.   Nevertheless,
the result has been an undue exaltation of wealth, an undue desire for its possession, and the use of undue means
for its acquisition.   This struggle for existence—for the
enjoyment by each of more than he himself produces—has per-
vaded all classes, and both led to, and been fostered by, the
inflated prosperity of the few years centring in 1871-72.
Society has become divided into unnatural extremes, and a
social condition grown up which is for the benefit of neither.
It is utterly impossible for it to continue without the infusion
of new life, or the obtaining of new support.   These are to be
found if sought for; but it is equally improbable that society
can either continue on its old lines or fall back upon them
again.   If trade and agricultural depression together drive
us into new channels of thought and action, prompt us to
give play to new motives, and inculcate upon us higher
principles by which to regulate our conduct ; they will prove
the seed of a richer harvest of happiness, honour, and real
glory, than all the accumulations of the past have ever
yielded.

XIII.

EXTENDED COLONIZATION A NECESSITY TO THE MOTHER COUNTRY.[1]

THE Paper which I have had the pleasure and privilege of preparing for this evening's meeting differs somewhat from those which are usually presented to the members of the Colonial Institute, inasmuch as it neither contains information respecting any portion of our Colonial Empire, nor does it treat of the subject from a Colonial point of view. It is the sequel to a series of papers read in other places on the trading condition and prospects of this country, out of which it would seem that there arises a necessity for action, with special reference to the advantages the Colonies offer as helps to the Parent State. Yet so closely are the interests of the children bound up with those of the parent, that whatever may prove to be for its welfare should also be the source or occasion of benefit to them. Some apology is needed from one who has so recently become a member of the Institute for attempting to deal with so wide and important a subject. I throw myself on your indulgence for the incomplete manner in which it is treated, with the full expectation that it may at least serve to promote a discussion that will have some influence in guiding public opinion, and it may be, in invoking legislative action towards effecting the desired end.

I. The population of the United Kingdom in the year

[1] Read at the Opening Meeting of Session 1879-80, of The Royal Colonial Institute, November 25, 1879.

1871, that in which the last census was taken, numbered
31,484,661. The estimated increase since that time has
been 2,671,452, and a like rate of growth between this and
1881, when the next enumeration will take place, would
give a further increase of 727,965, bringing up the total to
very close upon 35 millions, for whom food, raiment, and
shelter must necessarily be found.   In 1871 there were
3,831,054 acres of land appropriated to the growth of wheat,
the calculated produce of which being 53,620,000 cwts., was
supplemented by importations from abroad to the extent of
43,310,000 cwts.   Last year there were 3,381,701 acres,
yielding, it is supposed, 55,350,000 cwts., and the foreign
supplies were 58,760,000 cwts.   This year the cultivation
has been reduced to 3,056,428 acres, and it is probable that,
owing to the bad harvest, the whole yield will not much exceed
the half of last year's production; whilst the foreign importations have already reached to 57,000,000 cwts., and there
are yet two months of the year to run.   Mr. Caird puts the
annual home produce at 55,000,000 cwts., and the quantity
taken from abroad at an equal weight, thus giving 110,000,000
cwts. as the present consumption.

Other cereal products to some extent aid the supply of
wheat, but, roughly speaking, they may be said to about
compensate for the wheat devoted to other uses than that
of human food; and some 3,000,000 cwts. of rice are imported, of which, however, only a portion is eaten.

Of meat it is supposed that 25,370,000 cwts. were raised
in 1871, and an additional quantity of 3,960,000 cwts. imported.   The same calculation gives 25,000,000 cwts. of
home produce for last year, and 6,990,000 cwts. obtained
from abroad.   Butter and cheese may probably be taken at
3,000,000 cwts., both now and for 1871, and the milk consumed as equivalent to 6,000,000 cwts. more.   Adding this
to the meat may make the weight of home-raised animal
food 34,000,000 cwts.   Of foreign butter and cheese, including lard, the importations were 2,930,000 cwts. in 1871,
and 4,580,000 cwts. in 1878; together affording a present

annual weight of 39,000,000 cwts. of animal food furnished for the use of the whole population.

Potatoes are another important article of diet, of which probably 100,000,000 cwts. are usually grown at home, whilst the importations were, in 1871, 850,000 cwts., and in 1878, 8,745,000 cwts.

If we go back for another ten years to 1861 it will be seen that the population was then only 28,974,362, the importations of foreign wheat 36,260,000 cwts., of meat 1,810,000 cwts., of butter, &c., 2,010,000 cwts., and of potatoes 112,374 cwts. There are no records from which it is practicable—very satisfactorily—to calculate the various home products for that year, but it may be assumed that there were no great variations from the present average amounts.

These several descriptions of food, however, have varying degrees of life-sustaining powers, according as they are rich or otherwise in the flesh-forming constituents they contain. For instance, it is generally admitted that 480 lbs. of wheat per annum are capable of supporting one person, whilst 550 lbs. of meat would be necessary for the same purpose, and that 10 lbs. of potatoes go no further than 1 lb. of wheat. In estimating, therefore, the extent to which the whole will avail in feeding our population, as well as in ascertaining the proportion in which we are dependent upon home and foreign supplies, it becomes necessary to reduce them to a common standard, and thus to express their worth as food in that of wheat. It is not necessary here to show the several calculations. The basis on which these, as well as the estimates of quantities, rest, will be found in several papers by Mr. Caird, Mr. H. Thompson, and Dr. Playfair. Of their experience and judgment I availed myself in preparing a paper containing copious details, which will be found in the "Transactions of the Manchester Statistical Society for 1877."[1] Some extracts from tables given in a recent treatise published by Mr. Caird, near the close of last year, form the following table, and I may perhaps be allowed

[1] Ante, pp. 76-102.

to appeal with some confidence to the figures set forth in my
own paper when they are corroborated to so great an extent
by the calculations of one who is justly deemed an authority
in these matters :—

*Quantities and Values of Home and Foreign Agricultural Food Produce
consumed annually, as estimated by Mr. Caird.*[1]

[In million £'s to two decimals.]

	Quantities.			Values.		
	Home.	Foreign.	Total.	Home.	Foreign.	Total.
	cwts.	cwts.	cwts.	£	£	£
Wheat	55·00	55·00	110·00	32·19	32·19	64·38
Barley	44·00	11·00	55·00	19·80	4·95	24·75
Oats	64·00	12·00	76·00	28·80	5·40	34·20
Peas and Beans	14·00	5·00	19·00	6·30	2·25	8·55
Indian Corn	—	20·00	20·00	—	7·00	7·00
Total Corn	177·00	103·00	280·00	87·09	51·79	138·88
Potatoes	111·00	5·00	116·00	16·65	·75	17·40
Meat, &c.	24·50	6·30	30·80	87·00	22·05	109·05
Cheese and Butter.	3·00	3·10	6·10	13·50	14·00	27·50
Milk	—	—	—	26·00	—	26·00
				230·24	88·59	318·83

Reducing, then, the other articles to their equivalents in
wheat, and adding the whole together, it will be seen that
the two years 1871 and 1878 compare thus :—

[1] " The Landed Interest and its Supply of Food."   By James Caird,
C.B., F.R.S.   1879.

[In million cwts. to two decimals.]

	Home.	Foreign.	Total.	Per cent.	
				Home.	Foreign.
1871.					
Wheat..........................	53·62	43·31	96·93	55·32	44·68
Meat....................equal to	22·16	3·45	25·61	86·53	13·47
Dairy produce......... ,,	8·00	2·58	10·58	77·07	22·93
Potatoes.............. ,,	10·00	·09	10·09	99·11	·89
Wheat—value of total.........	94·	49·	143·	66·	34·
1878.					
Wheat..........................	55·35	58·76	114·11	48·50	51·50
Meat....................equal to	21·82	5·74	27·56	79·17	20·83
Dairy produce......... ,,	8·0	3·72	11·72	68·26	31·74
Potatoes.............. ,,	10·00	·87	10·87	92·00	8·00
Wheat—value of total.........	95·	69·	164·	58·	42·

For 1861 the totals would probably be :

96·	39·	135·	71·	29·

Dividing these totals of 135, 143, and 164 million cwts. amongst the existing population, they would show a supply of nutriment equivalent to wheat for each individual of 522 lbs. in 1861; 512 lbs. in 1871; and 538 lbs. in 1878; or an average of 524 lbs. Allowing for the export in various forms of prepared food, of perhaps 5 per cent., and for some waste, this weight comes singularly near to the 480 lbs. computed to be necessary for each person, thus supporting the presumed accuracy of the calculations.

But besides these principal articles of food there are many others of smaller importance—eggs, vegetables, fruit, &c.—both of home and foreign production, which aid in supporting life ; and many, such as beverages, both alcoholic and other, without which, according to the habits of the people, life would be scarcely endurable. The former class is chiefly of home growth, although the foreign is rapidly increasing in relative importance. The latter are mostly of foreign production. These are not capable of being dealt with in quantities, as we have previously done with the staple articles, yet a comparison of their collected values at the two periods may be serviceable; always remembering that for specific dates the money value is not an altogether safe guide, because of fluctuations in prices. For a series of years they are safer. A table of these extracted from the paper already referred to, and continued to 1879, will be found at page 79. One of a similar character taken from the Agricultural Statistics of the Board of Trade recently issued, which has this year for the first time thus grouped the various articles of food and shown their value, is as follows :—

Values of Food Imports from 1859-78, arranged in Groups, as shown in Official Abstract of Agricultural Returns, prepared by Mr. Giffen, of the Board of Trade.

[In million £'s to two decimals.]

Year.	Total Value.	Live Animals. I.	Meat, Cheese, &c. II.	Wheat and Flour. III.	Cereal, Sugar, Spices, &c. IV.	Beverages. V.	Fruit and Vegetables. VI.	Miscellaneous. VII.
1859	56·66	1·63	5·18	11·11	20·98	13·21	3·09	1·46
'60	78·79	2·12	9·05	20·87	25·45	16·06	2·93	2·31
'61	84·67	2·21	10·37	24·00	27·13	15·44	3·47	2·05
'62	91·00	1·89	11·82	28·59	24·47	18·21	3·60	2·42
'63	83·62	2·65	12·07	15·54	25·61	21·47	4·02	2·26
'64	82·83	4·28	13·08	13·51	25·61	20·63	3·64	2·08
'65	83·04	6·55	13·65	12·40	23·68	20·55	3·50	2·71
'66	94·63	5·84	14·93	16·78	28·06	22·70	3·79	2·53
'67	104·65	4·15	13·39	28·50	28·97	21·94	4·20	3·50
'68	98·13	2·70	14·17	24·90	33·77	15·38	4·64	2·57
'69	110·72	5·30	16·55	23·30	34·42	23·01	4·82	3·32
'70	106·42	4·66	16·19	19·65	35·75	23·53	4·27	2·37
'71	125·68	5·66	18·56	26·82	38·20	27·53	5·32	3·59
'72	141·53	4·39	19·35	30·26	47·93	28·77	7·96	2·87
'73	149·48	5·42	24·38	34·39	43·60	31·00	7·43	3·26
'74	147·20	5·26	26·33	30·92	45·69	28·72	7·10	3·18
'75	158·65	7·33	28·04	32·38	47·75	31·61	7·55	3·99
'76	158·77	7·26	31·45	27·92	49·25	30·81	8·77	3·31
'77	178·23	6·01	31·23	40·69	55·50	30·45	10·22	4·13
'78	167·36	7·45	33·98	34·22	50·97	28·08	9·48	3·18
Total..	2,302·06	92·76	363·77	496·75	712·79	469·10	109·80	57·09

Note.—The above Table includes all Imported Produce, whether for Home Consumption or Export, and does not comprise articles such as Guano and Chemicals, employed in the production of Food.

The totals which the table (page 79) displays for the two years stand thus :—

[In million £'s to two decimals.]

	1871.	1878.
Animal Food	£23·53	£39·98
Cereals	42·60 or 30·86	60·11 or 47·11
Sugar, fruit, &c.	22·05	29·15
Beverages, alcoholic	9·39 or 21·13	7·84 or 20·84
„ other	9·40	12·08
Miscellaneous	11·03	17·84
	£118·00	£167·00

The corrected figures for cereal and alcoholic are the result of a deduction from the one and addition to the other of the value of the grain employed in distillation and brewing, thereby entirely changing its character.

Mr. Caird thus compares certain of the above articles for the past year with those of home growth :—

	Home.	Foreign.
Corn	£87·09	£51·79
Potatoes	16·65	·75
Meat	87·00	22·05
Cheese and butter	13·50	14·00
	£204·24	£88·59

In one respect these figures fail to convey an accurate idea of the dependence upon foreign supplies, since a large portion of the home meat and dairy produce is fed upon imported corn and other food, or on grass and roots which owe much to the aid of the manures and chemicals included under the head of miscellaneous in my foreign estimate. It may not be too much to say that one-half of the two items, cereal and miscellaneous, say £38 millions, should be deducted from Mr. Caird's home estimate, thereby reducing the total to £166 millions—very nearly the amount at which the foreign supplies are valued by me.

Mr. Caird himself says in the book from which these particulars are quoted : " We now receive our bread in equal proportions from our own fields and those of the

stranger ; " and again : " This country thus derives from
foreign lands not only half its bread and nearly one-fourth
of its dairy produce, but must also depend on the foreigner
for almost the entire addition that may be further required
by an increase of its population." Nearly two years previously it had been stated by myself : " It may be safely
inferred that our bread is equally of home and foreign
origin ; " and, " The conclusion thus arrived at would appear to be that for absolute sustenance we rely upon home
and foreign produce in somewhere about the proportion
of three to two fifths." Also : " On this computation, of
the 33 million inhabitants of the United Kingdom, 18 millions may be sustained on food grown at home, and 15
millions on that received from abroad." Since that date
the proportions have somewhat altered, with increased
numbers and larger supplies.

Fortified by this concurrent testimony and the figures
which have been adduced—at a length and in detail
which must have been somewhat tedious, and would have
been unnecessary but for the extreme importance of attaining to right conclusions on the subject—it is not too much
to say that of the 35 millions which the next census will
show as inhabiting these islands, at least 17 millions must
be fed on food which is not produced at home. Furthermore, that if the present rate of increase continue—since
the whole of it must rely upon foreign supplies—in another
ten years (and such a term is not too long for our statesmen
to forecast) the seventeen will have grown to twenty, and
thus fully if not more than one-half the inhabitants of the
United Kingdom will be absolutely dependent for their
existence upon foreign food.

II. If, then, the food produced at home suffices for the
wants of little more than half its inhabitants, two questions arise : first, whether it is possible so to economize its
use as to make it serve for the sustenance of a larger
number ; secondly, what probability there is of success in
attempting to increase its amount.

There can be little or no doubt that the prosperity which marked our trading and manufacturing progress for many years has tended to much waste. Luxurious living on the part of the rich has in many ways led to the consumption or destruction of some amount of food, the distribution of which would have supported more lives, and in many households there is an actual waste which it is painful to observe whilst there is any real destitution in the land. The extremes of high and low living are far greater than they ought to be, yet it is pretty clear that any changes in this respect would but equalize consumption, since for those who consume unduly there are surely as many who suffer real deprivation or absolute want. We are not concerned now with the causes or the remedy, simply with the fact, and whether it have any bearing on the extent of available supplies. There is also an extravagant waste of food from ignorance, and indifference of and to the best kinds of food, the best mode of cooking it, and the proper seasons for its enjoyment; but here, again, it is doubtful whether the diffusion of sound information or the adoption of right principles would produce any other result than equalization. If there are many who are badly fed from misuse, there are surely as many who are underfed because what they have is not wholesome or sufficient. Adversity may enforce the judicious use of the food we possess, and it is certain that there is enough supplied, were it properly employed, to support vigorous life in all our people, but not more than may be beneficially consumed by the whole. The gain would be great in health and strength, and the prolongation of life, more than in any power to sustain a larger number. One exception, however, must be made to these remarks—they do not apply to the wasteful destruction of food by its conversion into alcoholic drink. A series of elaborate calculations show that during the twenty years ending with 1876, 584,000,000 cwts., giving an average of nearly 30,000,000 cwts. per annum of grain were thus converted into beer and spirits. A considerable portion of this would be wheat and oats, capable of direct application for human food—all of it might have been converted into meat and eggs for the same purpose. Chemists tell us that the actual amount of nutriment left when thus changed in its character is insignificant, and we are justified in assuming that as food the quantity thus destroyed would be ample to maintain healthy life at the very least in some 3,000,000 persons. Could a change to this extent only— which would still leave untouched all the imported alcoholic drinks—be effected in the drinking customs of our country, this number might be transferred from the foreign to the home-supported portion of the population. Further than this, it does not appear that any better employment or more equal distribution of the existing home-raised food would assist the land in providing for the wants of those who occupy it.

The question whether any alterations in the conditions under which agricultural operations are carried on would enable the land to support a greater number, is one of much wider range, and involves, as does also the one we have just left, not only the possibility, but, still more, the probability of such changes being affected.

There are many who believe that amendment of the land laws would be followed by increased productiveness of the soil, because of the greater facilities which might be afforded for its profitable working, and hence the larger amount of capital which might be drawn to this class of investments. Granted that this would be the effect of the desired legislation, it does not therefore follow that a larger number of people would be thereby sustained. More would depend upon the kind of produce which would be raised in enlarged· quantity. Of all the edibles for the growth of which our soils and climate are suited, the potato is that which will feed the greatest number per acre; but then the race it produces and sustains is deficient in power, and if measured not by numbers but by capacity for work it yields less than others. The legumes are coming into credit as admirably adapted for economically sustaining both life and strength;

but, taken altogether, there is little likelihood that wheat will be deposed from its supremacy as the staff of life, whether from the weight which each acre will produce as compared with other descriptions of food, or from its fitness for man's consumption. Now, this is just the kind of crop which seems the most likely of all to be displaced by that of foreign growth. The acreage devoted to its cultivation has for years past been gradually diminishing, and the tendency of the present day is towards its restriction, if not its abandonment, as an article for the home farmer to raise. In 1871 there were 3,831,054 acres growing wheat, in 1879 only 3,056,428, and of this diminution 325,273 took place as between this and the last year. The throwing of land out of wheat culture into that of any other description of food, however desirable or profitable it may be for the cultivator, lessens the number per acre which it can feed. This is especially the case with a change from arable to grazing purposes, since for every acre of land on which wheat is grown, eight will be required to give the same amount of nourishment in the shape of meat. Fruit and vegetables, again, however desirable it may be on the score of health and enjoyment to extend their use, will not contribute anything like the same degree of sustenance as would be afforded by the wheat of which they take the place. A prosperous and happy people will seek for more meat and green food, and be enabled to obtain more wheat from distant places, thus materially diminishing the sustaining power of the home soil.

Again, an increasing population and thriving trade absorb more land for the erection of buildings, the means of transit, and open spaces for recreation, all of which must be obtained at the expense of the food the land can bring forth. There is thus every reason to wish for a restriction in the extent of surface thus employed, unless indeed it can be obtained by the reclamation of that which is waste; and there is no reason to expect more will be done in this direction than will be absorbed in others.

It is as yet open to doubt whether high farming and improved machinery or modes of cultivation will hold their ground against the vast tracts of unoccupied land being every day rendered available in other countries, and the increased facilities for bringing their produce to our markets. If they do, it will almost certainly be by the production of such foods as need to be raised near at hand, which are just those that require the larger space for growth in proportion to their food-value.

There is one direction in which we are sadly deficient, namely, in not retaining and returning to the soil that which we have taken from it after its purpose has been served. True husbandry would teach that all refuse, whether animal or human, should be replaced rather than be sent to poison our water-courses and then be lost in the sea. Nature destroys nothing, simply changes its constitution ; and with all the inorganic matter we are continually bringing to the surface, where it can, through the instrumentality of vegetable life, be organized, and all the organic matter we are continually bringing from abroad, our soil ought to be growing richer instead of poorer, and in this way be able to minister more largely to our wants.

On the whole, therefore, we cannot expect the life-sustaining capabilities of the land to increase. Unless continued adversity should drive us to the use of simpler food, there is little reason to expect that an actually larger amount of nutriment will be raised at home; but rather, every reason for believing that each succeeding year will diminish our power to support increasing numbers upon the food which our own islands are able to give us.

Nor are we better able, without resorting to the produce of other countries, to clothe than to feed our people. All the cotton, as well as silk and jute, are of foreign growth, and so is a large proportion of the flax, leather, and wool employed in the manufacture of wearing apparel and household requisites. The following figures show the value, on an average of the past twelve years, of the imports of

materials retained for use and manufacture, with the portion
of them left after deduction of the estimated value contained
in the exported articles, and the corresponding values of
the home produce :—

[In million £'s to two decimals.]

| | Foreign. | | Home Produce. |
	Imports.	Home Consumption.	
	£	£	£
Cotton...........................	42·23	9·72	nil.
Flax.............................	5·16	3·02	2·00
Jute.............................	2·47	2·19	nil.
Silk	15·18	12·40	nil.
Wool............................	15·55	5·06	8·50
	80·59	32·39	10·50

It thus appears that probably one-fourth only of the
materials from which our clothing is manufactured are of
home growth. For the erection of buildings and manufacture of furniture, we are more than ever compelled to use
wood of foreign growth.

III. Before passing to the consideration of the sources
from which the deficiency in our home supplies is met, we
may briefly inquire whether there is any probability of
lessened demands upon these supplies in coming years, or
whether, in truth, the present rate of increase of consumers
is not lower than we have every reason to expect it will be
in the future.

Dr. Farr, in his report to the Registrar-General of the
mortality in England during the ten years 1861-70, points
out that in the healthy districts of England the annual deaths
are only 17 to the 1,000 living ; and though the number
for the whole kingdom raises the average to 22 per 1,000,
there is a gradual approximation to the lower rate, any
excess over which " is not due to the mortality incident to
human nature, but to foreign causes to be repelled, and by

hygienic expedients conquered : " the overplus due to the operation of these preventable causes being 115,833 out of 479,450, or very nearly one-fourth.   With the rapid spread of sounder views on subjects relating to health and the preservation of life, together with the greater attention now being paid to sanitary arrangements, it is not too much to hope that the diminution by death will be less than it has been ; nor is it altogether utopian to expect that the remarkable progress of public opinion in favour of temperance will not only liberate from destruction a considerable amount of food, but that the devotion of this food to its proper uses will tend to the conservation of life, and thus to swell the numbers for whom provision has to be made.   Furthermore, if the nation is at all to advance in morality and religion its rate of increase in population will assuredly not be thereby lowered.   On every ground we may expect that the causes at present in operation, and their probable extension, will lead to the multiplication rather than the diminution of the human species.

It is important here to notice that unless some means be found for adding to the number of those to whom agricultural operations furnish employment, whatever increase does take place in the population must all serve to swell the ranks of those who depend upon trading and manufacturing pursuits for their means of subsistence.   Of the 31,484,661 enumerated at the last census, 2,989,154 are classified as agricultural, and 6,425,137 as industrial; these numbers including not only the actual workers, but also their wives, children, or other dependents.   In the next census the industrial may probably amount to eight millions, if we include a fair proportion of the commercial class who have to deal with the products of industrial occupations.   A growth of population at the same rate during the succeeding ten years would raise the number to twelve millions, requiring for their employment that every branch of manufacturing industry must be extended at least fifty per cent.   The enormous surplus of goods thus created to seek for purchasers, would require our export trade to be doubled or trebled. Such an enlargement is quite within the bounds of possibility; but would it be so much for the prosperity of the country generally thus to convert it into one huge workshop, with all its attendant overcrowding and other evils at the seat of manufacture, rather than to disperse its inhabitants to found free and happy colonial homes?

IV. The next stage, then, in our investigation must be into the methods by which those for whom our own soil fails to produce the needful food are supplied with this and the other necessaries of life, and how far those or other methods are likely to continue sufficient for the present population, and to keep pace with its future growth.

It clearly matters little towards this end in what manner individual labour is employed, so long as its purpose is to procure what is required, and that this aim is realized. A ton of coal or of iron, though useless in itself as food, is of equal value to a hundredweight of wheat or of meat, so long as the one is interchangeable for the other; but loses all its value when this ceases. In the earlier stages of our commercial history, this country not only produced food enough for all its inhabitants, but had some to spare wherewith it could procure the various articles it chose to obtain from abroad; and up to the period when the food produced or retained at home sufficed for all who had to eat it, it was not their existence, but their comfort, their welfare, or their wealth which depended upon the continuance of the nation's trade. From the moment when it became necessary to make use of foreign food, it also became essential that our foreign trade should be made, and its extension with the same rapidity as the population increased could alone save us from starvation. The following figures, taken from the official tables for the last twelve years, will show that our exports (of all articles) attained their maximum in 1872, and our imports not till 1877, so that between these years we had a continually increasing balance against us. Since 1878 both have been decreasing, the imports more

than the exports, thus slightly decreasing the balance.
Certain corrections, however, have to be made by deductions
from the imports, because we do not really pay for them
the whole sum at which they are valued on arrival; and
additions to the exports, because we receive for them more
than their cost on departure.   It is well, therefore, to show
side by side the official figures and the revised estimate.
There is room for difference of opinion as to how far the
revision given is correct, and much controversy has arisen
on this subject, but substantially there is not much difference
of variation amongst those who have given most attention
to the calculations.

[In millions of £'s sterling.]

Year.	Official Values.		Revised Estimate.		
	Imports.	Exports.	Imports.	Exports.	Excess of Imports.
1867	230	181	205	188	17
'68	247	180	220	187	33
'69	248	190	221	196	25
'70	259	199	231	207	24
'71	271	223	240	230	10
'72	296	256	263	266	—3
'73	315	255	281	267	14
'74	312	240	278	251	27
'75	316	223	281	233	48
'76	319	201	284	209	75
'77	341	199	304	208	96
'78	316	193	281	202	79
'79	306	192	272	201	71

It was contended by the extreme school of political
economists that the imports, however much in excess,
must really be paid for by the exports, and therefore, that
their magnitude only shows the profit that accrues from the
exchange.   But the events of the last few years, and the
extreme depression of our trade, must surely show the
fallacy of this theory.   It is now generally admitted that
we have been liquidating the balances against us by the

sale of bonds and other securities accumulated in the times of our prosperity; and the recent rise in the Bank rate is due to the apprehension that America, from whom we are large purchasers, especially of food, whilst she buys little or nothing from us, having re-obtained possession of her bonds, &c., will now demand payment in gold.

Others, again, assert that the dividends and earnings accruing to this country from its Colonial and Foreign investments and trade are equivalent to the deficiency. There are no means of ascertaining even approximately to how much these receipts may amount ; no doubt they are large, but it is more than probable that, as our Colonial investments are continually going on, very much of that which would otherwise be applicable to payment for our purchased imports is really expended on loans and goods invested abroad, and thus they become additions to our capital rather than disposable income.

The important bearing which these questions have upon the ability of this country to sustain its people by its foreign trade will be seen in the figures, which show how largely the increase in our imports arises from our purchases of food ; this increase in the later years being really greater than it appears to be, on account of the low prices which have prevailed :—

[In millions of £'s sterling.]

1867	101	1871	118	1875	157
1868	105	1872	136	1876	159
1869	106	1873	147	1877	177
1870	100	1874	143	1878	167

It will be specially noted that whereas in 1867 our exports of British produce and manufacture exceeded our imports of food by £80,000,000, last year the excess was but £26,000,000, a sum quite insufficient to pay for the raw materials of foreign growth which are worked up into so large a portion of the manufactured goods we export.   In short, that at the present time the whole products of the labour expended and the capital employed in British industries for exportation, fail to realize enough to pay for the food we import for consumption. Let the figures be examined and their import scrutinized in what way we will, the conclusion is irresistibly forced upon us, that at the present moment England is unable to provide food for her people either from the produce of her own soil, or by the exchange of her manufactures and produce.

But it will be answered that these are times of universal depression; the whole world is suffering as well as we. That we have a great advantage, in that the savings of the past will tide us over the time of ebb, and that a glorious flood of prosperity awaits us in the future. The reply is twofold. Even if it be true that others are suffering as well as we, it is not to the same extent, nor is it so likely to continue with them as with us. It is not to the same extent, for, with few exceptions, the trading and manufacturing interests in other countries are the minority, with us they are the majority. We are essentially a productive and commercial nation; we have been the manufacturers for the world, but are every day becoming less exclusively so since others have discovered that they possess the same sources of mineral wealth as we do. They have increased in numbers and grown in wealth; they have learnt by our experience, profited by our skill, are copying and improving upon our processes, and are determined no longer to be dependent upon us for that which they can produce for themselves. There may be some revival of trade; let us welcome the gladdening symptoms which are showing themselves at the present moment, but not deceive ourselves by over-estimating their importance or believing that the inflation of 1872-3 is about to return. If the figures which have been produced, and the arguments by which they have been supported, are of any value, they can scarcely fail to establish the fact, that on financial grounds alone there is a necessity for extended emigration. We have hitherto been parting with thousands; it must now be by hundreds of thousands, even if not by millions.

V. Weighty reasons also why an extensive emigration is necessary, are to be drawn from the social and moral condition in which large masses of our population are found to exist. The rapid and continuous expansion of our manufacturing concerns, together with the consequent growth of our trade, have caused a continual drain from the country; and the congregation of increasing numbers in the towns, which both on the sea-coasts and in the centres of industry, have been growing with unexampled rapidity. It is in these that the additions to the population mostly take place; and to find employment year by year for those who are swelling the ranks of our artisans and labourers will require not only the maintenance of our present trade and manufactures, but such an enlargement as the most sanguine can scarcely expect to see. The healthy arrangement of dwelling-houses, and the adoption of sanitary improvements, become more difficult in proportion to the density of the population congregated within limited areas, and demand an expenditure the burden of which has been unwillingly borne even in times of the greatest prosperity, and in adverse times becomes the occasion of much outcry from the ratepayers. The crowding together of large numbers, and the distance from open spaces and fresh air, have a most injurious effect upon both health and character. Something has been done of late by the widening of streets and the multiplication of breathing-grounds, but these require continued expenditure, and after all scarcely keep pace with the additional necessity. It is only those who make it their business to visit the haunts of the poor, and the homes of even the better class of our labouring population, who know the wretchedness of overcrowding, insufficient ventilation, and deficient means for the removal of refuse; or understand how these undermine the health and lower the moral standard of those who exist rather than live. To these are to be attributed most of the addiction to drink and the want of morality that fill our poor-houses and hospitals, our gaols and lunatic asylums. There are

festering sores here which all our costly efforts fail to heal.
There are hot-beds of vice, infidelity, and disaffection which
may lie dormant whilst work is tolerably plentiful and wages
reasonably good ; but may become active under the strain
of long-continued depression such as we have lately passed
through, and from the recurrence of which we are by no
means safe.   We are wisely erecting schools, and giving
better training to the young, but education, while it cannot
cure these evils, will but render more dangerous to the
welfare of society those who, lacking employment and
suffering want, have every inducement to discontent and
disloyalty.   It is painful to think how much time and
money, how much philanthropic effort and heartfelt sym-
pathy, how much religious zeal and untiring energy, are
absolutely wasted in merely palliating the evils they are
powerless to overcome.   It may be doubted whether anything but a general breaking up of associations such as
extensive emigration would cause, will prevent the growth,
and ultimately the manifestation, of such disorders as are
utterly inconsistent with real national prosperity.

VI. Such being the condition of our agricultural and
manufacturing industries at home, as well as of our trading
relations with the rest of the world, let us for a moment
consider what would happen supposing that through some
extraordinary convulsion of nature there were an upheaval
in the Western Ocean of a cluster of islands, or even a
whole continent, whose situation should be as contiguous
to the shores of Ireland as the Emerald Isle itself is to the
Mersey.   Let us imagine further, that amongst these
islands were to be found some with a tropical climate suited
for the production of the sweets and the spices that we get
from the East and the West; some with broad acres of
pasture capable of supporting and fattening the cattle and
sheep our Englishmen cannot well do without; others with
the soil of California or Manitoba, bringing forth luxurious
crops of wheat, and the various cereals without which we
can scarcely live; others dotted with magnificent forest

trees, or the humbler plants which, whether for food or medicine, minister so much to our needs, and furnish the raw materials from which we manufacture our clothing and drape our apartments; that in others, beneath the soil, or cropping to the surface, were seen minerals like those which constitute so large a portion of our wealth. Let us again conceive of these new-found lands as tenanted by flocks and herds, their rivers teeming with life, the air swarming with fowl and game, in fact, with every form of animated nature known to man, but all destitute of human beings, and thus waiting the advent of him for whose use they were all created. And that nothing might be wanting to complete the attractions of these favoured spots, that they had hills and mountains reaching to the very sky, sloping valleys stretching till they meet the sea, rolling rivers and sparkling fountains, sights and sounds and scents to satisfy all the senses and charm the most fastidious tastes. Would such places remain long unoccupied? Would not our surplus labourers rush thither to till the soil or gather its fruits, our capitalists find the means of transport, and our ships bring back their products? Would there not be a speedy exodus from our shores, till all at least who failed to find profitable employment here, had transferred themselves to such enticing spheres for labour and enjoyment?

Once again, let us suppose that an adjoining continent, possessing every natural advantage, had for its inhabitants multitudes already used to gaining their own food, but satisfied with scanty clothing and rude shelter; yet willing to be taught the arts of husbandry and tillage which would increase their produce, and to exchange these for better clothing and all the articles which natural or artificial want requires to be supplied with. Would not our manufacturers set their looms and forges at work to meet the demands upon their stocks; our traders hasten to cultivate amicable relations with the several people, our men of money furnishing the means and sharing the profits of trade?

Should we not, as our American brethren are doing, move on to the Far West ?

Wherein, then, lies the difference between the picture which fancy draws, and that which our maps exhibit and our books of geography and travels show us ; for we have, in truth, all these places in our possession or easily attainable so soon as we need them ? Simply in the distance by which they are separated from us. But surely this is far from being an insuperable obstacle. Australia is now almost as easily reached as Ireland was in the days when first colonized ; and the passage scarcely costs more money than it did when vessels first traded thither. If it pays to bring bullocks across the Atlantic only to be slaughtered, it ought not to be unremunerative to transport human beings to places where they may work to repay the outlay. This outlay, too, it must be remembered, would all be spent in furnishing employment to our shipbuilders, clothiers, provision dealers, sailors, and other labourers. The only real loss is that of the time spent in the transit, and devoted to the first settlement. Once settled and thriving, those who go out will require supplies of clothing from our manufactories at home, and send in return food, &c., to support those who produce them.

One grave objection is often started—that emigration takes from us the wisest and the strongest, leaving behind the foolish and the feeble. This is a real difficulty, but if, on the one hand, we have inherited the wealth previously acquired, we must not, on the other, complain of the charges with which it is encumbered. Nor can we escape the evil by suffering those who might grow up wise and strong in homes of freedom and plenty, to become enfeebled and debased from overcrowding and want of food in their present abodes. Besides which, experience proves that those who are successful abroad do not forget the aged and the young whom they have left at home ; they make large remittances for the support of parents, and the bringing out of the brothers and sisters when old enough to come.

Hitherto many have looked forward to returning to spend their last days in the old country, and this will still be the case with the most fortunate; but when colonization becomes more general it will be a permanent settlement for most, and it is well that it should be. Attachment to the mother country may and will continue, but the centre of attraction to the majority will be the homes and the surroundings in the new country.

Colonization will necessarily be of two kinds. The one that which brings into cultivation unoccupied territories: this will absorb the larger number of emigrants. The other that which cultivates intercourse and trade with the uncivilized inhabitants in possession of lands which may yield us food; this will provide employment and sustenance for the greater number at home. Both should proceed simultaneously, and together not only lessen the population which may be superabundant, but also largely increase the power of the mother country to support successive additions to its numbers.

There is a wide contrast between the advantage to be derived from the sending of emigrants to our own colonies and to foreign countries. Apart from all other considerations they are better customers in the one than they are in the other. The following figures, showing the values of our exports, prove that whilst our trade has been expanding to the former, it has been contracting to the latter. The value of British produce and manufacture exported since 1871 has been to—

[In million £'s to two decimals.]

Year.	British Possessions.	Foreign Countries.	Total.	Per Cent.	
				British.	Foreign.
	£	£	£		
1871	51·25	171·82	223·07	23·	77·
'72	60·56	195·70	256·26	24·	76·
'73	66·33	188·83	255·16	26·	74·
'74	72·28	167·28	239·56	30·	70·
'75	71·09	152·37	223·46	32·	68·
'76	64·86	135·78	200·64	32·	68·
'77	69·92	128·97	198·89	35·	65·
'78	66·24	126·61	192·85	34·	66·
	522·53	1,267·36	1.789·89	29·	71·

Upon every ground, therefore, efforts should be made to direct the stream to our own possessions, and away from other countries, especially from those adopting hostile tariffs. We may then fairly claim and expect from our own Colonies the utter abandonment of all protective legislation, and the freest admission of our own products for the use of our own people.

VII. Thus far we have been treating the matter as one of compulsion, of stern necessity, enforcing upon the mother-country the duty of providing the necessaries of life for the children whom she can no longer feed from her own bosom, and for whom she has increasing difficulty in procuring supplies from extraneous sources. It requires no little courage to maintain these views in face of the revival of trade, which is at this time kindling the hopes of all save those who are immediately dependent on agricultural prosperity; but the truth still remains that a country, depending so largely for the means of existence upon the proceeds of its foreign trade, cannot look with complacency upon an insufficiency in its exports, or be satisfied with diminishing sale of out-goings, accompanied by more extensive purchases of in-comings. At present the additional cost of our food imports is fourfold that of our increased exports, and the artisan who gets fuller work or ampler wages has to pay far higher for the food he consumes. The recent activity in the trade of the United States is chiefly in its exports, the result of deficient crops on this side the Atlantic, which their abundance of wheat enables them to supply; and at the same time by their own increased consumption of dairy produce and other articles to raise the prices which we have hitherto paid. Anticipation of continued demands on our part are leading to the extension of their railway system, which brings them as customers to our markets, and hence the orders with which our manufacturers' books are filled. Should this continue it will furnish our people with means for the purchase of food, and thus support our trade; but it would be a great calamity should attention be diverted from the far more enduring basis of prosperity, which the extension of our Colonies is fitted to afford. The essential difference between our home and foreign or colonial trade must never be put out of sight. The employment of labour in the production of articles which minister to our comfort or enjoyment, and the distribution of wealth which it promotes, are results of the highest value; but so far as sustenance is concerned it does nothing to procure the supplies we need. It may be well to turn gold into stocks of iron or chemicals, but unless these are exported they cannot purchase more beef or bread than are raised at home.

The necessity of which we have been speaking might be received with alarm, were it not for the truth of the old adage that " necessity is the mother of invention." It is quite consonant with the Anglo-Saxon character to evolve prosperity from adverse conditions, to thrive best when combating trials and overcoming difficulties. Nowhere is this more clearly displayed than in the history of our American cousins. Necessity for economy of power has led them to become pre-eminent in the invention of labour-saving machines. Necessity for economy of money to repair the waste of intestine commotions, has led them to find out the value of patient self-denial, and of paying off the debt incurred in their time of trouble. Our necessities will become real blessings if they enable us to find out the true value of our Colonies, and in no respect greater than in teaching us the extreme importance of maintaining and multiplying human life, as the surest method for the acquisition of wealth.

The question is often asked, wherein lies the source of wealth ? The answer frequently given is that it comes from the soil. This is strictly true, though but in a limited sense. Gems and gold, the most precious substances derived from the soil, are only the representatives of real wealth, and this they owe to the trouble of obtaining them, or the scarcity in which they exist. Did the alchemy of nature produce them in profusion they would cease to be deemed wealth. Whatever of real worth is extracted from the soil owes its chief, if not its only, value to the labour which brings it forth.

Is labour, then, the source of wealth ? Not altogether, for it may be expended in the destruction as well as creation of wealth ; and wealth is often formed—as in the fruits which the earth spontaneously produces—without its agency. The true source of wealth is to be found in life, and life alone. Without life the earth would be barren and deso-late, as it was in the remotest period to which history reaches, " without form and void." Take the lowest form in which it is manifested, that of vegetable life. By its agency inert matter assumes the various forms and characteristics which make it capable of supporting the higher grades of life and furnish other substances of real wealth. In the next stage, animal life still further carries on the processes of conver-sion, until through the instrumentality of the living power inherent in man, the brain becomes fitted for the exercise of thought and power by the direct gift of the Creator, im-parted when he became a living soul. It is by the exercise of these gifts through which man wields dominion over animate and inanimate nature that the higher forms of wealth are called into existence. In limiting life we lessen the production of wealth ; by its preservation and multiplication, we may best increase our store of riches. We think and act thus with our fields and our flocks; ought it to be less true with respect to our families? There must be something radically wrong in our social or political condition when the words of Scripture, " happy is the man who has his quiver full of them," cease to be true; and that wrong may be set right if we will only properly use the unbounded means for the support of life which our Colonial Possessions place within our grasp.

Two illustrations may serve to establish this proposition. The Registrar-General in his last annual report, after calculating the average earnings of each inhabitant of Great Britain, and likewise the average cost of his maintenance through life, comes to the conclusion that the money value of each is £159, this being the difference between the wages received or money earned, and that necessarily expended for the support of life. In the period which has elapsed since first accurate registration took place, the kingdom has parted with some eight million of its people, which Dr. Farr sets down as a money gift to the world of £1,400,000,000. Of these, some 2½ millions have settled in Colonies, and 5½ millions gone to the United States. Further than this, he considers that even in this country, under proper hygienic regulation, the rate of increase which is now 1·3 per cent. should be 1·8, so that the population, instead of doubling itself in fifty-five years, should do so in every thirty-nine.

It is to be regretted that the Colonial records afford very meagre information by which to judge of the relative rate at which the population increases from natural causes in the Colonies as contrasted with that at home. For the Australian Colonies the accounts of the last five years do show the numbers of births and deaths from which the increase can be ascertained, and thus compared with similar results obtained for the United Kingdom:—

[In million £'s to two decimals.]

Year.	United Kingdom.			Australia.		
	Pop.	Inc.	Per Cent.	Pop.	Inc.	Per Cent.
1873	32·12	·43	1·33	2·12	·048	2·26
'74	32·43	·42	1·30	2·23	·045	2·02
'75	32·75	·39	1·18	2·33	·039	1·67
'76	33·09	·48	1·44	2·41	·047	1·95
'77	33·45	·49	1·45	2·52	·051	2·02

Total increase in five years U.K. 2,199.013 = 6·85 per cent.
,,   ,,   Australia 230,408 = 10·81   ,,
Average annual rate of increase U. K. 1·34
,,   ,,   Australia 1·98

The only available statistics from Canada, though insufficient for arriving at any accurate conclusion, yet help to show that this superior rate of increase is not confined to Australia, but extends to other colonies in a like manner.

To view this part of the subject in another aspect. Some calculations regarding the division and employments of the people of this country in 1877, which will be found in the Transactions of the British Association for that year,[1] show that in the then circumstances of the United Kingdom some 40 per cent. of the actual workers supplied food for the whole population, and some 25 to 30 per cent. more, other necessaries, leaving 30 to 35 per cent. free to provide the luxuries of life and to accumulate wealth. The fact seems thus to be established that each individual life is, or ought to be, of actual money value to the State. Were it not so, there could be no growth of substance or wealth. In the earlier days of settling, no doubt the whole time of every worker needs to be occupied in provision for daily wants; but after a short period there is more to spare for enjoyment or acquisition than is possible in the old country, with all its concentration of power and machinery for economizing labour.

[1] Ante, page 116 et seq.

VIII. One other motive which should induce the mother-country to foster the further colonization of her dependencies remains to be noticed—it is the sense of responsibility arising from the relationship in which she stands towards them. It is not only that her own soil fails to provide sufficient for the wants of her growing population; that there seems little likelihood of greater or improved cultivation increasing her produce to the necessary extent; that our manufacturing and trading operations, which have hitherto procured supplies from abroad, now fail to keep pace with the growth of those whom they have to support, and our producing power appears to be overtaking the demands of our customers. These are urgent reasons why we should send forth a large number of our people. It is not only that the conditions of existence which have grown up amongst us, the modes of life fostered alternately by inflated prosperity and seasons of depression, require the breaking up of many connections, the changing of many habits, the infusion of new life into the several classes of society; these offer many inducements to place our people in altered circumstances, and to surround them with new influences. Neither is it solely because by the diffusion of our people, the fresh start they may make and the development of multiplied life, there is much wealth to be gained. These are encouragements to the occupation of new lands and the enlargement of our intercourse with the natives occupying many of our possessions. It is that, above all these, there should be the conviction that we have solemn duties to perform and sacred trusts to execute.

If we trace the various means by which England has become lord of the vast territories which already own our Sovereign's sway, and those which it seems we cannot avoid acquiring—at one time by right of discovery, and another by that of conquest; at others for the purpose of restoring order or preserving peace; at one period in pursuance of selfish policy dictated by the greed of gain; at another from motives of the purest philanthropy and the most earnest desire to benefit those whom we have brought under control—we cannot fail to see that it is neither by accident nor for useless ends that we have thus been led to appropriate so vast a portion of the earth's surface.   What-ever our past policy may have been, we cannot ignore our present obligations, nor refuse to admit our responsibilities in the future.   Whether for good or evil the burden rests upon us, and we cannot cast it off.   The destinies of many nations are in our keeping, and the peopling of many countries at our disposal.   If we have been enabled to settle our own freedom on a firm foundation, we have to secure the same liberty and to give the same relief to those who are as yet unable to claim, or unfit to exercise the full privileges of British subjects.   If we have drawn to our shores the wealth created in our Colonies or obtained by trade from other nations, we have to employ our capital in fostering commerce and manufactures for their benefit.   If we have arrived at so great a knowledge of, and obtained so great a mastery over the powers by which the earth's products may be utilized, we have to impart these gifts to those who are yet in ignorance, and therefore in poverty. If we have joined the ends of the earth together for our own convenience, we have to unite the whole of our possessions together and to ourselves by yet closer links and more en-during ties.   If we are in the enjoyment of all the comforts and benefits which a high state of civilization confers, we have to train our dependents to secure the same advantages. If the principles and the practices of morality are to prevail, we must introduce them where they are unknown, and fill our lands with those who will aid in their propagation.   If we ourselves are blessed with the light of religious truth, we must strive to cast the reflection of that light over the dark places of the earth, and seek to raise up a seed to serve Him by whom it has been bestowed.   These are solemn duties we dare not decline; glorious privileges we would not lose.

    IX. It does not fall within the scope of this paper to

discuss the various methods by which the desired ends may
be attained. Its purpose is rather to prove the necessity
which exists, and to stimulate all, home-residents and colo-
nists alike, to determined efforts to meet that necessity.
The times and the circumstances are every way favourable.
At home we have the people, and the money wherewith to
assist their removal. We have the ships to carry them,
and the power to build more if wanted. We have capital
seeking for investment, which may be advantageously employed either directly by its owners, or indirectly through
the agency of public companies, in making harbours, laying
down railways, clearing lands, and building habitations in
the colonies with far better hopes of success than in many
of the wild schemes in which we are so prone to embark.
We have abundance of implements and tools for every description of agricultural, mining, and building operations, the
manufacture of which would furnish immediate employment
for many of our artisans, and give an impetus to many
trades. We have been educating the young, so that they
at least need not go out unprepared for entrance into new
life. The ranks of every profession are over-filled, so
that we have teachers—religious and secular—physicians,
engineers, lawyers, clerks, together with farmers, tradesmen, mechanics, all in sufficient numbers to direct and care
for the families and individuals who may cross the seas.
Facilities exist and may be provided such as never before
were to be found in so great a degree; and really nothing
seems to stand in the way but want of knowledge, desire,
and will.

In the Colonies there is abundance of unoccupied land,
every variety of climate, every description of food and of
material for clothing. Pioneers have gone forward to prepare the paths for those who are to come after them, so that
there are few places in which friends and companions are not
to be found; whilst postal and telegraph communications
keep up constant and close intercourse with those who
may be separated by wide continents or broad seas. In

many of our possessions, and in other uncivilized parts
which are ready for forming attachments with us, there are
large bodies who would soon become our customers for
merchandise and our growers of food with whom a profitable trade will in time be developed, if only we send as
settlers amongst them those who are prepared to cultivate
amicable relations, rather than to extort from them the
goods or the labour they have to give; to carry the gifts
of civilization, rather than those of the sword.

In former times two classes were disposed to emigrate—
those whose spirit of enterprise and desire for wealth led
them to brave hardships, in the hope of returning home
to spend their later days in ease and plenty; and those
who, having misconducted themselves or otherwise broken
down at home, found it desirable to seek new places to live
in. Hence Colonial life was rude and rough. Few cared
to become steady settlers, or to cultivate the comforts and
happiness of home. These may still go out in considerable numbers, but we also want those who, with settled
intention and hearty desire, change their country, but carry
with them or speedily make permanent homes wherever
they may go. The increasing numbers and the rapidity
with which these are added to in newer countries forbid the
expectation of return. The many must, once for all, transfer themselves to the fresh locality, seeking to make it as
much like the old one in everything that is good, and as
much unlike it in everything that is ill, as they possibly
can. The feeling must not be that of expatriation, but that
of extending the borders of the fatherland.

This, too, should be the spirit to actuate the Home Government in all its relations with existing or yet to be
formed Colonial possessions. All distinctions of laws and
customs should be swept away, and the same principles and
methods of rule should be adopted, or only withheld for a
time in the case of untutored natives. Whatever institu-
tions, religious, educational, scientific, or philanthropic, have
been found to work well at home, should be founded,

improved, and adapted to the special requirements of each place. Whether it would be possible to form an entire federal union of all parts of the British Empire, so as to have the same fiscal laws and regulations, is too wide a subject to be entered upon on this occasion; but there can be no question that if practicable it should be adopted, and if not altogether feasible, that no unnecessary obstacles should be placed in its way, or any departure from its spirit encouraged. If it be necessary for revenue purposes, on account of the different positions in which they are placed, to have different rates of duties on the importation of goods, they should undoubtedly differ as little as possible, and every attempt to establish Protection on either side as against the other be utterly repudiated.

It is the duty of the mother country to set the example and exercise her authority for the general welfare, but it is also the duty of the children to follow and acquiesce in that which is for the benefit of both. The idea of separate interests or independence of each other is utterly inadmissible. The object on all sides should be to draw tighter the bonds of union, to weld every portion of our Dominions together into one harmonious whole, to make everyone within the bounds of the British Empire feel and act as an inhabitant of the *one* United Kingdom.

I have spoken of the necessity imposed upon the mother country that she should extend and perfect the colonization of her numerous possessions, but is it not equally a necessity to those possessions that they should be fully colonized? She has more than an abundance; they, with few exceptions, a paucity of population. She is unable to raise her own food, they can raise more than they can consume. She has a plethora of wealth which seeks employment in foreign lands: they have need of more than she can give to develop their untold resources. She has the knowledge, the refinement, the treasures of art and science, accumulated in the course of the years that are past; they have yet to obtain these invaluable possessions in the years that are to come. The necessity is mutual: let both be gainers by its being met and supplied. These are considerations which can no longer be neglected or evaded. They force themselves upon us in our homes and our offices, in solitude and society, in the palace and the hovel; they will tax our intellects and should lie near our hearts. When these sentiments prevail, and—presumptuous though it may be in me to say so—not till then, will there be any solid return of national prosperity. Whensoever they are held by the leaders of public opinion, and responded to alike by the voice of those at home and those in our colonies, the work will be viewed as the most important that can occupy public attention, and all together will join in its performance. Then the most important and influential member of the Government will not be the Minister who sits at the Home Office, not the one who presides over War, not even he who rules at the Exchequer, but the honoured individual into whose hands Her Most Gracious Majesty commits the affairs of the Colonial Office.

XIV.

Drinking and Depression.[1]

THERE is every indication that the winter upon which we have now entered will be one of much privation, and it may be of severe suffering to a large portion of the labouring classes. The proposed reduction of wages in the agricultural district of Kent and Sussex, which is resisted there—though, we believe, tacitly accepted in other parts of the kingdom—cannot be without effect upon the comfort of many homes. Even that, however, is better than strikes and locks-out at a season of the year when work is always scanty, though the wants of the workers are increased. Nor are things any better in other quarters. In the coal district there are accumulations of stocks. Lord Londonderry speaks of having 60,000 tons lying on the banks for want of purchasers. In the Cleveland district, as well as the Scotch and other centres of the iron trades, numbers of furnaces are blown out, and mills are standing idle. The same tale is told in Lancashire as regards the cotton mills, which are working short time, and the condition of manufacture is very nearly alike in the woollen district of Yorkshire. Everywhere there is lessened opportunity for working—consequently smaller earnings for the support of the families, and there seems no prospect at present of a favourable change. The demand for the products of our manufacturing industry has fallen off; other nations are producing for themselves, and hence prices have been lowered below those which

---

[1] "The Church of England Temperance Chronicle," November 30th, December 7th and 14th, 1878.

yield profit, and it cannot be expected that employers will
continue to increase their losses by continuing to give
wages that raise the cost of the goods beyond that which
customers will give.   In the agricultural counties the cause
is somewhat different, though the result is the same.   The
abundant supplies which pour in from all parts of the world
so reduce the price as to leave little or no profit to the
farmers, and there is no doubt that they are compelled to seek
relief in reduction at both ends, the rents they are charged
and the wages they pay.   However much we may sympathize with the poor who suffer, there would appear no possibility of avoiding the reduction, nor any immediate hope of
the necessity passing away.

Now, it is just because we do most deeply feel for those
who are thus deprived of their usual amount of earnings,
that we would point out to them one effectual means of
meeting the evil; that is, by reducing the consumption of
beer and other alcoholic liquors; or, better still, cutting it
off altogether; for the strongest advocate for the moderate
use of these will admit that where retrenchment is necessary it may better begin with drink than meat, with beer
than bread.   The estimated average value of the intoxicants consumed by each individual being 90s., and the
average number of each family being five, of which two at
the most are bread-winners, and one of these not able to
earn more than half a full worker's wages; it follows that
the average charge upon each income must be 90s. multiplied by 5 divided by $1\frac{1}{2} = £15$, fully 6s. for each week of
work throughout the year.   This is the average for the
whole kingdom and for all classes, but we believe that the
poor do really consume their full share, for though some
families amongst the rich may expend much more, they are
not sufficient in number to actually lower the average to a
great extent.   Besides this, if the large number of abstainers
—all of whom are included in the calculation which produces the average—were left out, it would have fewer consumers amongst whom to divide the total consumption.   If,

further, it be admitted that the agricultural labourers from their lower wages, and country as opposed to town life, are more abstemious than the mining and factory workers— the self-imposed tax by reason of the amount spent in liquor is yet far more than equivalent to the reduction in wages which the Kent and Sussex labourers are crying out against. Thus the complaint inscribed on one of the banners carried in procession to the Exeter Hall meeting becomes the chief ground of offence: " We grow the hops, but we must not drink the beer." Let but the beer be cut off, and the reduced wages will go as far as those hitherto received in providing solid substance for the labourer and his family. To the operatives in other kinds of employment the same means of compensation for lower earnings lies open. We very much doubt if all the recent reductions in wages amount to nearly the sum which might be saved by the abandonment of excess in the consumption of drink.

To one class immediately above the labourers and operatives, that of shopkeepers and dealers, the reduction of wages or earnings has scarcely yet arrived, for the wholesale prices of all articles of food—excepting meat and milk— have been much lower than they were, whilst the retail prices have not fallen in proportion. But it cannot be long before diminished power of spending reaches them also; indeed it has done so already where, as in Wales and Durham, the number of persons in employment has diminished; and if not so, they have probably, through loss of work, more claimants amongst whom to divide their means or profits. To these, however, the same course, namely, abstinence, wholly or in part, is open, and they have thus the power of mitigating, if not of altogether averting, the present or threatened evils.

But is it in truth an evil? The prophet tells us, " When Thy judgments are in the earth, the inhabitants of the world will learn righteousness." We as a people have " grown and become strong," and in our pride have said, " Is not this great Babylon that I have built by the might of my power?"

May we not hope that the judgments which are even now in the earth will render counsel acceptable to us, so that we may "break off our sins by righteousness?" Amongst the sins which our nation has to break off, that of intemperance holds a prominent position, and where it exists righteousness can find no place.

We would earnestly press upon our workers and friends the consideration whether these are not times in which self-denying and vigorous effort in the temperance cause is most imperatively called for, and full of promise. There is already a perceptible decrease in the quantities of wine, beer, and spirits which are taken out for consumption. This may be attributed to two causes—one, we hope, is the spreading influence of sound knowledge and right principles; the other, the lessened means wherewith to purchase. Whatever is due to the former is an encouragement to go forward in the work we have undertaken; whatever to the latter renders the continuance of that work easier and more likely to succeed; for when abstinence is enforced by necessity, its benefits may be understood and appreciated, so that the habit, once broken, may not be resumed when prosperity returns.

2.

We alluded last week to retrenchment in expenditure on alcoholic liquors as an effectual means for mitigating the privations attendant upon the general reduction in wages which agricultural labourers and others have to accept. This diminution of earnings has its origin in the long-continued depression of trade which the country has to sustain; and until its removal there is little prospect of any class of labourers or operatives being able to obtain the wages they have until very recently enjoyed. It would, however, appear that this depression of trade is in some measure the result of, or is at least enhanced by, the undue consumption of alcohol, as was pretty clearly proved by some figures produced by one of the speakers at the recent great temperance meeting in Manchester. The details of this question are too elaborate for quotation or discussion in these columns—some of them will be found in the Appendix to Canon Ellison's evidence before the Lords' Committee—but it may not be uninteresting to state the general results of this and other investigations.

Owing partly to the growth of population, but still more to the increase in the average consumption of food, beverages, and tobacco, amongst all classes of society, it has come to pass that Great Britain and Ireland do not produce much more than half the supplies which their inhabitants consume. The remainder has to be supplied from foreign sources, and must be paid for with the products of the skill and industry of those who in one shape or other labour for the support of themselves and those dependent upon them. There is much difference of opinion among statisticians and political economists as to the causes and effects of the disproportion which late years have manifested in the quantities and values of the goods imported and exported into and from this country. But there is no room for questioning that want of economy in the use of what we have to purchase, and a diminution in the receipts for such articles as we have to sell, cannot add to the nation's wealth or the spending power of its people. That intemperance acts prejudicially in both directions it is not difficult to prove.

It is admitted that some six years ago, when trading and manufacturing prosperity was at its height, the goods we sent out of the country fully paid for those we brought into it; whereas now the value of the one is at least £96,000,000 a year less than the other. Those who take an interest in these particulars will find much of information and discussion in the Transactions of the Statistical Societies of London and Manchester. The important points for temperance advocates to bear in mind are, as regards the imports, that fully £25,000,000 out of the hundred is expended on the purchase either of alcoholic liquors them-

selves, of the grain used in the manufacture of beer and
spirits in this country, or of that which is needed to compensate for the barley, &c. of home growth which is thus
consumed.   Now, just in proportion as we lessen or extinguish the payments made for such beverages, or the materials
from which they are formed, may we retain in the country
for our own use the goods we give in exchange for them, or
the money which arises from their sale.   The whole of the
£25,000,000 or more thus annually parted with is absolutely lost to the country.   All that we get in return is the
life (?), health (?), and strength (?) which its consumption
creates, or the poverty (!), sickness (!), and vice (!) which
follow upon its being thus used up.   This is an altogether
different matter from the amounts taken out of the pockets
of the consumers in payment for what they drink, on the
one hand, and the money which flows into the exchequer
as the result of duties levied on these drinks, or the earnings of those who manufacture or deal in these articles, on
the other.   We are here speaking only of that which is
actually transported out of the country in payment or
exchange for the intoxicants or their materials brought
into it.

It may doubtless be argued that the traffic in the goods
which this twenty-five millions represents does bring profit
to our merchants and shopkeepers ; and their manufacture,
wages and profits to some of our labourers and their employers ; but to this it may be answered that the same
expenditure for any articles of absolute utility would yield
equal or greater profit.   The real question is, what do we
gain in return for this payment, and how does it act in
elevating or depressing the trade of the country ? Those
who see in the moderate use of these beverages a real benefit to such as partake of them, must admit that their im-
moderate use destroys instead of creating.   Food, which
maintains life, forms the bones and muscles, strengthens the
nerves, and fits the brain for action ; creates the power of
production, and increases the numbers and wants of the

consumers. It thus encourages manufacture and stimulates trade. Drink, which destroys life, enfeebles the constitution, and paralyzes the mind and heart; lessens the power of production, imposes a dead weight upon those who do produce, diminishes the numbers and the means of spending to those who might be consumers, and so checks manufacture and depresses trade. We had our cycle of prosperous years, and have had the folly to waste much of our substance in the extravagant consumption of alcohol. We have now our period of adverse seasons, shall we learn the wisdom of husbanding our means by retrenching in the expenditure on alcohol? Or shall we as a nation pursue the path of prodigality, till trade, manufacture, and commerce recede from our shore to those of nations more temperate, and therefore wiser, than we? Our hope lies in the spread of temperance principles, and our trust is in the Lord, who is thus owning, encouraging, and blessing the servants whom He calls to His help against the mighty power of evil which has overspread our land.

We must reserve for another number the endeavour to show how the same cause which increases our outlay for imports, diminishes the quantity and value of the exports with which we have to meet this expenditure.

3.

If it be true, as we essayed to prove a fortnight since, that there is to be found in a retrenchment in the consumption of alcoholic liquors an ample equivalent for any reduction which has taken place in the wages of agricultural and other labourers; and if the curtailment of the nation's expenditure on these articles would go far to rectify the balance against us in our dealings with the rest of the world, it is not less certain that the same measure would have a most powerful effect in quickening our export trade, and thus in finding the means of payment for the food and other necessaries which we are compelled to procure from

abroad. This truth may not at first sight be so apparent
as the others, nor is it so easy to explain within a limited
compass, but a little consideration will demonstrate the fact.

A reference to the Registrar-General's report upon the
last census will show that in the four great industries of our
country, the raising of coal, the manufacture of iron, and
the spinning and weaving of cotton and wool, and in dealing with these productions, there are some million and a
half of people employed. On the computation already made
the dependents upon these, will raise the number who have
to be supported by their earnings to some five millions—
amongst whom the consumption of beer, spirits, &c., must
entail an expenditure of say £22,500,000 per annum, a
sum which the most strenuous advocate for the moderate
use of these articles must admit to be some twenty millions
more than is needed.

If, then, we turn to the records of our foreign trade it will
be seen that our exports of coal, iron, cotton and woollen
manufactures for last year were valued at £120,000,000, on
which a charge of £20,000,000 is equal to 16 per cent.
It may of course be argued that the operatives by whom
this amount is assumed to be expended on alcohol, produce
a larger value of goods than that named for export, inasmuch as they manufacture for their own wants as well as
for home use by others.   But then their own direct consumption of alcohol by no means includes the whole charge
their earnings have to bear; for the houses they live in
have been built and furnished by those who have been like
consumers; the bread and meat they eat, the clothes they
wear, the comforts they enjoy, the rates they pay, have all
in the same manner been enhanced in cost by the value of
the liquor consumed by those engaged in their production.
In fact, this expenditure so runs through everything that it
is impossible to say where it begins or where it ends.   It
imposes a tax upon whatever is grown or made, used or enjoyed, and its reduction or extinction would lower the cost
of everything, so that a diminution of earnings or profits

would really leave the recipient no worse off than at present; to say nothing of the absolute saving of the outlay on the crime, sickness, and poverty which are the sure attendants on the habitual use of intoxicants.

If, then, we are not wrong in charging this £120,000,000 of export with the £20,000,000 of unnecessary expenditure, it is clear that if the prices at which we sell our goods can be maintained, there might be so much more money to be shared between those by whose capital, skill, and labour they are produced; to be applied to purposes which in themselves would require more labour, support a larger population, and employ more persons to supply their wants. If, on the other hand, our foreign customers fall off in their demands for our manufactures, as they have of late been doing, the surest way to bring them back will be by a reduction in price, such as might be done without injury, at least to the extent of the amount saved on alcohol. Dependent as we are upon other countries for the help we find needed for the maintenance of our population, it is a matter of vital importance for us to maintain our present markets, and to extend rather than contract the sale of our manufactures.

Whether, therefore, we look to the facility there exists for reducing the cost of home produce and the expenditure in foreign markets, or to the advantages to be derived from lowering the expense of our manufactures for abroad, we see most urgent reasons for the disuse in part, or even wholly, of the present amount of stimulants. We do not say that the present depression of trade is to be attributed to this cause alone—far from it—but we do say that it is an important factor in the case, and that its removal is one of the surest and safest remedies to which recourse may be had. The subject may be somewhat difficult to elucidate or to gain attention for, but the facts on which it rests and the arguments by which it may be supported are not beyond the reach of our intelligent working men and women, nor by the elder boys and girls in our schools. To none of these will they be wanting in interest when fairly brought to their notice.

In these and the previous remarks we have been seeking to derive instruction from the statistics of the past, for the surroundings of the present are none the less gloomy. Nor are there many appearances of brightness in the prospects of the future. We fear that there are hard lessons yet to be learnt. It is not alone the vice of drunkenness which has overspread the land, but the insidious habit of relying upon stimulants to sustain forced exertions and continuous labour, which is wasting so much money and sacrificing so much power. It is this which prepares the way and leads on to the more open evil. We rejoice, therefore, in the awakening perception to the truth in this matter, and trust that the financial arguments, though not the highest ground to be taken, may in the present juncture of affairs prove conclusive to many minds. Amidst all the distress and anxiety which is causing "men's hearts to fail them for fear and for looking after those things which are coming on the earth," we are reminded of the prophet's question, "Shall there be evil in the city and the Lord have not done it?" May not these evil results of intemperance be permitted to the end that we may see more clearly its enormity and hasten to put away the accursed thing from among us?

[This paper has been inadvertently placed out of order; it should have stood No. X., p. 199.]

XV

On the Recent Revival in Trade.[1]

THE latest issued official accounts of the foreign and colonial trade of the United Kingdom, together with those of the several preceding months, bear testimony to a very considerable increase in the quantity and value of both imports and exports. The figures in which these are set forth have been received as evidence that a real revival of trade has set in, and is about to extend beyond the bounds which have been reached in former years. Such an analysis of these figures as may serve to indicate their real bearing on the welfare of the country—both present and future—will not, therefore, be uninteresting; either to those engaged in trade or manufacture, or to those who are any way concerned to understand the position in which we stand, or that to which we may look forward.

It was during the sitting of the British Association in the manufacturing town of Sheffield last year, that the first gleams of returning prosperity were distinctly seen. There had been for some months previously more frequent appearances of "paper" in the London Money Market of American origin, which were taken as indications that there was a stir in American trade; and many proofs that the depression into which trade on the other side of the Atlantic had fallen was passing away. Not a few hopes were expressed that this country would in like manner

---

[1] Read in Section F of the British Association, Swansea, Aug. 27, 1880.

emerge from the depth into which its trade had fallen, so soon as prosperity was again brightening the prospects of the United States. The receipt, therefore, of orders for various descriptions of our iron products—and especially for rails—was immediately viewed as a precurser to manufacturing activity. Nor was the expectation unwarranted by the results. A spirit of confidence at once sprung up, and prices rose so high as to show that in addition to that which had a sound basis, much speculative business was going on. Thus a stimulus was given to production. Higher prices were asked and given, and for a time there seemed to be no lack of buoyancy in almost every market. Prices again gave way, but are now being partially recovered, and the opinion is almost universally entertained that a new era of prosperity is being entered upon. Such being the case, it may be worth while to compare a year's transactions with those of the preceding one. The early date at which the monthly accounts are now issued from the Custom House gives us the means of compiling for such comparison the twelvemonth ended July 31 last with those which came to a conclusion on the last day of July in 1879. We can thus place side by side the figures for the worst year of depression and the first year of recovery.

Before entering into an examination of the details of the last two years, it may be well to state the totals for each year since 1871—that is, so far back as they were collected, on the same system as now exists; and to show the difference in value between the goods imported and those exported, as follows:—

[In million £'s to two decimals.]

Year ending	Imports.	Exports.	Excess of Imports.
	£	£	£
July 31, 1880	404·31	271·24	133·07
,, '79	345·78	239·86	105·92
,, '78	387·35	250·59	136·76
,, '77	389·76	254·31	135·45
,, '76	372·37	266·81	105·56
,, '75	369·48	288·87	80·61
,, '74	375·12	301·23	73·89
,, '73	366·43	320·72	45·71
,, '72	349·85	304·73	45·12

It will thus be seen that of the imports the twelve months just ended were the highest, and those of the preceding twelve the lowest of the whole series. Of the exports, the period ending in 1879 was likewise the lowest, but that just ended was by no means the highest; whilst as regards the preponderance of imports, the most recent is very nearly the greatest, there having been, until 1880, a progressive decline in the value of the exports. Comparing the years ending in 1880 and 1879 together, they differ in all these particulars more widely from each other than any of the preceding years, the growth in imports having been £58·53, in exports £31·38, and in the excess of the former £27·15. These figures include the whole of the imports —those again sent away, as well as those retained for home consumption; and of the exports both the re-exports and the articles of British produce and manufacture.

Separating the one class of exports from the other, it appears that in the latter year they have amounted in value to £214,000,000 British, and about £57,000,000 foreign and colonial, as against £187,000,000 of the one and £53,000,000 of the other. These figures are not exact, for the accounts of the foreign goods are only shown in total at the proper end of each year, but they are accurate enough for the present purpose, and tell the increase of

British to have been 27, and of foreign between 4 and 5 millions of pounds.   These foreign and colonial goods show the activity of trade, and add to the national receipts by the commissions and profits on their sale ; but, as regards the employment of labour and capital, are of inferior importance to the British.

In estimating the worth of this increase, very much depends upon whether it has taken place in the quantities of the goods that have been sold, or in the prices they have realized.   From so many of the articles being shown in the accounts in value only, it is not possible to say how this may have been as regards the whole, but by abstracting the principal articles that are stated in both quantity and value, the relation of the one to the other may be ascertained for such portion of the exports, and it is not likely that the proportions of the remainder will vary greatly. Classifying the articles so abstracted, and calculating how far the difference in value is due to greater quantities or altered values, the following results appear.   As before, in million pounds to two decimals :—

[In million £'s to two decimals.]

	Value of Exports, 1879-80.	More or less than 1878-79.	Increase or decrease due to	
			Quantity.	Price.
	£	£	£	£
Coals......................	8·01	·96	1·13	—·17
Copper....................	3·16	·24	·10	·14
Iron	26·12	8·44	7·63	·81
Mineral....................	37·29	9·64	8·86	·78
Cotton Piece Goods........	53·42	7·30	7·59	—·29
Jute ,, ,, ...	2·12	·30	·26	·04
Linen ,, ,, ...	5·03	·49	·44	·05
Woollen ,, ,, ...	15·95	1·19	1·83	—·64
Textile	76·52	9·28	10·12	—·84
Cotton and other yarns......	19·02	·01	—·58	·59
Alkali	2·32	·38	·24	·14
Beer......................	1·73	—·09	—·09	—
Leather...................	2·92	—·09	—·23	·14
Seed-oil..................	1·61	·01	—·03	·04
Sundry	27·60	·22	—·69	·91
Total specified.............	141·41	19·14	18·29	·85

Since the full value of all the British manufactures exported for the year is 214 millions, and that of these specified articles is nearly 142, the evidence thus afforded relates to two-thirds of the whole. In like manner with the increase, 27 millions for the whole and 19 for the enumerated.

Examining these particulars more closely, it will be seen that the increase of £19·14 is between 15 and 16 per cent. on the exports of the previous twelve months, and that of this amount £18·29, or 95½ per cent., is owing to the quantities having been greater, and only £·85, or 4½ per cent., has arisen from better prices having been obtained. But whilst these are the proportions of the whole, the rates on the different classes of goods differ very much. Thus in coals and metals the increase has been 35 per cent., on textile manufactures 14 per cent., and in the miscellaneous less than 1 per cent. So in respect to the gain in quantities, the minerals are greater by 92 per cent., and the prices are better by 8 per cent. In textile fabrics the increased quantities should have given 9 per cent. more money than was actually credited, but failed to do so because the prices were less to this extent. On the contrary, in the few miscellaneous articles shown above there was a real diminution of quantity, but an increase in price, whereby what would have been a loss of $2\frac{1}{2}$ per cent. became converted into a gain of something less than 1 per cent. Descending more into detail, iron figures for very nearly one-third of the whole year's gain, viz., £8·44 out of £27, and cotton piece goods for £7·30, or one-fourth. Of the gain in iron, one-tenth only is due to price, whilst cotton goods have sold for a trifle less than the previous price. On the other hand, cotton yarn has decreased in quantity but somewhat gained in price, and woollen piece goods, though increasing 13 per cent. in quantity have fallen 4 per cent. in price.

Taking the whole of the exports together, these figures establish the fact that the very low prices of manufactured goods which prevailed in the latter part of 1878 and the earlier part of 1879, have continued to rule since that time ; and that for very nearly all the addition to the values of that which left our shores before the revival, we have had to give extra quantities, the advantage in point of prices obtained having been inconsiderable. If, therefore, the business of selling has yielded any better return, it must have been because the manufacturer received less ; and if the manufacturer gained at all, it must have been either from the lesser value of money or a reduction in the wages of his labourers. Further, as will be shown in dealing with the imports, in the cost of the raw materials from abroad, from which most of our textile fabrics are woven, there has been, especially in cotton, a decided increase.

Turning now to the imports, and separating those retained at home from those re-exported, we find a total value
of about £347,000,000, as against £293,000,000 in 1879.
Abstracting, as with the exports, the chief articles, and
classifying them according to their uses, the following
figures present themselves :—

[In million £'s to two decimals.]

	Value of Imports, 1879-80.	More or less than 1878-79.	Increase or decrease due to	
			Quantity.	Price.
	£	£	£	£
Meat, live and dead.........	23·72	+·06	3·70	·36
Butter and cheese...........	15·34	1·18	1·15	·03
Corn and flour...............	64·35	13·96	6·32	7·64
Potatoes.....................	3·68	1·93	1·95	—·02
Coffee, tea, and sugar.......	32·66	·26	—·68	·94
Spirits and wine............	8·24	1·69	1·18	·51
Tobacco.....................	1·95	—·58	—·18	—·40
Food.....................	149·94	22·50	13·44	9·06
Cotton, raw.................	37·63	10·50	7·21	3·29
Flax, hemp, and jute	9·31	2·66	2·03	·63
Silk, raw	2·64	·76	·92	—·16
Wool, sheep's	11·77	1·79	2·02	—·23
Textile	61·35	15·71	12·18	3·53
Iron ore and manufacture...	5·80	1·86	1·78	·08
Copper......	4·13	·34	—	·34
Wood	12·38	2·03	2·28	—·25
Hides and leather	5·02	1·36	1·03	·33
Metals, &c.................	27·33	5·59	5·09	·50
Total specified.............	238·62	43·80	30·71	13·09

As with the exports, these selected articles form about
two-thirds of the whole of the importations retained for
home consumption or manufacture—namely, 238 millions

out of 347; but they absorb more than that proportion of the increase over the previous year—namely, 44 out of 54, which is equal to four-fifths.

Coming to details, it will be seen that this increase of 43·80 is 22½ per cent. on the value of the previous year, whereas on the exports it was not much more than 15 per cent., from which it is clear that the value of the additional goods received for home use has exceeded that of the deliveries for sale abroad in the proportion of very nearly 3 to 2. Of this amount £30·71, or 70 per cent., is owing to the quantities having been greater, and £13·09, or 30 per cent., from better prices having been obtained.

The first division in the foregoing table, consisting of food, with which are included beverages and tobacco, is by far the largest, taking more than one-half of the whole sum —150 millions out of 239; and its share of the increase for the year is nearly in the same proportion (22½ out of 44), the increase itself being 17½ per cent. beyond last year's supplies. In the raw material for textile manufactures— £61·35, which is rather more than a fourth of the whole, shows an increase over last year of £15·71, equal to 34 per cent. In the remaining class, including the principal metals, wood, and leather, £27·33, comprising one-sixth of the whole, the increase in the year is £5·59, or 26 per cent. Dividing, then, the surplus between volume and value, it appears that of the increase, that in food has been from 60 per cent., in textile materials 77 per cent., and in the others 91 per cent. on the quantities. So, in respect to the prices paid, which have been 40 per cent. on food, 23 on textile materials, and 9 per cent. on metals, &c.

It needs no very close observation of these figures to discover the marked contrast they present to those for the exports, in that, whilst those showed the rise of prices to have been comparatively little, these manifest a decided advance, particularly in almost every article of food proper. We have not only consumed more, but that consumption has been more costly, as well as more abundant. In proof that this is really the case, two articles may be singled out, sharing between them in nearly equal portions rather more than half the whole increase in outlay. These are wheat—the food for the body, that on which more than on anything else we depend for the power to manufacture; and cotton, the food for our mills, on which vastly more than on any other article we depend for the maintenance of our power to produce that which we can exchange for food. Of wheat we have within the year consumed, or are storing up for consumption, that which has cost us £12,000,000 more than in the previous year; and of this amount £7,000,000 has been spent because our growth at home was deficient in quantity, and £5,000,000 because that deficiency enhanced the price the consumers have had to pay. Of cotton wool we have imported and kept that which has cost us £10,500,000; and of this £7,250,000 has gone to provide the additional weight, and ₤3,250,000 the extra price at which it has been procured. Of this additional cotton as near as possible one-half has gone away again in the shape of manufactured goods, the other half being added to the stocks on hand, or consumed for home purposes.

Thus far we have been considering the articles in which the country has traded, and the money value they represent; but an important branch of the inquiry relates to the countries with which that trade has been carried on, and the altered conditions in which it stands. The figures that may serve to illustrate these points are not so complete as those with which we have been dealing, for it is only at the close of each year that the necessary accounts are published, and these do not show the transactions of the respective months which must form a portion of any period ending otherwise than on December 31. The quarterly accounts furnish materials for compiling the value of the whole imports for the twelve months ending in June, but not for those re-exported; and those for the exports contain only the values of British produce and manufacture. From these data, however, it is possible to obtain a pretty clear idea of the directions which the trade has been taking, and the differences between its progress during each of the twelve months completed on June 30, 1879 and 1880.

The following is a condensed account of the value of the United Kingdom manufactures which have been exported to the British possessions and foreign countries.

[In million £'s to two decimals.]

	1879-80.	1878-79.	Excess of former.
	£	£	£
To British India...............	28·68	23·39	5·29
„ Africa..................	8·46	8·05	·41
„ Australia...............	15·48	18·46	—2·98
„ North America.........	6·50	5·70	·80
„ Other Possessions......	8·67	7·53	1·14
	67·79	63·13	4·66
To Foreign Countries in Europe......	79·88	80·72	—·84
„ „ Asia.........	11·20	8·78	2·42
„ „ Africa.......	4·26	3·97	·29
„ United States of America...........	30·49	15·14	15·35
„ Other Countries in „	17·05	16·43	·62
	142·88	125·04	17·84
Total to British Possessions and foreign countries................	210·67	188·17	22·50

If we except Australia, to which there has been so marked a decline—the effect, doubtless, of her protective tariff—the only countries that show a great difference in the two years—and these both in the way of increase—are British India and the United States of America. India has taken from us in cotton yarn and piece goods to the value of £18·99 against £14·72, thus nearly accounting for the above excess, and going far towards repaying us for the raw cotton purchased from her. The United States

have drawn upon us for iron and other metals to the value
of £11·03 against £3·14, and for cotton and other textiles
£9·56 against £5·34, thus more than returning the increased sums paid by us for her wheat and flour.

Following the same arrangement, the imports for the
same periods show thus:— .

[In million £'s to two decimals.]

	1879 80.	1878-9.	Excess of former.
	£	£	£
From British India.....................	35·51	31·64	3·87
„ Africa.....................	6·67	6·01	·66
„ Australia.................	23·26	22·80	·46
„ North America...........	10·69	9·71	·98
„ Other Possessions........	10·30	8·42	1·88
	86·43	78·58	7·85
From Foreign countries of Europe.....	161·88	146·50	15·38
„ Asia........	17·35	16·23	1·12
„ Africa......	14·19	8·67	5·52
United States of America...............	100·92	81·63	19·29
Other countries in „	20·62	19·74	·88
	314·96	272·77	42·19
Total from British Possessions and Foreign Countries...................	401·39	351·35	50·04

These figures indicate that the expansion of our import
trade has been a benefit to almost every country, though
here India and the United States, with Egypt, have been
the most prominent.   In all these the two great articles of
corn and cotton have had the principal part.   That with
the various countries of Europe is so large that a slight
addition to each, arising in great measure from our demands for corn, makes up a considerable total.   The chief
interest, however, centres in the supplies we have drawn
from the United States.   Wheat and flour together

Y

amounted in 1878-9 to £17·46, and in 1879-80 to £26·58; cotton to £22·68 in the former, to £28·37 in the latter.

The analysis to which these figures have been submitted serves to bring out many points of especial interest connected with the present revival, and should afford much food for thought as regards its probable course and duration.

In the first place, it shows that, great as has been the increase in our exportations, that in our import trade is far greater. If we have sold in the last twelve months to the value of £32,000,000 more than we did in the previous twelve, we have also received more goods to the value of £59,000,000, thus leaving a greater balance to be provided for. No doubt a considerable portion of that £27,000,000 will remain with us in payment for freights, commissions earned, or profits realized; but an ample allowance for these must still leave a large amount to be met either by payments in bullion, the transfer of securities, or as deferred obligations. Nor must it be forgotten that there is a continual stream of capital flowing from this country for investment in our colonies and in foreign lands, which going out mostly in goods or in bills which serve as payment for goods, the actual receipts for our exports are lessened thereby. There is, on the other hand, capital returning for investment here, which in like manner is represented by imports; but all our experience justifies the supposition that the influx from this cause is less than the efflux. Much of the former is held here on foreign account, liable at any moment to be withdrawn; hence the doubts so freely expressed at the present moment whether a drain of gold may not soon set in.

Secondly, it is evident that on the whole the prices obtained for our exports are only to a trifling extent better than they were, whilst the prices paid for our imports are considerably enhanced. Thus the revival has been much more to the advantage of the sellers of the goods we have consumed than to that of those who sold our own produce or manufacture. In the complicated state of trade transactions it is impossible to say whether any or how much of this advantage belongs to our merchants, since this depends upon the ownership at the time when the sales are effected. As between the actual producers and consumers it is clear that a higher rate of payments for imports, with nearly stationary receipts for exports, cannot increase the prosperity of either one or the other. It would seem to be the case that sales are effected because prices are low, and that purchases are made because we need them, although prices are high. Take, for instance, the fact that the cotton used up in the manufacture of our piece-goods has failed to bring in the higher price which the advanced cost of the raw material would justify or require.

Thirdly, the whole excess in the value of the exports is scarcely equivalent to the extra cost of the food we have imported. Unless we can suppose that large stocks of produce and manufacture, or the means of producing them, are prepared for future sale, in readiness to obtain a profit when parted with, it follows that, as a whole, all the gain of extended foreign outward trade has but gone in the sustenance of those by whom the goods have been produced, leaving nothing wherewith to recompense capital or for the accumulation of wealth.

This brings us to the really important consideration whether the food question is not truly at the bottom of the recent fluctuations in trade. For a series of years our own supplies have been scanty, and the bad harvest of last year rendered us more than ever dependent upon the produce of foreign countries, particularly of America. Purchasing largely from the western growers, and giving them remunerative prices, they have large profits to expend upon our manufactures. Encouraged by the successive annually increasing quantities they were able to sell, they have been laying themselves out to meet our wants, and, anticipating an ever-growing call for their produce, they have determined by means of new railways to bring larger quantities and at lesser cost, from the distant fields in the west to the seaboard in the east. Hence the sudden demand for rails and for the iron to make them which the pits and the mills of their own country could not supply, but which the diminution of prices here enabled them to obtain sufficiently low to counteract the otherwise prohibitory duties of their own tariff. Trade thus started in one direction speedily spread in others, and extended far beyond the boundaries in which it emanated. The repeated adversities of former years have caused the depression of 1878-9 to be greater than the causes warranted, and with the changes of last autumn confidence became restored, and this of itself creates trade.

The supposition that this revival is greatly owing to the failure of our home crops derives much confirmation from the fact, that whilst the best authorities estimate the diminished growth of wheat last year at from five to six million quarters, worth some eleven or twelve millions of money, our purchases of corn from the United States alone were fully that amount in excess; to compensate for which they took from us iron and other metals and textile manufactures together to the value of twelve millions more than in 1878-9. We have here a beautiful illustration of the way in which Nature, rather let us say the Author of Nature's laws, the Divine Ruler, who orders the course of Nature for the welfare of His creatures, counteracts one disturbing element by the restorative power of another. When the fertilizing influence of the sun's heat failed us last year, vegetation languished and our fields failed to yield their accustomed supplies. From whence did relief come but from the latent heat, which ages back became imprisoned in the depths of our coal pits, being brought forth and utilized for the production of those manufactures wherewith we purchased corn elsewhere? Where can we look for a more convincing argument in favour of free trade than is to be found in the blessings it procured for us in permitting this unrestricted exchange of the commodities

absolutely necessary to our existence, and of special importance to our brethren in America ?   Whilst we sympathize
with our agriculturists in the loss of their substance and the
severe trials which they are enduring, let us rejoice that
the evil was stayed from spreading to our manufacturers
and traders, and thereby involving them in the like suffering.   Let us not, however, be led away by undue expectations for the future.   A good harvest at home—still more,
a succession of them, if combined with greater productiveness abroad—would so far depress prices as to lessen the
purchasing power of the food-growers at home, whilst we
should not need to buy so largely from abroad.   Thus those
who have latterly supported our markets will fail to purchase as they have done, and if our manufacturing industries
are to be sustained we must not rely on a repetition of the
demands that have latterly been made upon them.

There is too much danger at present that we shall be
drawn into wild speculations and expectations, such as led
up to the fictitious prosperity of seven years back, and cul-
minated in the depression of more recent years.   Let us
not delude ourselves with the belief that the inflation of
1871-3 is about to return—that fortunes are going to be
made as rapidly as then, or wages to rise to the same level.
Let us not, however, give way to gloomy fears.   Cheap food
will foster cheap production, and though our old customers
may under its influence be enabled to supply their own
wants, there are new races of purchasers to be found or
called into being, and new homes to be founded by those
who are cumbering the ground here rather than tilling it in
the distant parts of the Empire.   The judicious transferal
of much of our capital and labour to places abroad, where
there is ample room for its profitable employment, together
with greater thrift—individual, family, and national—at
home, are the true sources on which to rely for the maintenance or restoration of our manufacturing and commercial supremacy.

XVI.

The Finance of " National Insurance." [1]

THE scheme for the prevention of pauperism propounded by the Rev. W. L. Blackley, in the pages of the " Nineteenth Century," of November, 1878, and so ably defended and enforced in his sermon in Westminster Abbey on September 28th, 1879, and on numerous subsequent occasions, commends itself to the sympathies of many who cannot altogether acquiesce in the conclusions at which he arrives, or see the matter to be one so easy of settlement as many of those who support the plan believe it to be. The formation of the " National Providence League for Promoting National Compulsory Insurance against destitution, or sickness, infirmity, and old age," Lord Shaftesbury being its president, with a goodly array of clerical dignitaries and well-known philanthropists as its Council, has removed the subject from the region of speculative theory to that of proposed practical application ; and the warm advocacy of the project by Lord Carnarvon in the House of Lords, together with the influential support it has received, and the active exertions made towards securing Parliamentary sanction for the establishment of a National Club, all justify a close examination into the merits of the scheme, in order that if practicable its adoption may be generally promoted, or if impracticable, it may be discarded.

The plan itself may be stated as one which provides—

[1] Read before the Social Science Congress at Edinburgh, Oct., 1880.

1st. That every male should be compelled at some period previous to arriving at full age to contribute the sum of £10 to the funds of a National Club, established under Government guarantee.

2nd. That for this payment he should be entitled to receive "aid in sickness to the amount of 8s. per week till he reaches seventy years of age, and a pension of 4s. weekly from that age till his death."

The organized arrangements for receiving and paying these amounts, it is not intended to discuss on the present occasion, nor yet to enter upon the disputed points as to whether such compulsion can or ought to be exercised. It is proposed simply to inquire into the financial soundness of the scheme; that is, whether the proposed contribution, if made, would suffice to provide for the proposed grants contingent upon sickness during the working years of life, and of definite pensions to the survivors when these years are past. The latter portion of the inquiry is simple enough, for the average duration of life is well ascertained, and the sums necessary for the purchase through the P. O. Savings' Bank of annuities for life to commence at the age of seventy, are published in every number of the " Postal Guide," or are to be obtained from any life assurance office which deals in this branch of business. But it is not so easy to calculate the expected claims on account of sickness, for the average periods during which incapacity for work from this cause prevail at the different ages of life have never yet been accurately determined. The only basis on which such calculations can rest is the experience derived from the records of the various Clubs and Friendly Societies already in existence. There are many reasons why absolute reliance cannot be placed upon them; but before alluding to some of these, it may be well to see how far the computations based upon the information furnished from this source will serve to show that the enforced payment will be sufficient for the ends proposed.

Mr. Blackley assumes that the proposed £10 will be

paid either in one sum or by instalments during one, two, or three years, so that it may be completed before the age of 20 years is attained, say on an average at 19. Let us then suppose that such a scheme had been in operation some ten or twelve years, and taking the census figures of 1871 for England and Wales as a guide, calculate the growth of a fund arising from the payment of £10 from each lad of 19 alive in that year, subjected to the anticipated payments for sick allowances through fifty-one successive years, when those who survive would be at the age of 70, and become claimants for the promised weekly pensions.

Table showing for England and Wales (a) number of males living in 1871 at each age from 19 to 70; (b), estimated average period of incapacity from sickness in each year; (c), total number of weeks' sickness for existing lives; (d), net amount of sick allowances to be provided.

[In million and decimals.]

Ages.	Number living.	Sickness.		Total amount of sick allowances.	Year of Fund.
		Average in Weeks.			
		Per head.	Total.		
	(a)	(b)	(c)	(d)	
19—20	·205692	·7022	·145	£·058	1st
—21	·201047	·7223	·145	·058	2nd
—22	·196061	·7405	·145	·058	3rd
—23	·193070	·7565	·145	·058	4th
—24	·188790	·7699	·145	·058	5th
—25	·184184	·7803	·144	·058	6th
—26	·179723	·7913	·141	·056	7th
—27	·174938	·8061	·141	·056	8th
—28	·170191	·8240	·140	·056	9th
—29	·165541	·8444	·139	·056	10th
—30	·161023	·8668	·140	·056	11th
—31	·156734	·8971	·140	·056	12th
—32	·152545	·9258	·141	·056	13th
—33	·148492	·9522	·142	·057	14th
—34	·144536	·9811	·142	·057	15th
—35	·140790	1·0115	·142	·057	16th
—36	·137307	1·0339	·143	·057	17th
—37	·133962	1·0613	·142	·057	18th
—38	·130758	1·0956	·143	·057	19th
—39	·127662	1·1327	·145	·058	20th
—40	·124611	1·1747	·146	·058	21st
—41	·121709	1·2217	·151	·060	22nd
—42	·118745	1·2766	·151	·060	23rd
Car. forward	3·658111		3·298	£1·318	

Ages.	Number living.	Sickness.		Total amount of sick allowances.	Year of Fund.
		Average in Weeks. Per head.	Total.		
	(a)	(b)	(c)	(d)	
Brht. forward	3·658111		3·298	£1·318	
—43	·115906	1·3395	·155	·062	24th
—44	·113264	1·4104	·159	·064	25th
45	·110797	1·4893	·164	·065	26th
46	·108537	1·5761	·170	·068	27th
—47	·106541	1·6695	·177	·071	28th
48	·104603	1·7693	·185	·074	29th
—49	·102047	1·8758	·192	·077	30th
50	·099074	1·9887	·198	·079	31st
—51	·095888	2·1082	·202	·080	32nd
52	·092460	2·2219	·205	·082	33rd
53	·088996	2·5899	·210	·084	34th
—54	·085525	2·5523	·218	·087	35th
—55	·082040	? 2·70	·222	·089	36th
—56	·078620	? 2·86	·226	·090	37th
—57	·075247	? 3·03	·228	·091	38th
—58	·071936	? 3·21	·230	·092	39th
—59	·068695	? 3·40	·235	·094	40th
—60	·065527	? 3·60	·236	·094	41st
—61	·062434	? 3·81	·240	·096	42nd
—62	·059410	? 4·03	·240	·096	43rd
—63	·056451	? 4·27	·240	·096	44th
—64	·053548	? 4·51	·241	·096	45th
—65	·050694	? 4·85	·246	·098	46th
—66	·047880	? 5·14	·240	·092	47th
—67	·045096	? 5·34	·241	·096	48th
—68	·042340	? 5·66	·240	·096	49th
—69	·039603	? 6·09	·239	·096	50th
—70	·036884	? 6·45	·240	·096	51st
	5·818154		9·317	£3·719	
70 and upwards	·035535	@ £76 2s. each.		£2·704	In perpetuity.
	5·853689			£6·423	

In the foregoing table the first and second columns show for each year of age from 19 to 70, the exact number of males then alive; and assuming the rate of mortality to remain unchanged, the yearly diminution of numbers, and consequently of claimants for sick allowances in each year of the fund's existence will be seen. The third column contains the estimated average extent of sickness, in decimals of a week or whole weeks. The fourth column brings out the number of weeks for the whole existing number, and the fifth the sum to which 8s. for each week

would amount in each year up to 70 ; and for that age the
cost of a life annuity equivalent to the 4s. of weekly pension.
Each line will therefore show the amount for the payment
of which the fund would be liable in each successive year,
and the total the full amount of liability incurred during its
whole duration.

Dealing, then, in the first instance, with the £10 per head
paid by those who in 1871 had completed their nineteenth
but not their twentieth year, the fund would start with a
capital sum of £2,056,920, the annual interest on which at
3 per cent. would yield £61,708, wherewith to provide the
8s. per week during the sickness of the next fifty years, and
4s. per week for the remainder of life. In the first year the
expected sickness per head being ·7022 of a week, would
for the whole number amount to 145,000 weeks, absorbing
£58,000 ; that is, allowing but a moderate sum for expenses of
management, not far short of the whole accruing interest.
In the following years the number of claimants would be
diminished by death to the numbers shown in the table, but
the average of sickness increasing with age would for several
years keep pace with this diminution, and thus still leave
no room for accumulation.   In fact, it would seem that the
charge on the fund would be the same at the age of forty as
at twenty.   From that time forward the increase in sickness
would overbalance the decrease by death, and the claims
begin to exceed the income ; and this with considerable
rapidity up to the age of fifty-four, when, including expenses,
the payments cannot be taken at less than £90,000 per
annum, one-third of which would have to be paid out of the
capital, as a smaller proportion had been for the previous
years since forty-one or forty-two. From the age of fifty-five
upwards it is believed that no trustworthy information as to
the extent of sickness is to be obtained, but taking the
same progressive increase as before, which must certainly
err on the side of being too little, the annual claims would
probably stand as in the table at about £96,000 per annum
for the years between sixty and seventy. Now these succes-

sive inroads upon the capital with which the fund originally started would, with the accruing compound interest at the rates given, have reached to £1,047,000, or rather more than one-half the commencing sum. Then according to the table the number of those living to pass the age of seventy would be 35,635, each of whom would become entitled to an annuity of 4s. per week, or £10 8s. per annum; to purchase which, according to the price given for the Post Office Savings' Bank, would require £76 2s. per head, or a total of £2,704,000. To meet this there would be less than one million of money left. A fund, therefore, formed upon these conditions would become bankrupt before all the claimants upon it had expired. If we suppose that in each year a fresh batch of payments were made by those arriving at the required age, we have but to multiply each of these by the number of years that have elapsed to ascertain exactly how much would have been contributed at any given year, and to add together the successive claims in the table up to the same period, to know what would then constitute the outgoings. If we take the state of the fund at seventy years we shall find that £2,056,920 × 51 = £104,902,920 will have been paid, of which a large portion, though not the half, will have been sunk to supply the deficiencies in the amount received as interest; and that the annual claims for sick allowance, and the purchase of pensions would require £6,423,000, or more than double the income the fund would produce, even if it had suffered no diminution in its progress.

These figures relate only to England and Wales; the population of Scotland is about 15 per cent., and that of Ireland some 24 per cent. of the English, and assuming their relative number at the respective ages to be the same, it would need at least £9,000,000 to provide for all. But this is not its full extent, for in these days, when women are so greatly earners of wages, there can be no reason why they should not be called upon in like manner to contribute. Pauperism prevails far more with them than with men, and needs the same provision for sickness and infirmity.

Mr. Blackley, however, in fixing the required contribution from each young man at £10, does not calculate upon its being sufficient to provide for sickness and old age in all, for this he would name £15. The calculation is based upon two suppositions—first that whilst all, rich and poor alike, would be compelled to pay, a large number would fail to claim either allowance. Again, he expects that the funds would be invested at 4 instead of 3 per cent. Both these expectations need to be carefully examined.

There can be no manner of doubt that, although in justice, every individual who had contributed would be entitled to come upon the fund, many would not do so; but the abstainers would scarcely be so large a number as might be anticipated. The feeling would be pretty general that the allowances having been fairly purchased might be justly taken. No charitable emotions would interfere, since Government would be paymaster; and in a great many cases it would be the trouble of obtaining the grant, not any thought of shame, which would preclude its being asked for. For a few years the stigma of taking a pauper's allowance would attach to the dole; but this would soon wear off, and pride would not be wounded by the assertion of a purchased right. But any saving thus obtained—and it would, after all, be a very considerable one—would probably be counterbalanced by the extra numbers who would be found amongst the very class for whose wants the fund was founded to make provision. The tables of sickness on which the calculations have been made are derived from the experience of clubs and friendly societies in actual existence, and all of these require proof of good health on entrance. No such barrier could be opposed to joining the National Club. The constitutionally weak and the permanently disabled would be just the class—so far as they possessed the means—who would be but too ready to join. In multitudes of cases the parent would have to provide the money for the son, and it is not for a moment to be expected that he would omit paying for the disabled ones—nor could they with any justice be excluded. Even those who were seriously ill would but be too ready if within their power, to pay a sum which it would take but six or nine months' illness to return to them, and the rich man who paid without any reasonable chance of having to accept the benefit, would at once demand that the weak and sickly should be those to partake of it in his stead. Neither is it likely that any Government inspection could so effectually guard against deception as the agency of existing societies does. There is thus no reason to anticipate that the claims would on the whole fall short of the calculated amount.

Nor is there any better reason to rely upon a permanent gain from a higher rate of interest than 3 per cent. If 4 could be obtained the difference would be immense, for in the case we have supposed the annual income, instead of being but just enough to meet the sick allowances, would leave a surplus of some £20,000 a year for more than the first twenty years, and of gradually lessening amounts for ten or twelve more—so that the survivors at the ages of seventy would find more than enough to provide their pensions. It is, however, far more probable that the fund would fail to obtain investments so high as three, than that they would be found at four or higher. It is quite clear that any national club or fund must be guaranteed by Government, and therefore that no securities should be taken but such as are absolutely certain. Private persons or bodies, and public also may, without undue risk, make loans on various descriptions of property and receive higher rates; but the very fact that these rates are given when Government can obtain loans at very little more than three, is an evidence that the security is not so perfect; for whenever any investments approaching to the security of those of the Government are offered—such, for instance, as that of the Public Works Board—the money is obtainable at 3¼ or little more. When so large a lender as the National Club would be, came into the market, it would help to keep down the interest obtainable. In fact it would be impracticable for Government to be largely borrowing and lending at different rates, and in practice it would come to this, that no higher interest could be obtained than Consols or the other Government Stocks would yield. The result would be as it is with the Savings' Banks—the insurance funds would go towards absorbing the National Debt—thus helping to keep the interest down, and ultimately enabling the Chancellor of the Exchequer to force upon the nation's creditors the acceptance of even lower interest than 3 per cent.

The calculations in the foregoing table are not put forward with any pretensions to the close accuracy that would govern actuarial figures, for which indeed there is not yet sufficient data to base them upon, and the estimate of sickness from the age of fifty-five upwards, rests upon an assumption that the progressive increase would be in the same ratio in the later years as the previous ones, which is probably below the truth rather than above it. It is convenient also in considering the progress of the fund, to capitalize the payments after seventy, at the rate for which the requisite annuities may be purchased through the Post Office Savings' Bank, rather than to carry on the calculation to the extreme limit of life. We thus, in the fifty-first year of its duration, arrive at that stage in the history of the fund when all who first became contributors to it, will have passed off, and there will be a regular sequence of new members coming on and old ones passing away ; and were the number of the population to remain stationary, it would stand thus :—

Provision against sickness would be made for 5,818,154, being the whole of the male population of England and Wales who had completed their nineteenth year and not passed beyond their seventieth ; the estimated incapacity in each year being 9·3 millions of weeks, for which the allowance of 8s. per week would constitute a yearly amount of £3·72 millions : to this must be added £2·71 for the purchase of annuities of 4s. per week for those exceeding seventy years, together requiring that the fund should

have an income of £6·43 millions of money. Towards this
the payment of new contributors would produce £2·06,
and for the remainder reliance must be placed on the interest from the accumulations of previous years. This, however, would only meet the wants of the English and Welsh
male population, numbering 11·09 million persons. That of
Scotland, being 1·58, and of Ireland 2·64, a provision for these
at the same rates would require £2·45 annually, of which
the contributors coming into the fund would supply £·78.
If then to these we add fifty per cent. for the females,
who being engaged in occupations and earning wages, cannot
on any principle of right be treated otherwise than the
males ; we shall have a total annual charge amounting to
£13·32 millions of money, and a receipt from the young
persons under compulsion to pay, of £4·26, leaving some
nine millions to be provided from the investment of previous accumulations. That is, supposing compulsion to
have been applied to all the young men and one-half the
young women of the United Kingdom, and thus all so paying to have acquired a right to relief in sickness and old
age to the extent proposed—nothing short of an accumulated fund of £300,000,000, if interest be reckoned at 3 per
cent., would be a sufficient security for the due payment of
these allowances. If the money could be invested at 4 per
cent., 225 millions would suffice ; but should only 2½ per
cent. be obtainable, 360 millions would be requisite. We
thus see somewhat of the gigantic proportions of the question with which we have to deal. An accumulated fund of
from two to four hundred millions, created and maintained
by an enforced levy on the wages earned by the youths
between seventeen and twenty-one years of age, to the extent of five if not six or seven millions annually, and
furnishing the means for dispensing weekly allowances in
the aggregate amounting to thirteen millions in each year.

In this estimate it is assumed that the population would
remain stationary in numbers, whereas it is evidently increasing ; if it continued to grow as at present, at the end

of fifty years it would be doubled or trebled, and the £13,000,000 would be at least £30,000,000, or more.

It is obvious that such a fund could only be administered by the Government of the country, not solely because of its magnitude, but also from the impossibility of granting compulsory contributions without State guarantee ; or the payment of allowances being thus secured, excepting under State control. The responsibility of conducting all the operations of receipt, investment, and payment, whether through the Post Office, the Local Government Board, the National Debt Commissioners, or a special department to be formed for the purpose, would exceed that of any existing Department, and necessarily involve a large expenditure; for though it might not be difficult to arrange for collecting the receipts, the organization for distributing the grants would be far more intricate than the present Poor Law arrangements. It is true that in the first commencement a limited number of transactions would have to take place, and that they would only grow by slow degrees, thus affording time to perfect plans and develope the requisite machinery; but the extent to which that growth would ultimately reach must not be lost sight of in considering the practicability of the scheme, or determining the course to be taken in the institution of its working. A real difficulty arises at the very commencement in providing such an instrumentality as may be capable of gradual but certain expansion through the years to elapse before its arrival at full maturity.

But a much graver difficulty will be found in providing any investment for the monies received other than in the Public Stocks (Consols or 3 per Cents), and this is one on the overcoming of which, it depends how much must be contributed by each insurer. Mr. Blackley supposes that 4 per cent. will be easily procured, and on this supposition bases his estimate that £10 per head will be sufficient, or even more than enough. If this be so, and the total allowances should be as the previous calculations show, there is

no doubt that this opinion is correct, but if only 3 per cent.
be obtained, £15 or even more, would certainly be required.
Private insurance offices may often be enabled to place
their monies at 4 per cent., and public bodies borrowing
for buildings or drainage works, have frequently to give as
much, but not for very large sums. The Board of Works
is able to borrow at 3½ per cent., and most of the money so
borrowed is invested by insurance and other offices. It
will not therefore be safe to calculate or expect that the
National Insurance funds could be put out so as to yield
more than 3 per cent., and the result would be that as
with the savings' bank monies, they would have to be
absorbed in the reduction of the National Debt, and thus
yield only a trifle beyond the lower rate of interest. Nor
is it likely that even this would be maintained : there are
already symptoms that the holders of Consols will ere long
have to accept, it may be as little as 2½ per cent., and the
diminution of this stock offering for actual sale in the
market, would tend to raise the price, and thus facilitate
the conversion of the 3 per Cents. into a lower paying stock.
Were the saving thus effected applied from time to time,
in addition to that shortly to arise from the falling in of
terminable annuities, together with the provision already
made for a sinking fund, a perceptible decrease in the
National Debt would be going on. Thus by the time that
National Insurance came fully into play, or even long
before the term of fifty years was completed, it might happen
that the whole of the National Debt would come to be held
on this account. Already trustees, both public and private,
experience the greatest difficulty in finding safe securities
that will yield more than Consols. It is this which helps
to drive the price for purchase up so high, and with so
much more money to be thus invested, this upward movement will be greatly accelerated. It is the absence of higher
paying securities on which implicit reliance can be placed,
that leads to the introduction of so many unstable projects
and causes so much loss to unwary investors. A curious

state of things would result should successive decreases of
the National Debt, and successive increases of the National
Insurance Fund bring the two to the same level. The
State would then be debtor in one capacity and creditor in
another, and the simple course would be to abolish the
fiction of both separate funds, and transfer the charges
on the Insurance Fund, present and prospective, to the same
category as that for the interest of the National Debt,
namely, the general revenue of the country provided for by
taxation in one shape or another. We should thus be
establishing another kind of poor relief of far larger extent
than that at present afforded, inasmuch as the proposed
allowances would exceed the grants at present given; and
the recipients would not as now be paupers, but actual
creditors of the State, having purchased by specific payments in early life, specific grants for sickness and old
age.

Two fallacies appear to underlie the calculations, or it
may rather be said the expectations upon which the scheme
of National Insurance is based. First, an undue reliance
upon the power for accumulation of compound interest.
This is only true as regards that portion of the contributions
to the fund which go to provide for old age; but as the
figures in the table show, the claims on account of sickness
will at once commence to accrue, and probably swallow up
the whole of the interest intended to be re-invested. The
fund thus would not grow with anything like the rapidity
anticipated, unless the primary contributions were fixed at
a higher rate. Secondly, it is forgotten that money has no
power of increase apart from judicious employment in conjunction with labour, either that which is put forth in
agricultural or manufacturing occupations, or saved, as
when public works, such as docks, bridges, &c., render it
advantageous to those by whom these are used to pay some
portion of their earnings as an equivalent for the labour
they would otherwise have to bestow. Such opportunities
are limited in number and extent, and therefore there is a

limited field for the appropriation of the funds proposed to
be raised.

A question far too wide and deep to be treated within
the limits of this paper is here opened up—namely, the
expediency of thus divorcing capital from the labour which
alone can cause it to fructify, and the encouragement of
those who possess money in trusting its employment to
others, and spending their own lives in expending the interest they receive for its use. The policy of tying up so much
money in settlements, loans, and employments unconnected
with its owners, is clearly not one of unmixed good, and it
may fairly be debated whether in this country we have
not already gone too far in this direction. The nation is
divided into two classes of debtors and creditors, producers
and non-producers, to a degree which may perhaps very
soon prove to be fatal to its continued prosperity. But
this theme must not now be farther pursued, although there
is in it enough of importance to awake anxious thought and
prompt to careful inquiry.

Again, taking into consideration the magnitude and
duration of the engagements into which it is proposed to
enter, it is scarcely consistent with sound economical principles to make contracts of this nature to bind our succes-
sors in future and distant years. Whenever money is now
lent by the State, or borrowed under its sanction, for the
promotion of public works, it is usually arranged that the
loan shall expire by the repayment of both principal and
interest within thirty years. The National Club, were it
established to-day, would become bound for twice that
period, by receiving money now, the whole of which would
not be repaid till every life now under nineteen had expired; and its solvency would depend upon the same
rates of interest and other conditions existing unchanged
throughout the whole intervening time. It is true that this
is already done whenever a Government deferred annuity
is sold; but such transactions are so limited in number and
amount, as to render it impossible for serious inconvenience

to arise, whereas these would within twenty years embrace
two-thirds of our population. Nor are the circumstances
analogous to those which occur when new Stocks, Consols,
or Three per Cents. are issued. Then what in effect takes
place is the creation of a rent-charge upon the freehold and
other property of the kingdom, to the extent of £3 per
annum for every £100 of stock. It is called a perpetual
annuity, but can at any moment be cancelled by the payment of the principal; whereas in national insurance no
power can be given to terminate the contract save by the
decease of the individual contributor. The object in view
is to prevent his becoming a pauper, and while life lasts,
the State, which has taken payment, must be bound to provide for his incapacity from sickness or old age. Yet even
then there is no security that the object sought will with
certainty be attained; for who shall say whether half or
three-quarters of a century hence, the specified sums of 8s.
and 4s. a week will meet the necessities of the case? With
the rapid changes going on in the value of money and in
our social condition, these sums may be wholly insufficient
or vastly too much. Money is now abundant at three per
cent., it may then be scarce at double or treble that amount,
or not be loanable at a half or third of that rate.

On all these and many other grounds which might be
specified, the financial aspect of the scheme is scarcely such
as to commend it to the sober sense of statesmen.

Thus far we have been considering the matter as affect-
ing the interests and the prospects of the State; let us see
whether its features are more attractive to the individuals
whom it is proposed to subject to compulsion. Every such
scheme must necessarily have two sides—the one possessed
of advantages, the other the reverse. In this one all the
disadvantages would appear to fall on the thrifty, and its
chief value to be to the thriftless. This is assumed at the
very outset: it supposes that the contributors are disinclined
to save, for if the disposition existed—always supposing that
the benefits to be received are not more than the enforced

contribution will fairly purchase—the man who can and will restrict his expenditure, has other openings for the investment of his savings. A policy of insurance or a deferred annuity he can already purchase through the Post Office on as favourable terms as the fund could safely grant him, whilst for sickness the £10 or £15 which it is proposed to take from him, would, if deposited in the Savings' Bank, serve as a fund on which to draw during incapacity to earn wages; which in the case of the healthy and the prudent, who, because they are so, suffer less than the average amount of illness, would rarely be exhausted before by restoration to health the power to replenish it was regained. Besides this, there are sound and well conducted sick funds springing into existence—there is no reason why there should not be more—whose terms are better suited to his · circumstances than those of the National Club, adapted as they must be for the imprudent and the fraudulent, could possibly be. One great disadvantage amongst the many that might be mentioned, would be that the man who wished to emigrate could not carry with him to his adopted country the rights and privileges of the fund, secured to him whilst remaining at home. With our ever-increasing population and declining or stationary production, it must be the lot of many to seek employment abroad: numbers of our young people are saving up their earnings with this in view, and it would be cruel to drag from them the product of their self-denial and industry to preserve them from becoming paupers in a land they never intend to inhabit permanently.

Again, to the man (or woman) who is striving to improve his position, it is all important that his earnings should not be taken from him. The true incentive to thrift is the power which money gives to render labour valuable. Tools with which to work; materials for manufacture, goods for sale, houses to live in, or land to cultivate, nay, even appliances for health and comfort, or means for the acquisition of knowledge, are all of infinitely more pecuniary value to the wise and the prudent than the paltry 2½ or 3 per cent., which is all that the borrowing State can afford to give him. It cannot be too strongly impressed upon our youth of both sexes and of all classes, that in the use of capital, in conjunction with physical or mental power rightly employed, lies the secret of success in life, of that advancement which should be to all a lawful and laudable object of desire. Once more, the proposed compulsory investment would fall with peculiar hardship on students, apprentices, tor hose who are working without earning, in prospect of future returns for their labour. How many parents are there, petty tradesmen or small mechanics, to say nothing of clergymen, professional men, government servants, clerks, and others of small means and large families, whose sons, and daughters too, need every penny that can be saved for their maintenance and education or training, to whom the abstraction of the £30, £50, or £100 would prove absolutely destructive. From how many homes like these would the wail of despair, if not curses loud and deep, arise, let those say who witness the hard struggles of suffering poverty.

But the chief weakness of the scheme lies in the fact that the reckless and improvident will participate in its advantages to the detriment of the industrious and careful. So far as it will operate in restraint of extravagant expenditure, enforce the laying by of something for the future, absorb the earnings which otherwise might be spent in folly and dissipation, and thus compel to the exercise of self-denial during the earlier years of life, its value would be great; but in the removal of incentive to exertion afterwards, and the security it would afford of subsistence during illness, although the result of misconduct, its effect must be prejudicial. To the dissolute, the amount of sick allowance would often be an inducement to magnify ailments and feign incapacity for labour, whilst to the right-minded it would be so small as to induce every effort to avoid the sacrifice of earnings by declaring on the fund. Whatever sum may be fixed upon as the contribution to be exacted,

it must be that which experience shows to be sufficient to
provide the sick and aged allowances. The reckless class
would by their claims upon it, both increase the average
and absorb the greater share—thus compelling the honest
ones to contribute more than would cover their own average,
whilst they would actually receive less.   It is no answer to
this to say that the present effect of our Poor Law is to
support or give relief to the undeserving out of funds provided by the deserving.   So long as the administration of
relief, whether in or out of doors, is vigilantly watched, and
granted only as a matter of necessity, much may be done
to check idleness and fraud ; when the allowance can be
claimed as a right, no amount of care in dispensing it will
altogether prevent a considerable amount of malingering, or
prevent its bestowal on those whose only title to claim it
arises out of their own improvidence.   This danger or
difficulty is inseparable from the condition of a payment
once for all, whereas the periodical subscription to a
friendly society or sick club, brings the conduct of the
members under review, and those who are unworthy of its
benefits are constantly losing their rights by inability or
unwillingness to keep up their payments.   Yet it is doubtful whether, on the whole, even the unworthy class would
really be benefited by such a fund.   The ease with which
they could shuffle through seasons of incapacity would have
a demoralizing influence, probably leading to such further loss
of time and health as to more than counterbalance the value
of their actual receipts, and this, in addition to the moral
evil produced, would in fact be financially injurious.

It is with no desire to find fault with a plan suggestive
of so much good, that this criticism has been undertaken.
The evils it proposes to remove are so deep-seated, and so
detrimental to our national prosperity, that any mode of
satisfactorily dealing with them would be hailed with joy
by philanthropists and statesmen of every class or party.
Neither is there any reason to regret that it has received so
large a share of public attention, for it may stimulate many

to voluntary efforts for their own provision, to learn the channels through which they may be made, and the value of early economy for the purpose of judicious investment. It may encourage a spirit of self-reliance, and go far to determine the course of life of many by showing them the money-value of small savings, and the ease with which those who have the will may likewise find the way to secure themselves against the worst trials of incapacity for labour when sick, or entire dependence upon others in old age. The author of the plan has done good service by evoking discussion, and is to be applauded for his earnest efforts to carry it into practice, although he may have failed to demonstrate its financial soundness, or that it is otherwise capable of being adopted. Yet if the figures now produced are correct and the reasoning based upon them be sound, it will be a national evil to waste further time or exhaust further philanthropic effort in endeavouring to procure legislative sanction for a measure which, when treated in all its bearings, and traced through all its probable results, must be financially unsatisfactory alike for the thoughtless, the thrifty, and the State.

P.S. Should the scheme be made to embrace all of both sexes, as was assumed in a discussion at the Church Congress held at Leicester since the foregoing was in type, the annual charge on the fund would be more than proportionately increased on account of the superior numbers and greater tenacity of life in females at the later ages. This raises the value of the annuities to be provided for at 70 by at least 30 per cent. The difficult question would also arise as to provision for incapacity to work during the sickness incident to maternity, so that altogether the charge could not be estimated at less than £20,000,000 instead of £13,000,000 per annum.

INDEX.

www.ingramcontent.com/pod-product-compliance
Lightning Source LLC
Chambersburg PA
CBHW030908270326
41929CB00008B/614